*Shakespeare's Romances
and the Royal Family*

The Family of James I (1622–24), by Willem van de Passe.
Courtesy of Folger Shakespeare Library.

DAVID M. BERGERON

Shakespeare's Romances and the Royal Family

UNIVERSITY PRESS OF KANSAS

Published by the University Press of Kansas (Lawrence, Kansas 66045),
which was organized by the Kansas Board of Regents
and is operated and funded by Emporia State University, Fort Hays State
University, Kansas State University, Pittsburg State
University, the University of Kansas, and Wichita State University

Library of Congress Cataloging in Publication Data

Bergeron, David Moore.
   Shakespeare's romances and the royal family.

   Bibliography: p.
   Includes index.
   1. Shakespeare, William, 1564–1616—Characters—Kings
and rulers. 2. Kings and rulers in literature.
3. James I, King of England, 1566–1625. 4. Family in
literature. 5. Shakespeare, William, 1564–1616—Tragi-
comedies. 6. Shakespeare, William, 1564–1616—Political
and social views. I. Title. II. Title: Royal family.
PR2992.K5B47   1985   822.3′3   85-689
ISBN 0-7006-0271-2

Printed in the United States of America

For my Mother,
Geraldo, and Frank

Contents

List of Illustrations

Preface

I began thinking about the topic of Shakespeare's Romances and the family of James I after reading Glynne Wickham's essays on the subject. Though I eventually disagreed with some of his interpretations, I see his work as the begetter of my own study. He also kindly sent me offprints of essays, and we had the chance to discuss the matter briefly. When I was seriously beginning to formulate my ideas, I learned of the then forthcoming book by Gary Schmidgall. He generously sent me advance page proofs, thereby reassuring me that I had not already been preempted. As readers will find, I also disagree with Schmidgall's analysis, even as I am influenced by his effort.

Enumerating those people and institutions that have assisted me in specific ways prompts joy for me. G. Douglas Atkins shared his considerable knowledge of current literary theory, and Stephen Orgel read *The Tempest* section with his usual candor and keen analysis. He forced me to rethink parts of my position on that play. Jonathan Goldberg's work on King James and the literature of the period has been an inspiration and a model to me. His reading of part of the manuscript, his advice, his bibliographical information all enriched me and my work. Early in the process, my friend Jeanne Roberts read the beginning chapters and offered her helpful criticism and encouragement; she eventually read the entire manuscript, providing even more assistance. I am particularly indebted to Henry Jacobs, who read the manuscript and wrote an exemplary and extraordinarily valuable report. He will recognize some of his ideas here.

So will four rare and priceless friends who read the entire manuscript in varying stages of revision. To Jean Atkins, Geraldo Udex de Sousa, Richard Hardin, and Frank Murphy, I owe an embarrassingly large but wonderful debt. Each not only provided sound criticism of what I had written, but each also gave me encouragement when I needed it most. One friend, the Rev. Homer D. Henderson, who has not read a word of this book, nevertheless unwittingly gave me many valuable ideas as well as nurture and inspiration.

It is a pleasure to offer other special thanks. None of this book would have been possible without the kind cooperation of the libraries where I conducted my research: the British Library, the Folger Shakespeare Library, Watson Library of the University of Kansas (especially the Interlibrary Services department), and the Department of Special Collections, Spencer Research Library of the University of Kansas. The University of Kansas has generously supported this project by three grants from the General Research Fund, by awarding me a sabbatical leave for 1982/83, and by a grant to assist publication of this book from the Scholarly Publications Revolving Fund. Pam LeRow as the typist, or more precisely the word processor, of several drafts of this manuscript performed with her usual exceptional skill and extraordinary cheerfulness. I owe her much.

I am grateful to the History Department of the University of Tennessee, Knoxville, which invited me to speak in 1983 on the fact and fiction of Renaissance families at a departmental colloquium. Participants at the Central Renaissance Conference in 1983 and at the Iowa State University Shakespeare Symposium in 1984 heard pieces of this book. Responses from all these groups added to my understanding. I should also single out for thanks the graduate students in my Shakespeare seminar in the fall semester of 1983; they patiently bore up under barrages of information about James and families, and they challenged me to think yet once again about the Romances.

The dedication of this book to my mother, Geraldo Sousa, and Frank Murphy constitutes a small effort to repay an enormous debt. Each has enriched my life in special ways too priceless to be enumerated in the mere preface to a book. No taffeta phrases, silken terms precise, or three-piled hyperboles will suffice. But I rejoice beyond a common joy in my good fortune and grapple these people to my heart with hoops of steel.

As I get ready to turn loose this book, two statements hang somewhat ominously in my mind. The first, from Spenser, reminds me of inherent limitations in my topic: ''My narrow leaves cannot in them containe / The large discourse of royall Princes state'' (*The Faerie Queene*, I.xii.14). The second, from Shakespeare, reminds me of the risk of my subject and of the need to get on with it nevertheless:

"Your time's expir'd: / Either expound now or receive your sentence" (Antiochus to Pericles, I.i.90–91).

David M. Bergeron

November 1984
Lawrence, Kansas

1

Introduction

Writing to Ralph Winwood on 28 March 1605, Samuel Calvert observes: "The Plays do not forbear to present upon their Stages the whole Course of this present Time, not sparing either King, State or Religion, in so great Absurdity, and with such Liberty, that any would be afraid to hear them."[1] French diplomatic reports confirm such analysis of the English theater: for example, Count Harley de Beaumont records in April 1606: "One or two days before, they [players] had brought forward their own King, and all his favourites, in a very strange fashion. They made him curse and swear because he had been robbed of a bird, and beat a gentleman because he had called off the hounds from the scent. They represent him as drunk at least once a day, &c."[2] Whatever particular events these comments may refer to, the statements indicate the topicality of Jacobean drama, a quality difficult to understand from this distance. These contemporary accounts reveal how some people "read" (i.e., interpreted) the plays in light of current events and people. Those early audiences apparently saw reflected in and through the drama an immediate political and social reality. One might reach Jonathan Goldberg's conclusion that the theater "was a place for self-knowledge precisely because it mirrored state, because its re-presentations duplicated public life. It is there that Renaissance man went to know himself."[3]

My subject is Shakespeare's last plays, those generally called Romances, and my focus is on the royal families in those plays. What we need, I think, is to attempt a fresh "reading" of those plays as they were "read" by the initial audiences, at least insofar as we can approximate their experience. That is, we need a full awareness of the topicality of the plays, especially of how the Stuart royal family was perceived. I will argue that King James and his family constitute a "text" that Shakespeare read in gathering materials for the Romances

1

(more on this concept at the end of this chapter). James and his family were, after all, the only royal *family* that Shakespeare knew. I will attempt to assess the relevance of the presence and experiences of James's family for the late plays.

Though not its primary intention, this study may offer a partial answer to the perennial and vexing question of why Shakespeare wrote these plays *when* he did. Edward Dowden in the latter part of the nineteenth century popularized and institutionalized one answer: Shakespeare wrote these plays at this point in his career because he emerged, as Dowden says, from being "in the depths" (the time of the tragedies) to being "on the heights." A sunny disposition and outlook supplanted a bleak and gloomy view. Would that questions of artistic development could be answered so easily. Some critics have suggested that the acquisition of the Blackfriars Theatre by the King's Men had something to do with the design and writing of the Romances, but this matter is problematic because these plays, we know, were also performed at the Globe. Perhaps court masques, with their spectacle, prompted Shakespeare to write the Romances, which, indeed, contain many elements that correspond to masques. But again, we cannot be certain. Short of finding a handwritten autobiography by Shakespeare, we shall probably never know why these plays were written in the waning years of his professional career.

Studies continue, nevertheless, to posit answers, the latest full exploration being Gary Schmidgall's *Shakespeare and the Courtly Aesthetic*. Schmidgall, adding his own speculation about Shakespeare's motivation, writes:

> Shakespeare, a servant of the King and most likely a participant in the King's revels, could not have remained untouched by the Jacobean artistic efflorescence. My purpose in the following pages is to suggest ways the playwright might have been affected by the new fashions, and to observe the infuence of what might ᵤe called the new Jacobean royalism in the arts upon Shakespeare's working environment and, hence, upon his Late Plays.[4]

Schmidgall adds: "I find it plausible to imagine that he [Shakespeare] saw that the artistic mood of the time was changing and that different aesthetic fashions were catching on among the courtly avant-garde" (p. 43). Though this is not Dowden's "on the heights" theory, it has some of the same inherent problems; indeed, one might call this approach Shakespeare "on the bandwagon." Schmidgall suggests that with the establishment of the Stuart court the "literary iron age of 1600–04" had passed and "rose-colored spectacles" were put on, idealized heroes and heroines again predominating in literature (p. 44). Historically this view misleads since it ignores the satiric drama that spanned the first decade of James's reign; it also overlooks the personal attacks on James's policies and the growing cynicism about his reign.

Writing about the court masque, Schmidgall observes: "Glorification of the King and court was the *raison d'être* of the masque. It was an elaborate, pompous compliment to a social elite" (p. 137). But that is only half the story; for studies, such as those by Stephen Orgel, reveal that the masques could condemn as well as praise. "Because courtly art was obliged to reach happy conclusions," Schmidgall says, "it was essentially comic" (p. 145), history and tragedy thereby being of limited usefulness. What, then, does one make of the performances at court of a number of Shakespeare's tragedies? Schmidgall's view risks being simplistic both about the court and about Shakespeare. The Jacobean courtly aesthetic certainly warrants investigation. But whether Shakespeare embraced such a new fashion or resisted it is the question. The answer is more problematic than Schmidgall suggests.

Whatever the precise nature of the courtly aesthetic, we can recognize the obvious, that James and his family on the English throne offered a new experience for Shakespeare and his countrymen. I will attempt to establish the historical context in which the plays were written, primary emphasis being on the Stuart royal family and the royal families in the Romances. Shakespeare's pervasive interest in and preoccupation with families coalesce, I will argue, with the actual family of James. Awareness of the Stuart royal family helps explain these plays' fascination with politics and family matters.

Critical interest in Shakespeare's fictional families is on the increase, witness the several essays on the topic in the collection *Representing Shakespeare: New Psychoanalytic Essays.*[5] Attempting to survey the family in Shakespeare's drama, C. L. Barber writes in this collection: "Shakespeare's art is distinguished by the intensity of its investment in the human family, and especially in the continuity of the family across generations. This investment is extended out into society and up into the royal family" (p. 188). Barber explores, for example, the connection, especially in the tragedies, between the families there represented and "the religious worship of God and the

Holy Family" (p. 195). Barber's psychological focus is evident in his assessment of the Romances: "In the late romances, we have symbolic action that, instead of freeing sexuality from the ties of family, works to restore family ties by disassociating them from the threat of degradation by physical incest" (pp. 194–95). My approach will be historical rather than psychological, though neither rules out the other. Further, Louis Adrian Montrose has demonstrated Shakespeare's concern in *As You Like It* for problems in family relations, namely the tension between brothers and the position of the younger brother.[6] Montrose claims that Shakespeare is "not merely using something topical to get his comedy off to a lively start: the expression and resolution of sibling conflict and its social implications are integral to the play's form and function" (p. 33). Therefore, we may conclude with Montrose: "*As You Like It* is both a theatrical *reflection* of social conflict and a theatrical *source* of social conciliation" (p. 54). I think that the Romances are a theatrical reflection of the social circumstances of the Stuart royal family as they also portray the process of reconciliation.

Maynard Mack's lecture *Rescuing Shakespeare*, given at Stratford in August 1978, offers historical perspective on the families in Shakespeare. His focus is on the family "both as Shakespeare shapes it for his own structural and expressive purposes on stage and as it actually existed and functioned in the cities, towns, and villages of England, and in the manors and great houses of the squirearchy and aristocracy."[7] Mack proceeds by linking the families of the drama with actual examples from real life, focusing on such issues as life expectancy, average age at marriage, child-rearing customs, and married life. Mack's series of questions constitutes the heart of my own investigation:

> What, one wonders, were the vital interconnections of these two domesticities, historical and dramatic? At what points in which plays may one reasonably suppose that a contemporary spectator sensed cross-currents between the conflicts and configurations before him in the playhouse and those known from family life around him, or possibly from his own? Or to put these questions somewhat differently and in a form perhaps more manageable, what do we know about the family of history that might cast at least an oblique light on the Shakespearian family of art? (P. 6)

I believe that Mack has articulated the issues well, and I will attempt some answers to the question. My pervasive concern will be with the family of history and the family of art. Why? The answer lies in the assumption expressed in the conclusion of Mack's lecture: "Shakespeare keeps up an elusive but fascinating traffic between the world of history and the world of art, and . . . our chances of learning more about his achievement in the latter depend in large part on our learning more about the former" (p. 31). My approach differs from Mack's both because I do not propose to survey the canon and because I focus on the royal family of history and of art, an area unexplored by Mack.

One of the families of history that has a direct bearing on Shakespeare's family of art is, of course, his own family. I can only sketch some of the details that seem appropriate to the period of the Romances; for this information I depend primarily on S. Schoenbaum's *William Shakespeare: A Compact Documentary Life.*[8] This book reinforces the picture of William Shakespeare as playwright, entrepreneur, landowner, parent, and general middle-class citizen. (If there are any vestiges left somewhere of a romantic image of Shakespeare seated under a mulberry tree warbling his woodnotes wild, Schoenbaum's book should dispel such a notion.) My concern is with the fortunes of Shakespeare's family during the period of 1605 to 1613, the time that encompasses the last plays.

Without more information than we have, we are left to speculate about how the personal events of 1605–13 affected Shakespeare emotionally or artistically. Because so many important things did happen in his family during this period, it is far-fetched, if not perverse, to rule out some effect. As with many interesting issues involving artists, we remain in a state of teasing wonder. A simple rehearsal of facts, as provided by Schoenbaum's book, scarcely does justice to the presumed feelings of the artist, but of course we cannot know. What we can document is an undulating pattern of births and deaths, unmatched in any other period of Shakespeare's life.

These events center on his immediate family and the families of his sister, Joan Hart, and his brothers. In 1605, Joan and William Hart had their second child, Thomas; then, in 1607, their four-year-old daughter, Mary, died. Shakespeare's brother Edmund, apparently an occasional actor in London, was also buried in 1607 in late December; he was predeceased by his illegitimate son, who died in August. This was the same year in which Shakespeare's daughter Susanna married the physician John Hall of Stratford. Susanna gave birth in February 1608 to their only child, Elizabeth, who was to be the only grandchild Shakespeare would know in his lifetime. It is of at least passing interest to note that 1608 was the year in which King James's daughter Elizabeth officially arrived at court, having been residing at Combe Abbey in Warwickshire with the John Haringtons. Is it possible that Shakespeare's granddaughter was named for the princess, who resided nearby? Another nephew, Michael Hart, was born in 1608, which was also the year of the death of Shakespeare's mother, Mary. The birth of a granddaughter and death of his mother—profound evidence of the older generation passing away and the new one aborning. At the end of this period, Shakespeare's two remaining brothers died: Gilbert in February 1612, and Richard the following February (incidentally the time of the wedding of Princess Elizabeth to Frederick Elector Palatine).

These events in Shakespeare's family have been explicitly linked to the last phase of his dramatic career by several interpreters. R. E. Gajdusek, for example, finds in *Cymbeline*, particularly the story of Posthumus-Imogen, an analogue to Shakespeare's life. Posthumus's story, Gajdusek writes, "is a speculative history of Shakespeare, the Stratford boy become London wit, the wife-abandoning bard become incest-victim-cuckold who at last returns in disguise to rejoin his own."[9] Gajdusek suggests further that Shakespeare's return to Stratford and his close association with his daughters "was an active attempt to resolve in act what he was then at last attempting to resolve in art" (p. 127n), to "move his daughters into roles comparable to those he finds for them in the late plays." Under such circumstances life begins to imitate art.

Charles Hofling's task is no less than to explore "the psychological relationship of *Cymbeline* to its author."[10] For Hofling the play presents several matters of concern to "Shakespeare's own emotional life," especially the matter of the dramatist's relationship "with significant women" (p. 129). From his life several events stand out near the time of writing *Cymbeline:* the death of his mother (1608), the marriage of his daughter Susanna (1607), the return to his wife (which Hofling dates 1610—a dubious assumption), and even, with the publication of the Sonnets in 1609, some reminiscence of a relationship with the "Dark Lady." These events, plus concern for a male heir, pervade the final plays, especially *Cymbeline.*

Though I believe that the claims of Gajdusek and Hofling exceed the facts, I would not want to close out the possibility that Shakespeare's personal life found its way into his art, if not precisely in the terms indicated by some interpreters. Surely the births and deaths in Shakespeare's family resemble, if accidentally, the pattern of the

Romances. Though the final memorable image of these plays is the reunion of lost or separated families, we cannot forget the pain, suffering, and sometimes deaths that occur before that glorious final moment. The motto of these plays seems captured in the words of the Shepherd in *The Winter's Tale:* we meet with "things dying" and "with things new-born." So it is in Shakespeare's family: the family of history reflects the family of art. If we knew more about Shakespeare's personal life, we might find additional evidence for confirming the connection between his private life and his public art.

The historical family that occupies the center of this study is, of course, the royal family of James I; I will explore the connection between this particular family and Shakespeare's families of art in the Romances. Why should Shakespeare, or anyone else for that matter, have taken any special notice of the family of James? First, James was Shakespeare's official patron; the importance of this should be neither overestimated nor underestimated. But in 1603 the paths of Shakespeare and King James officially crossed when the dramatist's acting company came under royal patronage, to be known henceforth as the King's Men. Indeed, James had been in London scarcely a month when he took the unusual action, eventually bringing all the principal companies under royal patronage. Nothing in James's background fully prepares us for this official action regarding the public theaters, nor can we be sure of the precise implications or effects of this patronage. Of course, the King's Men performed at court, but that in itself is not unusual. And they were given red cloth with which to garb themselves as servants of the king's livery in order to be present at the magnificent royal entry of James into London, 15 March 1604, an extraordinary civic pageant by whatever measure one applies. Assessing the impact of royal patronage on the actors and the theater is one of the desirable but elusive goals of scholarship. Suffice it to say, Shakespeare could not have been unaware of or insensitive to his patron or to historical events, whatever he thought of them personally.

Like the general public, Shakespeare was probably struck by the simple fact of the advent of a royal family to the English throne. Lest this seem unremarkable, one need only recall that since Henry VIII, every English monarch had been childless. Edward VI and Mary left no child to succeed the royal parent, thereby dashing hope. With Elizabeth, of course, there had not even been a marriage, though negotiations for such continued far beyond the likely time for her to bear children. A kind of public grumpiness, induced by her own crankiness and the nagging realization that there was no clearly designated heir, set in during the last years of Elizabeth's reign. Only on her deathbed, or so the story goes, did Elizabeth give any feeble sign of who her successor should be, though, of course, Robert Cecil had been secretly paving the way for James for some time. Francis Bacon noted succinctly in a letter requesting gifts for the impending marriage of Princess Elizabeth in 1613: "Queen Elizabeth, Queen Mary, and King Edward had no children, and King Henry 8 died before his son was of the age of 15 or his daughters married."[11] A sense of incompleteness pervades such a statement. Suddenly, in 1603 a royal *family* occupies the throne—parents, two sons, and a daughter. Further, during the first years of James's reign, two more daughters, Sophia and Mary, were born, though both died in infancy. They were the first royal children born in England since 1537. Documents of the time reflect much excitement about the arrival of the family in the kingdom with particular interest in the royal births.

The first flush of enthusiasm for this Stuart family must surely have touched Shakespeare as it did his countrymen. Even the pattern of births and deaths, successes and failures observable in Shakespeare's family finds a strange parallel in James's family. What no one could have foreseen in the heady days of the spring of 1603 were the troubles that lay ahead for the king and his family: the Gunpowder Plot, the deaths of his two infant daughters, the unexpected and tragic death of Prince Henry, and James's ineptitude and waning popularity. Even the jubilant event of the wedding of Princess Elizabeth in early 1613 had its sad note; for she and her husband, Frederick, disappeared into the mists of the Thirty Years' War in Europe, she to become known as the "Winter Queen" and destined never to return to her beloved England during her father's lifetime. Thomas Fuller, commenting on the events of the winter of 1612–13, offers an image appropriate to the theater and the royal family:

> *One generation goeth and another generation cometh, but the earth remaineth for ever:* the Stage stands, the Actors alter. Prince HENRY's *Funerals* are followed with the Prince PALATINE's *Nuptials*, solemnized with great State, in hopes of happiness to both persons, though sad in the event thereof, and occasioning great revolution in Christendome.[12]

These poignant events vitiate the great hope and expectation that greeted the royal family's arrival in England—such is the plight of this family in its first decade in England.

Shakespeare has his eye on family relationships from the beginning of his career, families being fit subjects for drama from the Greeks onward. To generalize, family matters seem of less consequence in the early comedies than later; by the time of the major tragedies, they are of paramount concern—one thinks immediately of *King Lear*, the most intense tragedy of family relationships. Shakespeare could not, of course, write his history plays without focusing on families, since that is in fact the nature of English history itself. Parent-child relationships, however, do not receive much exploration in the histories; Shakespeare casts a broader net of kinship. In the Romances, on the other hand, Shakespeare focuses on parent-child ties with an intensity matching that of the tragedies but with happy results.

What is initially striking about the Romances, as distinct from the other plays, is the age of the father character. In no other group of plays, apart from the histories, can we be quite as sure. Lear tells us how old he is; but the ages of Claudius, Polonius, Brabantio, and Volumnia are difficult to determine. The ages of children help determine likely parental age in the Romances. Perdita in *The Winter's Tale* is sixteen at the play's end; and Leontes, probably forty-four or forty-six, a point reinforced by Leontes' early references in the play to the twenty-three years since he was roughly the age of Mamillius, thereby making him approximately thirty at the play's beginning. Marina and Miranda in *Pericles* and *The Tempest*, respectively, are fifteen, leading one to speculate that at the end of the plays their fathers are comparable in age to Leontes. In *Henry VIII* the king would be forty-two at the time of the birth of Elizabeth. *Cymbeline* is rather different—as it is in many ways—because Imogen is already married at the play's opening. One notes that these fathers are more or less the age that Shakespeare was when he wrote these plays. And, one can add, these fathers are also comparable to King James, who is two years younger than Shakespeare.

I think that Shakespeare has a special identification with Leontes, Pericles, Prospero, Henry VIII, and perhaps Cymbeline. Somewhere, at least on the edges of his consciousness, is the link to James, also a father of similar age. Like his countrymen, before 1603 Shakespeare had never known a royal family, but now this family occupies a position of major importance in the national life. Through their triumphs, problems, and failures, Shakespeare sees how an actual royal family functions; he absorbs their experience and gives it artistic shape in his fictional family of art. He does not, I think, set out consciously to imitate the Stuart royal family but to re-present it in these last plays.

John Keats wrote to the family of his brother George in a letter of 19 February 1819: "A Man's life of any worth is a continual allegory— and very few eyes can see the Mystery of his life—a life like the scriptures, figurative—which such people can no more make out than they can the hebrew Bible. . . . Shakespeare led a life of Allegory; his works are the comments on it—."[13] That Shakespeare the man is in his works is undeniable, but precisely where and how is the mystery. What did Shakespeare think about current events or prominent persons? In what follows, I will discuss particularly the topical approach to the Romances.

Why should these plays in particular evoke a response that attempts to see them in their immediate historical context? I think there are several reasons, beginning with a point already made that James was Shakespeare's patron and may have had an influence, at least indirectly, on the plays written in the latter part of Shake-speare's career. We know also that most of the Romances received court performances, *The Tempest* and *The Winter's Tale* being produced at court at least twice. Court masques illustrate the royal family's immediate involvement in drama, because they actively participated in them. These masques often consciously comment on the family, either with compliment or with criticism; in any event, they reflect current events. In other words, both dramatic climate and tradition respond to the royal family.

Historical events of considerable importance concerning James's family also correspond to the time of the Romances: I refer to the arrival at court in 1608 of Princess Elizabeth and the investiture of Prince Henry as Prince of Wales in 1610, both events attracting much attention and comment. Births of royal children occur here in the family of history and in the family of art. One of the distinguishing characteristics of the Romances is the birth of children: Marina, Perdita, and Elizabeth (in *Henry VIII*). Such procreation receives no comparable emphasis in the rest of Shakespeare's canon. Themes that emerge from the Romances also correspond to ideas and facts of the first decade of James's reign: the themes of deliverance, peaceful succession, royal lineage, union of the kingdom, expectations that rest with the younger generation, and concern for the marriage of the eligible royal children. Not surprisingly, then, the Romances have attracted topical investigation and analysis.

Other plays have been approached in this light as well, particularly *Measure for Measure*. Josephine Waters Bennett's book on that play epitomizes topical investigation, and I cite it as an example of this critical method. Stated simply, her idea rests on the assumption that *Measure for Measure* "contains much topical matter which indicates that it was written expressly for King James, and for this particular occasion [i.e., the beginning of the Christmas Revels, 1604]."[14] That it was performed as the first play in that season of entertainment may or may not be significant; one notes, for example, that *The Merchant of Venice* was performed at court on 10 February 1605 and again on the twelfth, apparently because James liked it so much. Should this fact evoke an investigation of this play as well? Bennett creates needless difficulty by arguing that *Measure for Measure* was written "expressly" for James; on this point there can be no proof.

For Bennett, *Measure for Measure* is topical on two counts: Shakespeare refers to his own works within the drama, and he embodies ideas of James in the Duke. Bennett's summary indicates the direction of her analysis:

> With Shakespeare as the Duke, his various styles of speech glance
> humorously at other plays he has written, and his principles of
> government can be borrowed out of the King's book [*Basilicon Doron*]
> without any danger of his seeming to impersonate the King. . . . [He
> produces] a play which exemplifies the highest ideals of justice and
> mercy which King James had prescribed for "myself and mine." Seen
> in this light, the play fits together like a nest of boxes, with
> Shakespeare, the master-dramatist, directing it as well as acting in it.
> (Pp. 148–49)

Would that *Measure for Measure* were so susceptible to this kind of unraveling or decoding. That the play may on occasion echo some of James's ideas on government does not demonstrate that it was written expressly for the king.

Taking to task this topical approach—and many others—Richard Levin analyzes in some detail what he refers to as "The King James Version" of *Measure for Measure*.[15] His attack is unrelenting and sometimes harsh. Among his targets is Bennett's book. He points out, for example, that those interpreters of the play who set out to find a link between ideas in the play and James's *Basilicon Doron* inevitably find such connections, ignoring the commonplace nature of these ideas on government and conduct. Even the absence of verbal parallels, for those unable to locate them, can be—indeed, has been—explained away (see p. 176). The circularity and reductive nature of some of the arguments Levin easily documents; he concludes:

> If, then, this is the strongest occasionalist case yet made for any play written by Shakespeare or his contemporaries, we can be spared the trouble of investigating the others. They all must fall with the "King James Version" of *Measure for Measure,* and so, too, must the entire approach, since this is the best it has to offer. Unlike the other approaches we have considered, there would seem to be nothing that can be said in its favor. (P. 191)

With this all-inclusive denunciation ringing in my ears, it takes not a little temerity to proceed to build a case for a connection between the family of James and Shakespeare's last plays. I think, however, that it is possible to negotiate successfully between the Scylla of doubt and the Charybdis of confidence about the links of James to Shakespeare's plays. Bennett presents, admittedly, a weak case; but the popularity of James's *Basilicon Doron* should not be discounted nor court performances discredited in interpreting *Measure for Measure.* Levin assumes, falsely I believe, that lurking behind these "occasionalist" attempts is the tacit but unspoken notion that the plays are more valuable if they have a presumed connection with a royal audience. Somehow we apparently want to believe, according to Levin, that Shakespeare moved in aristocratic circles and that, through his plays, he conducted "a kind of private conversation with the monarch" (p. 193). Levin is thereby in danger of trying to read the minds of critics, potentially guilty of the excesses he has so vigorously castigated.

A more compelling recent reading of *Measure for Measure* and its political/topical context is that provided by Jonathan Goldberg, who throughout his brilliant study of the relationship of King James to literature argues that language and politics "are mutually constitutive, that society shapes and is shaped by the possibilities in its language and discursive practices" (*James I,* p. xi). Goldberg also contends that the theater "was the public forum in which the royal style could be most fully displayed" (p. xiii). It is with such ideas that one may approach *Measure for Measure* and find in it not exact identification, as Bennett attempts, but rather in the Duke a representation of Shakespeare's "powers as playwright as coincident with the powers of the sovereign" (p. 232). Goldberg writes: "No exact replay of James at all, the play yet manages to catch at central concerns: in the disguised Duke, the king's divided self; in the relations between privacy and the public, the play between internal and external theaters of conscience; in the Duke's actions, the combination of absence and presence through which James claimed authority" (p. 235). For Goldberg this play provides the "clearest emblem for the relationship of literature and politics in the Jacobean period" because of its concern for representation (p. 239). The ambiguity that we may find in *Measure for Measure* is at one with the ambiguity of politics itself, a quality at the heart of political power.

Aware that Levin is out to debunk all historical criticism by dwelling on its shortcomings and that he does not like the idea of "themes" in dramas anyway, we need to see, with Goldberg and others, that drama, Shakespeare's in particular, is a constant interplay of ideas and action. The plays invite our contemplation about what and how they mean. Surely the reason that people still go to the theater to watch Shakespeare's plays is not necessarily to admire their structure but, rather, to be captured by the entire experience—the characters, the action, the poetry, and, yes, the ideas. As Maynard Mack has suggested, it is just possible that historical awareness may cast a light, however oblique, on the accomplishment of Shakespeare's art.

Thus far the only book-length excursion into the topicality of the Romances is Frances Yates's *Majesty and Magic in Shakespeare's Last Plays*,[16] originally a series of lectures given at University College, London. Dame Frances has for some time been bold in her claims; this book is no exception. This new title of the American edition reflects fairly accurately its subject matter: it is about the sovereign and his family as seen in the Romances, and it is about magic, specifically in *The Tempest*. Underlying the argument of most of Yates's book is the assumption of an Elizabethan revival in the Jacobean period, a deliberate harkening back to the earlier time, what Yates calls "an archaising revival" (p. 79). Such a movement centers on James's children, Prince Henry and Princess Elizabeth.

That the Jacobeans indulged in a growing nostalgia for Queen Elizabeth's reign with each passing year of James's rule is quite plausible. That is not, of course, quite the same thing as claiming a deliberate harkening back to the golden age of Elizabeth. Nor does such a presumed movement necessarily reveal anything about the shaping of Shakespeare's Romances. The truth may reside somewhere between Gary Schmidgall's idea of a new courtly aesthetic and

Yates's Elizabethan revival. Each is guilty of a partial truth that ignores inconvenient contradictory evidence. Yates's zeal gets the better of her when she claims that the famous "Rainbow Portrait" of Queen Elizabeth at Hatfield House, generally dated around 1600, "may reflect Princess Elizabeth as a bride, with her hair hanging down. . . . The intensely religious character of the allegory would remain extremely apposite for Princess Elizabeth as a bride representing a pure church" (p. 34). Unless there is some evidence, not mentioned, that the portrait is not of Queen Elizabeth and that its likely date is 1613, one has to regard this claim as a flight of fancy—a seeking after an Elizabethan revival with a vengeance.

An examination of Yates's argument for *Cymbeline* will suffice to indicate her topical approach to these plays; indeed, she has little to say about *Pericles* and *The Winter's Tale*, and her discussion of *The Tempest* strays off into magic. Part of the process is to identify James with Cymbeline and the three children of Cymbeline with James's children. Not much is said about Cymbeline's wicked queen. Yates writes: "If the youths in the cave [Cymbeline's long-lost two sons] called to mind Prince Henry and his brother, would not Imogen call to mind their sister, the Princess Elizabeth, expected to be the 'mother of nations'?" (p. 51)—possibly, but probably not. For every spark of illumination that such an identification may set off, dozens of sparks are snuffed out, robbing the play of its richness by reducing it to such terms. Yates sums up her view:

> I suggest that *Cymbeline* was written about 1611 when the masques were building up the British History in relation to James and his children, and that it was revised in 1612 to make it fit the rejoicings over Princess Elizabeth's engagement but *before the death of Prince Henry*. . . . When, at the end of *Cymbeline*, King Cymbeline-James presides over a family consisting of two sons, a daughter, a son-in-law, the play would reflect a moment in the history of James's family before the death of Henry but after it became certain that Elizabeth would marry the Elector Palatine. (P. 52)

Even when Yates acknowledges that the identifications do not fit very precisely, she can explain that nuisance away: "Shakespeare did not have time to rewrite the whole play" (p. 53). One question: where is the evidence for this revision; what, if anything, in the text suggests revision? A later statement is breathtaking in its implications: "Reading through this volume [*Calendar of State Papers Venetian*], one can play the game of choosing the date at which Shakespeare wrote *Cymbeline*, and the date at which he revised it" (p. 59). If the matter is merely one of "playing the game" of picking a date, then one need not put any credence in Yates's own arguments about the date of *Cymbeline* and its alleged revision. This rather cavalier approach sullies the accomplishment that such a topical analysis might produce.

One's confidence does not increase when one notes that Yates consistently has Prince Henry's death (or, as she calls it rather quaintly at one point, "Prince Henry's early disappearance" [p. 57]), on the wrong day and at the wrong age. Symptomatic of a fundamental problem in Yates's analysis is this claim: "The new interpretation of *Cymbeline* would seem to indicate that Shakespeare was a whole-hearted supporter of Prince Henry, and of Princess Elizabeth, the phoenix of a new Elizabethan age, leaders of the younger generation" (p. 59). Her assertion takes us beyond topical identification, itself questionable, to a claim about Shakespeare's apparent belief—a procedure fraught with dangers. Yates is right to seek out the historical context that lies behind the Romances, but she claims a precision that is unwarranted, I think. Cymbeline's three children superficially parallel the three royal children of James; but to press for identification of the two sets strains the evidence, risks diminishing the art of the play, and ignores the many ways in which the children are in fact not parallel.

Since 1969, Glynne Wickham has been publishing essays on the Romances and their topicality for the family of James. Two pieces on *The Winter's Tale* in 1969 began Wickham's investigation: the first explored the sixteen-year gap between the execution of Mary, Queen of Scots, and the accession of her son to the English throne and a similar gap in the play;[17] the second attempted to make the case for the play's having been written for the festivities in conjunction with the investiture of Prince Henry as Prince of Wales in 1610.[18] In the latter essay, Wickham suggests that Shakespeare "would either choose or be required" to make a contribution to the entertainments (*TLS*, 1456). Wickham's "evidence" consists of masques and pageants of the time that develop the theme of union, seen embodied in James. That *The Winter's Tale* echoes this theme is arguable, but this does not demonstrate anything about the likely date of the play. All we know on that score is that Forman saw it performed at the Globe in May 1611 and that it was performed at court in November 1611 and again for the wedding festivities in February 1613. Nothing that Wickham points out gives assurance that the play was written in the summer of 1610 as a contribution to Prince Henry's investiture. Wickham begs the question on this issue.

Constituting the linchpin to Wickham's topical approach is his essay published in *Shakespeare Survey* in 1973.[19] What Wickham offers, using *King Lear* as his starting point, is an explanation for the turn in the Jacobean period from revenge tragedy to the mode of tragicomedy, as in Shakespeare's Romances. Though Schmidgall accounts for this change in light of a new courtly aesthetic partly influenced by Italian models, Wickham argues that it comes about as a result of the "political consciousness" of the British. Three facts are crucial: the British have been "saved from foreign invasion and civil war by the peaceful accession of James I in 1603, by the timely discovery of the Gunpowder Plot in 1605, and the final ratification of the Union of the two Crowns by Act of Parliament in 1608" (p. 36). The perception of these events as miraculous leads to a "literature of a new messianic vision, with King James and his family at the centre of it" (p. 36). That Shakespeare "should have elected to co-operate in the active propagation of these ideas, *as far as his artistic conscience as poet and dramatist would permit*" (p. 37) strikes Wickham as being natural.

His important italicized qualifier lets Wickham off the hook of suggesting that Shakespeare rather mindlessly indulged in propaganda to suit the whim of the king. But in fact, what can we possibly know about Shakespeare's "artistic conscience"?—easy to imagine but impossible to explain or document. Wickham does not face adequately the limitations of our knowledge about what James's patronage meant to Shakespeare. Having Shakespeare elect to cooperate in "the active propagation" of themes that celebrate James and his family suggests for the dramatist a program that, I think, the facts do not support. In effect, Wickham offers another version of why Shakespeare wrote the Romances when he did.

Wickham makes much out of the presumed Union of the kingdoms by Act of Parliament in 1608; union in fact is the major theme that he sees working in these plays and the most immediate cause for the composition of them. Historical or literary events are gauged according to the date of this Union; thus, Heywood's *Troia Britannica* "was published a year after Parliament's final ratification of the Union" (p. 41). The Brutus/Troynovant myth that Wickham views as important in these plays takes a different shape after the Union: "In this sense Shakespeare's *King Lear* may be taken as the prologue to what he was later to do with the story *after* the

Gunpowder Plot had been averted and *after* Parliament had ratified the Act of Union" (p. 42). There is one fundamental and crucial problem with all of this: Parliament never approved such a Union.

Though from James's accession there had been much talk about an official Union ratified by Parliament, devoutly desired by James, there was in fact no such action taken by Parliament. The only union was the inherent one brought about because a Scottish king now sat on the English throne—a kind of de facto union but certainly not a de jure one. Investigation into this matter reveals year after year of debate in Parliament on the subject, much strategic maneuvering to scuttle the whole issue, much dragging of legislative feet, but no Act of Union. As Wallace Notestein reports, in one of the standard studies of Parliament in the early Jacobean years: "When Sir William Maurice, at the beginning of the session of 1610, brought up the question of union he was greeted by whistling. That subject the Commons were not inclined to revive."[20] So, two years after Wickham says there was an Act of Union, here is the House hooting at such a prospect; James was left to whistle in the dark. Official union by act of Parliament did not come until the eighteenth century.

Somewhat like those who move from James's *Basilicon Doron* to verbal parallels in *Measure for Measure*, Wickham sees in James's speeches to Parliament ideas and language captured in Shakespeare's Romances. For instance, he quotes part of the speech by James to Parliament in 1608 and concludes: "This is not the language of revenge tragedy, but it is the language of *Cymbeline, The Winter's Tale* and *The Tempest*" (p. 42). Since James is discussing his favorite topics of peace and union, one cannot reasonably expect to hear the language of revenge tragedy; therefore, there is no remarkable connection to the Romances. The problem is that Wickham demonstrates no actual verbal parallels. Of course, it is possible that the dramatist might pick up a phrase or an idea and echo it in his plays, but that must be substantiated in some way.

One thread that runs throughout Wickham's analyses is topical identification. In *Pericles,* for example, Shakespeare sought to provide audiences "with a romance that corresponded in its general shape with the hardships endured by James before attaining to the succession, the escape of King, Queen and royal children from assassination, and, finally, with the reunification both of the British Isles under a single crown and of father, mother, and daughter in Whitehall" (p. 44). This analysis ignores the sources that Shakespeare presumably used for this play. Like Yates on *Cymbeline,* Wickham says that "with

Imogen and the two boys out of Wales, audiences are expected to associate the Princess Elizabeth, Prince Henry, and Prince Charles" (p. 44). In his most recent essay on *Cymbeline*, Wickham identifies James with Cymbeline, without, one should note, ever citing Yates's work:

> James, like Cymbeline, spoke to the ambassadors of continental Europe with the voice of "the Empire of Great Britain"; and James, like Cymbeline, was in a position to refuse or sanction the marriage of his children to the heirs to Europe's crowns. Thus James, in real life, could aspire, like Cymbeline in the play, to be thought of and discussed in the familiar imperial imagery of Renaissance iconography.[21]

Certainly in a Shakespearean drama the matter of a father's having a hold over his children on the subject of marriage is commonplace. It remains unclear how Cymbeline's wicked queen fits these identifications. If James is Cymbeline and Princess Elizabeth is Imogen, we immediately have problems, because Imogen, who is already married, is banished by the king, none of which corresponds to the Stuart family.

This identification process carries over into the discussion of *The Winter's Tale*. Leontes in the second part of the play becomes James-like because he is "the second Brutus whose deeds of atonement as a bringer of peace and the provider of tombs and painted statues . . . have prepared the way for a double reunion" (*Shakespeare Survey*, p. 46). This reunion is the return of Hermione to Leontes and "the marriage of the heir-apparent to Great Britain, alias Perdita, lost by the first Brutus but restored in the fullness of time by Divine Providence to become Prince Henry's bride" (p. 46). It is difficult to unravel this because the analysis seems a bit confused between allegorical concepts and actual figures. If Perdita, the daughter of Leontes/James, marries Florizel/Henry, don't we encounter incest?

In *The Tempest* Miranda is Princess Elizabeth, Prospero is James, and Juno, in the masque, is Queen Anne. "The pressure," Wickham writes in another essay, "on audiences of the time to recognize within the figure of Juno that of Queen Anne was overwhelming."[22] If overwhelming, why has no one recognized it? In "Prospero's faith and magic powers deployed in substituting forgiveness, peace and reconcilement for revenge and the consequent tragedies for mankind of recurrent deaths and everlasting war" one may see the link to James (p. 12). In Caliban's plot may be "glimpsed" the threat of the

Gunpowder Plot. Prospero's island, somewhere in the Mediterranean, is in fact the Great Britain ''of James's making on whose shores the naval forces of its Catholic enemies were wrecked by storms, but . . . by the process of dynastic alliances in the marriage of children, reconcilement of former differences is to be achieved and a prosperous future ensured for all'' (p. 12). Surely if James understood the plays in this manner, he must have been quite pleased. Wickham's enumeration of themes in the Romances and his exploration of topicality in these plays are valuable contributions; some of his ideas I will pursue. He strays when he pushes the evidence too far, especially in the process of identification; but he does compel us to examine the last plays in light of their historical and dramatic contexts.

In view of what Levin would surely call the ''King James Version of the Romances,'' exemplified in the work of Yates and Wickham, one might ask Muriel Bradbrook's question: ''How then are we to read Shakespeare's last plays? As direct celebrations of the royal family, as suggested by Glynne Wickham and . . . by Frances Yates?''[23] Her answer points to one of the vexing problems of this analytical method: ''To me . . . they have too distinct an individual life to be treated as variants on the masque, emblems of Prince Henry, vehicles of Rosicrucian doctrine. The difficulty with such theories is that they can neither be proved nor disproved. The eye of faith will detect such latent meanings everywhere.''

The fundamental problem with the approach of Wickham and Yates is that they fail to acknowledge how Shakespeare uses his materials, whether these are other literary works or historical characters and events. In identifying characters from the Romances with members of James's family, critics ignore the process by which Shakespeare mediates his sources, depending on them and rejecting them in the same work. To insist on identification is to portray the artist as one who unimaginatively accepts his extraliterary materials and who reflects history in a narrow, literal manner. With effort and learning we can, as Rosalie Colie observes, ''see what went in and, from that recognition, can even begin to see *why* certain things went in.''[24] We also learn, of course, what is left out, thereby seeing how the artist differs from his presumed sources.

Avoiding the process of identification, I will instead regard James and his family as a ''text'' that Shakespeare ''read'' when writing the Romances; this text joins other texts, such as John Gower's *Confessio Amantis* and Robert Greene's *Pandosto*, in the fabric of the author's creative imagination. I agree with Maynard Mack's assessment that "discussions of Shakespeare's sources . . . have erred by defining the term too narrowly, paying almost exclusive attention to specific books . . . while virtually ignoring larger, admittedly vaguer, but equally cogent influences, which frequently determine the way in which the specific source is used."[25] Just as Shakespeare does not merely duplicate literary sources, so he does not set out to imitate or copy the royal family. The issue is not so much mimesis as it is re-presentation. Part of the cue for my approach is in Jonathan Goldberg's idea that "the aim of the Jacobean theater is not mimesis, representation, but *re*-presentation."[26] Such an argument is, of course, the focus of Howard Felperin's book on this topic. Felperin writes:

> For mimesis, the illusion of reality traditionally ascribed to literature in general and epitomized in Shakespeare's plays, arises not from the direct imitation of "nature" or "life" or "experience" but, as I try to show, from the *re-presentation*, with a difference, of inherited models or constructs of "nature," "life," and "experience." For the notion of "re-presentation," as something distinct from a presentation on the one hand and from a copy on the other, depends, like the notion of modernity, on the idea of difference after all.[27]

Shakespeare differs from his sources, whether literary or historical—a point insufficiently acknowledged by Wickham and Yates.

My approach to the Romances can be called "textual," but not in the bibliographical or editorial sense. The royal family does not constitute the typical written text; for I do not insist, as Wickham does, that Shakespeare read James's speeches. Rather, I argue that its actions and the attention afforded this family constitute a living text, writ large in the public consciousness. Given that James was acutely and self-consciously aware of his role as performer in the theater of the state, it seems all the more appropriate to think of the family as a kind of dramatic text. As Goldberg observes: "The theater pervaded the king's sense of self and role, and provides a defining term for the bifurcations that mark his language."[28] In his 1620 masque *News from the New World*, Ben Jonson links James and the idea of a text: " 'Read him as you would do the book / Of all perfection' (lines 310-11). The maker of the text is a text. James is written, a book with a full name: 'Say but James' (line 345), and all is said" (Goldberg, p. 65). By extension I suggest that the whole royal family constitutes a text, not because they, like James, have published, but because they contain material, experiences that one could know.

Texts have often been known without being literally read. One recalls that masses of people learned Biblical texts for centuries not from reading them but from hearing them. In a similar fashion they "read" the stained glass windows in churches. Medieval drama, without widely distributed texts, survived in part because people standing in the streets interpreted what they saw and heard, not what they read. Half of Shakespeare's plays were not available in printed texts during his lifetime; audiences nevertheless "read" them through performances of them. Pericles, in Shakespeare's play, looking at Antiochus's daughter, says of her: "Her face the book of praises, where is read / Nothing but curious pleasures . . ." (I.i.16–17). Pericles interprets this daughter as he will also read and interpret the riddle that Antiochus gives him. Perhaps Shakespeare through Pericles offers another hint for regarding James's family as a text. Coming to the realization of the sin of Antiochus and his daughter, Pericles observes: "Who has a book of all that monarchs do, / He's more secure to keep it shut than shown . . ." (95–96). My argument is that Shakespeare had access to just such a "book" for the royal family; he read it and used it. We, too, need to read the Romances, as they were doubtless written, in light of this historical, actual text.

Terms that describe my emphasis include "contextual" and "intertextual." Subsequent chapters offer extended treatments of James's family and of the other comic drama of the period so that we can appreciate the "text" of the royal family and understand Shakespeare's dramatic context. By "intertextual" I mean the common-sense understanding of that term: that is, the relationship among various texts. But there is a broader meaning, articulated by Jonathan Culler, which seems appropriate to my enterprise: "What makes possible reading and writing is not a single anterior action which serves as origin and moment of plenitude but an open series of acts, both identifiable and lost, which work together to constitute something like a language."[29] Regarding the Stuart royal family as a text is compatible with this understanding that all kinds of texts may be at work in a single poem or drama. No privileged texts, absolutely ruling out competing texts, exist; nor are there autonomous texts; all are dependent on pre-texts, written or observed.

We may reach Felperin's conclusion: "From the point of view of the audience, every work becomes a *déjà vu*, or as Roland Barthes puts it in another context, a *déjà lu*, and simultaneously a *jamais vu* or *jamais lu*" (p. 42). Standing in the Globe Theatre in the first audiences or attending today's modern theaters, spectators probably have a basis for understanding what unfolds on the stage. At the same time, these spectators see things that differ from what they know of the texts or from their expectations. We may come to regard the fiction of the drama, as Norman Rabkin suggests, "all at once as mere storytelling and realer than life itself."[30] The Romances evoke such a response.

These late plays are not mysteries to be decoded; they are not plays with some hidden allegory or myth to be exposed if we can just make the right topical analysis. If these plays are mysteries, it is because they show us a mystery about life and death, and they include the active involvement of the supernatural. Uppermost in my mind is Maynard Mack's question: "What do we know about the family of history that might cast at least an oblique light on the Shakespearian family of art?" What I will argue is that Shakespeare takes the experiences of the actual royal family (the "text"), internalizes them, and creates his fictional royal families, a new "text" that differs from the original. The events and characters in the plays may at moments resemble the actual royal family, but that hardly seems Shakespeare's purpose. I do not think the Romances constitute some kind of conversation with the sovereign. Indeed, if James and the other family members paid much attention to the performances of the Romances that they saw, they may have been aware of the discrepancy between these fictional royal families and themselves.

Shakespeare clearly offers a rather idealized view of his royal families, though this is not to say, of course, that they are without strife and difficulty. Shakespeare's text may contain an implicit criticism of the Stuart royal family, a claim hard to substantiate but not far-fetched. I think that one of the principal elements that Shakespeare derived from the historical royal family was a strong emphasis on the politics of the family, an emphasis, interestingly, not found in Shakespeare's other sources for these plays. Other themes in the late plays reflect topical ideas or events in a manner not apparent in the traditionally accepted literary sources. My task will be to interpret Shakespeare's plays in light of their contextual relationship to the drama of the era and of their intertextual relationship to James's family.

Gower tells us in the opening Chorus of *Pericles* that he has come "To sing a song that old was sung." Throughout the Romances, Shakespeare is forever singing an old song cast in the sometimes primitive, archaic mode of romance. Whatever else one may say, these plays certainly give the lie to any naïve expectations of literary history that the artist will move from crude materials to some kind of sophisticated naturalism. As Felperin notes, ''we should expect to encounter more fossils at the beginning of his twenty-year career than at the end'' (p. 58); but in fact, Shakespeare is more archaic at the end than at the beginning. In the old songs of romance, Shakespeare found a compatible mode for singing his new song, an overlay of old fiction and new or topical reality. If, as I suggest, Shakespeare re-presents the Stuart royal family in these plays, then romance seems to be especially appropriate, for it is capable of rendering both conflict and triumph in the families. Both the idyllic and the demonic night world of romance, articulated by Northrop Frye,[31] inhere in the fictions of these plays and in the actual world of the Stuart royal family. Surely part of the energy, strength, and beauty of these late plays grows precisely out of the intertextual relationship among the many sources for the plays. The open-ended nature of romance, lacking the awful finality of tragedy, corresponds to the lack of closure in the royal family: it is still very much in process as Shakespeare writes—a living, moving text, to be read afresh each new day.

From Pericles' quest in Antioch for a wife, so that he might propagate ''an issue,'' to Henry VIII's presence at the baptism of his daughter Elizabeth, Shakespeare examines the politics of royal families in the Romances. What I will be demonstrating is the pervasive quality of politics in these plays and how the political issues are inextricably linked to the royal family. The most prominent political issue is dynastic, the need for an heir and clear successor. With varying degrees of emphasis, each Romance confronts this fundamental political-familial problem. That James clearly had heirs and therefore offered an apparent future order for the kingdom may have prompted Shakespeare to explore this matter in much greater detail than he found in his generally acknowledged sources. That such security could fall apart is also evident in James's family: the death of Prince Henry and the marriage of Elizabeth completely redefined the line of anticipated succession. Each Romance ends with having the matter of succession clarified. Nothing reveals Shakespeare's political interest more, even though his fictions may be set in some remote time or place. The royal children redeem their kingdoms by providing much-desired stability. Like King James himself, the royal fathers in the Romances are both rulers and parents/husbands. Even at the most poignant moments of reunion of separated families, political issues intrude.

I believe, contrary to Levin, that awareness of this kind of historical context or topicality can expand and enrich our appreciation of Shakespeare's artistry, for we will see how the dramatist creates his fictional world out of the several texts available to him. Though these plays seem to be about the past, they in fact confront the present and the future. Like King James, Shakespeare was a father (and grandfather) in his mid forties, well beyond the usual life expectancy. From the vantage point of age, Shakespeare decides to peer into the political future, drawing assurance from the prospect of orderly succession and at the same time recognizing the fragile nature of such an assumed process. Only by perceiving the Stuart royal family re-presented in these plays can we apprehend their immediacy. Part of the achievement of the Romances derives from the blending of romance and political quest, the latter clarified, I believe, by knowledge of James's family.

The next chapter will focus on James and his family: James, Anne, Henry, Elizabeth, Charles, and, to some extent, Arbella Stuart—their personalities, attitudes, conflicts, and activities. Strain and confict, for example, are apparent in the relationship between Anne and James, who, for all of James's sage advice on the subject, were not particularly successful in their marriage, notwithstanding the opinion of one mid-seventeenth-century writer that they were a "matchless pair." The royal children occupied the attention and writings of many, the initial delight being that there were children, clear potential successors to the king. In a subsequent chapter, I will establish the dramatic context in which Shakespeare wrote the Romances. I will be examining in particular the other major strain of Jacobean comedy, the satiric drama, especially the works of Ben Jonson and Thomas Middleton. Certainly one of the main targets of the satiric drama is the institution of marriage and family. In these plays, children, when they exist, are generally insignificant, and family relationships corrupted (one thinks particularly of a play like Middleton's *A Chaste Maid in Cheapside*). The final section is an analysis of the Romances themselves. Primarily I will pursue the intertwined issues of politics and family. Because these are noble or royal families, one sees recurrent concern for the matter of succession, as one also finds the unmistakable expectation that rests with the next generation. Here, surely, the family of art resembles the royal family of history.

Since, as Jonathan Goldberg notes, the term "theater" derives from a Greek word meaning "to view" or "to see," it is appropriate to think of it as a place of speculation, of spectators, and of spectacle

(*James I,* p. 148). The Romances contain much spectacle and many spectators; I will provide the speculation. But we must remember that the idea of "conjecture" is only one of the meanings of the word "speculation." Our English word comes from the Latin and means to "spy out, watch, examine, observe." The Latin word "*specula*" means a "look-out, a watch-tower" (OED). From our vantage point of history we can peer backwards and speculate about the relationship of James's family to Shakespeare's last plays. The theater itself, I am suggesting, invites such searching out, such observation. The plays, I argue (to expose another dimension of the same Latin root), hold the mirror up to history and current events. As we see through the glass darkly, we may observe the sometimes elusive, fitful images and outlines of members of the Jacobean royal family. What we will see clearly is the general outline of the royal family and politics, the family's domestic and public life. This book, then, is a book of speculation.

Part of the justification for my approach is our distance from the past; we no longer immediately know what family life was like then, and we know little about royal families in particular. And yet, that was Shakespeare's context in which his daily life, both inside and outside the theater, collided with interest in and concern for the Stuart family, which was occupying the English throne. If I seem at moments to traffic in uncertainties about the precise connection of the family of James to the plays, that is because the subject is inherently problematical. To insist, as some have done, on seeing one-to-one identifications or on viewing the plays as consciously designed to celebrate the king and to perpetuate favorable myths about him is to lose sight of the complexity of Shakespeare's art and circumstances.

That we frequently need help in understanding the past is apparent in Peter Laslett's statement: "Time was when the whole of life went forward in the family, in a circle of loved, familiar faces, known and fondled objects, all to human size. That time has gone for ever. It makes us very different from our ancestors."[32] As we approach the end of the twentieth century, the institution of the family seems in disarray and under attack, the experiences of past centuries of families a vague recollection at best. As L. P. Hartley writes in his novel *The Go-Between:* "The past is a foreign country: they do things differently there."[33] As we journey together in the pages that follow, we will visit that foreign country of the past, not because we are antiquarians, but because we seek illumination, however oblique, on Shakespeare's art. I hope that the journey will strain no one's faith.

2

The Royal Family

"All I say is, kings is kings, and you got to
make allowances. Take them all round, they're
a mighty ornery lot. It's the way they're raised."
—Mark Twain, *The Adventures of Huckleberry Finn*

When King James I ascended the English throne, he brought
with him a metaphor that was to prevail at least during the
early part of his reign, namely that he was "father" of the country.
For James the state but reflected the construct of his own family, of
which he was proud father. Public focus thus shifted from Elizabeth,
an unmarried, childless sovereign, to one already married and father
of three living children. The appearance of a royal *family* in England
captured public attention and imagination, an initial asset that James
was to exploit. This chapter explores historical ideas about families
and the political and domestic life of the Stuart royal family from their
arrival in England to 1613. We shall examine not only the personal
attributes of those who formed James's family but also the pivotal
moments in the public and private life of this family. What emerges
from this family portrait constitutes the text that Shakespeare knew, a
text broad in its scope and rich in its content—a drama in its own
right.

In *Basilicon Doron*, written in Scotland but reissued in 1603 in time
for his arrival in England, James offers advice to Prince Henry, his
elder son, on a range of topics from kingship to marriage. He gives a
famous reminder to his son, that he should be thankful to God "for
that he made you a little God to sitte on his throne, and rule ouer
other men"[1]—an idea that James, to everyone's grief, was to take
rather too seriously. James tells Henry to honor his parents as a
dutiful son; and he outlines three reasons for marrying: "staying of
lust, for procreation of children, & that man should by his Wife get a

helper like himself" (p. 127). A king "must timouslie Marie for the weale of his people," and he must be sure that his wife is capable of bearing children. James made it fairly clear that he married Anne out of kingly duty and the desire to have heirs to the kingdom. Writing no doubt partly out of experience, James tells Henry: "First of all consider, that Mariage is the greatest earthly felicitie or miserie, that can come to a man" (p. 121). In his first address to Parliament on 19 March 1604, James likened himself to the husband of the kingdom: "What God hath conioyned then, let no man separate. I am the Husband, and all the whole Isle is my lawfull Wife; I am the head, and it is my Body."[2] Warming to the subject of kingship once again, James informed Parliament, meeting on 21 March 1610, that kings "are not only GODS Lieutenants vpon earth, and sit vpon GODS throne, but euen by GOD himselfe they are called Gods" (p. 307). Further, "Kings are also compared to Fathers of families: for a King is trewly *Parens patriae*, the politique father of his people" (p. 307).

Obviously, James relished his position as a kingly father; this afforded him an initial advantage over the memory of Queen Elizabeth. George Marcelline, writing in 1610, may well speak for many Englishmen, reflecting on the accession of James: "O happy English, that haue no more women and children for your King, but a King full of strength, a king participating the verdure of his youth, and ful ripeness of his age."[3] Not since the reign of Henry VIII could anyone have made such a statement. Equipped with a wife and royal children, James was in a position to captivate the public's attention and affection. Few living in 1603 had known what it was like to have a royal family on the English throne. Shakespeare, along with everyone else, took notice; in his case I think that this family's image helped shape his last plays.

Writing in the fifteenth century, Leon Battista Alberti, in a prose analysis of his own family, poses a question that continues to vex and fascinate scores of historians, psychologists, sociologists, anthropologists, and other interested sorts. In a dialogue exchange in Book 3 of *Della Famiglia*, Lionardo Alberti asks: "What do you mean by family?" And the answer comes from Giannozzo: "Children, wife, other relatives, retainers, and servants." To which Lionardo can respond: "I understand."[4] Such an answer, reflecting the idea of the extended family, corresponds also to fifteenth-century England as well as to Italy. It indicates how remote from this early period is the modern conception of what is called the "nuclear family"—father, mother, children. Alberti's concept of the "extended family" loses ground as we move into the sixteenth and seventeenth centuries, for reasons that many scholars have tried to determine. By Shakespeare's time it is appropriate to refer to the smaller unit of the family—parents and children—though clearly the larger concept has not completely vanished, especially in aristocratic families. To define the family by its organization overlooks, of course, the emotional and psychological bonds that operate within such units; such bonds have enticed literary writers from ancient to contemporary times. Tolstoy in the famous opening line of *Anna Karenina* asserts: "Happy families are all alike"—whereupon the novelist takes the next one thousand pages to explore interesting conflicts within families.

From our vantage point near the end of the twentieth century, it is exceedingly difficult to imagine what family life was like in the Middle Ages and the Renaissance. Yes, of course, we have evidence, but it is often contradictory. What were one's emotional ties to and feelings about other members of the family, however large or small that group might be? Fortunately, for our sake, a number of serious studies have been done on the history of the family. I find the work of Phillipe Ariès and Lawrence Stone to be particularly valuable for my purposes; Ariès emphasizes the centrality of the child, and Stone, the transient nature and patriarchal structure of the family.

The controlling idea in Ariès's book *Centuries of Childhood* is that the concept of the family is "inseparable from the concept of childhood."[5] Through an analysis of iconography—in this case pictures of families—Ariès concludes that the idea of the family "was unknown in the Middle Ages, that it originated in the fifteenth and sixteenth centuries, and that it reached its full expression in the seventeenth century" (p. 353). This does not mean, of course, that families did not exist; "but the family existed in silence: it did not awaken feelings strong enough to inspire poet or artist" (p. 364). On this score, one contrasts Chaucer and Shakespeare: Chaucer does not emphasize the family to the extent that Shakespeare does. In the latter the family constitutes a major preoccupation. The "discovery" of the child, as it were, reinforced the concept of the conjugal family. I think that Shakespeare's plays, especially the Romances, clearly reflect such an interest in children. These plays may be seen as "speaking pictures" to join Ariès's analysis of family portraits of the sixteenth and seventeenth centuries.

The triumph of the modern family, according to Ariès, derives in part because the family overcame obstacles that had hindered its development, mainly social demands of the larger community. Thus the "progress of the concept of the family followed the progress of private life, or domesticity" (p. 375). The possibility of privacy, an alien notion for centuries, greatly assisted the solidifying of the family group. As Ariès observes: "until the end of the seventeenth century, nobody was ever left alone" (p. 398). Life was lived out in public rooms and public streets. The architecture and construction of houses bear out this idea: there are no private places. The nearest thing to privacy was a curtained bed, but then one might be forced to share that bed with some other member of the family or a servant. Under such circumstances, one can readily understand Giannozzo Alberti's defining the family so as to include virtually everybody. It is probably impossible to be certain about which came first, the limited concept of family or privacy. Nevertheless, domesticity reinforces the idea of a nuclear family.

Ariès concludes thus, noting the impact of the child on family life:

> Between the end of the Middle Ages and the seventeenth century, the child had won a place beside his parents to which he could not lay claim at a time when it was customary to entrust him to strangers. This return of the children to the home was a great event: it gave the seventeenth-century family its principal characteristic, which distinguished it from the medieval family. The child became an indispensable element of everyday life, and his parents worried about his education, his career, his future. He was not yet the pivot of the whole system, but he had become a much more important character. (P. 403)

The last point is made with suitable caution, there being much contemporary evidence in England of the older pattern of child subordination. More compellingly than anyone else that I am aware of, Ariès calls attention to the central figure of the child as determining family relationships. So long as the child is one merely to be farmed out, or sent away from home, the cohesive emotional bonds that have come to characterize the modern family are hard to imagine.

A central idea in Lawrence Stone's *The Family, Sex and Marriage in England 1500–1800* is that the "pre-modern family" was, "statistically speaking, a transient and temporary association, both of husband and wife and of parents and children."[6] For Stone, the most striking feature that delineates the early modern family has nothing to do with marriage or birth: "it was the constant presence of death" (p. 66). Life expectancy was brief; infant mortality, very high. What follows from this, according to Stone, is a lack of "affect," a society of the sixteenth and seventeenth centuries "in which a majority of the individuals that composed it found it very difficult to establish close emotional ties to any other person" (p. 99). One thinks of *Troilus and Cressida*, where Cressida, when informed that she must leave Troilus and join her father in the Greek camp, resists: "I have forgot my father; / I know no touch of consanguinity— / No kin, no love, no blood, no soul so near me / As the sweet Troilus" (IV.ii.94–97). Such an attitude accounts in small part for the problematic nature of this play. Shakespeare does not show the reunion of this father and daughter.

Stone summarizes four practices that helped lead to what he sees as the lack of affect:

> These four factors, the lack of a unique mother figure in the first two years of life [the wet-nurse syndrome], the constant loss of close relatives, siblings, parents, nurses and friends through premature death, the physical imprisonment of the infant in tight swaddling-clothes in early months, and the deliberate breaking of the child's will all contributed to a "psychic numbing" which created many adults whose primary responses to others were at best a calculating indifference and at worst a mixture of suspicion and hostility, tyranny and submission, alienation and rage. (Pp. 101–2)

Stone may be correct in this general portrait of society; but as he is aware, there are wonderful exceptions to this bleak picture.

If, for example, one's knowledge of the Renaissance family derives only from Shakespeare's plays, as our knowledge of English history often does, then one might reach quite a different conclusion, as Lynda Boose observes: "Not the absence of affect but the possessive over-abundance of it is the force that both defines and threatens the family in Shakespeare."[7] To turn to the actual example of the Alberti family in Italy, one hears time and again a genuine, affectionate concern for children and other members of the family. Adovardo, in Book 1, reminds his listeners that the father "must worry on thinking that mortality is at its highest in childhood! Think how bitter it is for him to fear from moment to moment that he will be deprived of so much happiness" (*Della Famiglia*, p. 57). Lionardi later comments: "I believe it is shameful not to know how to gain the affection of one's family" (p. 209).

A particularly poignant instance of family affection is the reunion of the dying Lorenzo with his brother Ricciardo in the Alberti family:

> He [Lorenzo] heard Ricciardo and recognized his brother's voice as if awakening from his lethargy. He looked up and at the same time

raised one hand, leaving the arm bare. Then he let it fall back after moving it slightly, sighed, and turned toward his brother. He looked at him steadily and, although very weak, struggled to greet him. He gave him his hand. Ricciardo approached, and they embraced for a long time. It seemed that both wanted to greet each other and say many things but were unable to speak. They cried. (Pp. 163–64)

We doubtless agree with Giannozzo's response to this report: "How moving this is!"—the kind of experience and response that one gains at the end of many of Shakespeare's plays, especially the Romances. Gathering historical evidence, one must be careful not to exaggerate the "psychic numbing" that took place in the earlier centuries. It is logical, given the four conditions that Stone cites, that such "numbing" might take place, but emotional and human relationships rarely follow logic: "Reason and love keep little company together" (Bottom, *A Midsummer Night's Dream*). Absent the four conditions that Stone cites, our modern society should exhibit few examples of alienation and psychic numbing. We know better.

The Reformation, Stone suggests, gave new emphasis to the family with its domestic prayer and family Bible in the home, a movement carried even farther by the Puritans. At least one attribute remains fairly constant: the prominence of the father as head of the household. That position corresponds to the state itself, as Stone observes: "The growth of patriarchy was deliberately encouraged by the new Renaissance state on the traditional grounds that the subordination of the family to its head is analogous to . . . subordination of subjects to the sovereign" (p. 152). One scholar who has done extensive study of this subject notes: "It is no exaggeration to state that virtually all social relationships—not merely those between fathers and children and magistrates and subjects—were regarded as patriarchal or familial in essence."[8] James, as indicated earlier, seemed determined to exploit such a patriarchal relationship. Shakespeare's emphasis on fathers reflects this social pattern as it also serves practical theatrical constraints. Capturing the familial pattern, Alberti records the following exchange:

Giannozzo: I should want all my family to dwell under the same roof, warm themselves at the same fire, and eat at the same table.
Lionardo: I think you want this for your own happiness—not to be alone, but rather to see yourself seated every night in the midst of your family, father, lord, and teacher. . . . This is a pleasure which you old men prize very much.
Giannozzo: We certainly do, my dear Lionardo. But it is also good management to be all together under the same roof. . . . (P. 193)

I do not know of a better or more succinct statement of what holds families together, all problems and obstacles notwithstanding: emotional and practical bonds.

Using the work of Ariès and Stone as a backdrop, we can examine the Stuart royal family, seeing, for example, how it conforms in some measure to what these scholars have observed about families of this period. The increasing importance of children, the lack of affect, and the patriarchal structure of the family are all evident in James's family. As both Ariès and Stone recognize, exceptions to generalizations are plentiful, for families persist in carving out their own identity regardless of the normal pattern. Families are often contradictions, sometimes conforming to presumed norms, sometimes not: abandoning or embracing children, producing affection or psychic numbing. About royal families as such not much has been written. Despite the several books on members of James's family, none offers extended treatment of the sixteenth- or seventeenth-century English royal family as family. Evidence suggests that the pattern in such families typically corresponds to that of aristocratic families. In the discussion that follows, I will examine both the public and private dimensions of James's family—the politics of the family and the domestic life. They are ultimately, of course, inseparable.

By "politics of the family" I mean the domestic life of that family converted to state use. In James's case the simple fact that there was a royal family was a political reality that he exploited to his advantage. From the spring of 1603 to the winter of 1612–13, many events call attention to the public, political nature of this family, such as the royal entry through London in 1604, the births of royal children, the investiture of Henry as Prince of Wales, Henry's untimely death, and the festive wedding of Princess Elizabeth in 1613. Certainly all stratagems to resolve the marriage prospects of the royal children were more political than personal. One can speculate, though not prove, that James, if bereft of his family, might have had an even more difficult time as ruler; the other members of his family generated an interest, expectation, and enthusiasm in the political sphere that soon were lacking in James alone.

When James arrived in England, the public exhibited considerable interest in his family. As George Puttenham had written years earlier: "I say therefore, that the comfort of issue and procreation of children is so naturall and so great, not onely to all men but specially to Princes, as duetie and ciuilitie haue made it a common custome to reioyse at the birth of their noble children."[9] In many ways the

Simon van de Passe, *King James,* from *The Workes of James* (1616), Courtesy of the Department of Special Collections, Spencer Research Library, University of Kansas

appearance of a royal family was a relief; the historian William McElwee aptly observes: "A virgin queen of Elizabeth's calibre was a phenomenon to be proud of, but in many ways it was a comfort to have a man with a wife and young family and with the ordinary, obvious human weaknesses."[10] In his fragmentary *History of Great Britain*, Francis Bacon thus described the arrival of James: "A king, in the strength of years, supported with great alliances abroad, established with royal issue at home, at peace with all the established world."[11]

Bacon reminded the recipients of a letter in 1612, in which he wrote to collect "aid" for Princess Elizabeth's impending wedding: "Then may you declare the reasons why the like hath not been demanded of late time . . . : which are apparent: for that Queen Elizabeth, Queen Mary, and King Edward had no children, and King Henry 8 died before his son was of the age of 15 or his daughters married."[12] Now there is a royal family with marriageable children, a situation not faced in England for decades. In 1610 Marcelline, in *The Triumphs of King James*, writes that James is "the Common *Father* of all his people" (p. 14) and later enumerates the advantages of the royal children. These children make the kingdoms happy "whereon dependeth their peace and freedom from strife . . . which wanting before in that Empires felicity, makes it now an Empire abounding in felicity" (p. 46). Anne has helped make this situation possible by giving birth to the children; she has thereby "set vs aboue the winds, as safe sheltred from all stormes, by the firme assurances of so faire a succession" (p. 47). Here the confidence, not possible since Henry VIII's reign, is political, revealing little of personal feelings about the family.

Writing to the Privy Council a few days after word had reached him of his proclamation as King of England, James noted: ". . . forasmuch as we do intend to bring into this Realme, as soone as possibly we can, both the Queene our Wyfe and our two elder Children, . . . we must recommend . . . the sending hither of such Jewells and other furnyture which did appertaine to the late Queene, as you shall thincke to be meet."[13] James reminded the council not only of his family but also of the need to provide for them in what became an ongoing, somewhat irksome financial problem. Greeting James outside of London on 7 May 1603, Richard Martin welcomed him with praise and observed that James's "Princely offspring" may sit "upon the throne of their fathers for evermore" (Nichols, 1:*132). The recorder of Southampton made similar remarks later in 1603, when James visited that city; here the recorder referred to the "most noble Progenie of your Royall Children" (Nichols, 1:277). To call attention to the parents and children echoes political concern about succession. Having lived through the worrisome problem of who would succeed Elizabeth, Englishmen were evidently enormously relieved to know that this political problem was resolved by the advent of James and his family.

In the spring of 1603, James made his steady, slow, and triumphal way from Edinburgh to London; soon thereafter came Anne and Prince Henry, gathering adulation along the way. Seemingly wave after wave of royal family hit the English shores, each changing place with that which went before, as Elizabeth and eventually Charles also joined the family. Probably the first time that Londoners saw the family together (or most of it) in public display was the spectacular royal entry into London on 15 March 1604, coronation festivities having been curtailed by the plague. The Venetian ambassador, Nicolo Molin, captures the form of the royal family procession:

> The Prince [Henry] was on horseback, ten paces ahead of the King, who rode under a canopy borne over his head by four-and-twenty gentlemen, splendidly dressed. . . . The Queen followed twenty paces behind; she was seated on a royal throne, drawn by two white mules . . . ; in a richly furnished carriage behind her Majesty came the Lady Arabella, with certain maids of honour in attendance.[14]

Princess Elizabeth was deemed too young for the entry, and Prince Charles was still in Scotland. Striking was the presence of James's cousin, Arbella Stuart, kept virtual prisoner by Queen Elizabeth, but now given new prominence by James and included as a member of his family—one of James's politically wise and genuinely generous actions.

We find an eyewitness account of this 1604 civic pageant in Gilbert Dugdale's *The Time Triumphant*. In this quarto text, Dugdale praises James, Anne, and the children; he calls Anne "pierles," "Her Sonne a Prince, / Her Children since / All royal borne, / Whom Crownes addorne."[15] Near Cheapside an apprentice spoke to James, or at least attempted to, in words not recorded in any of the printed texts of this pageant. Dugdale records the apprentice's praise of the family, including the children: "Thy sonnes and daughters, princely all compleat, / Royall in bloud, children of high Renowne" (sig. B4). Dugdale also describes the Queen and Prince Henry in the procession: "Our gratious *Queene Ann*, milde and curteous plaste in a Chariot, of exceeding beauty, did all the way so humbly and with mildenes, salute her subiects, . . . that women and men in my sights wept with ioy" (sig. B2ᵛ). The "young hopeful *Henry Fredericke*" smiled "as ouer-ioyde to the peoples eternall comfort" and acknowledged the crowd's cheers (sigs. B2ᵛ-B3). The speech of Genius at the first triumphal arch, in words written by Jonson, greeted the royal family in Fenchurch, praising Anne who has the title of mother, "In which one title you drown all your other. / Instance be that fair shoot [Henry] is gone before, / Your eldest joy and top of all your store, / With those, whose sight to us is yet denied [Charles and Elizabeth], / But not our zeal to them . . ." (Nichols, 1:387).

Dugdale closes his pamphlet with a benediction: "I beseech the Almighty God of his infinite mercy and goodnes, so keepe our *King Queene* and *Prince*, and all their princely progenie" (sig. B4ᵛ). Such a prayer may well have been in the hearts of all Englishmen that spectacular day. Such a prayer did rise from the lips of the bishop of London during the Hampton Court Conference late in 1604: "*Gods goodnesse be blessed for your Majesty, and give health and prosperity to Your Highnesse, your Gracious Queene, the young Prince, and all the Royall Issue.*"[16] Shakespeare, standing in the streets of London on that March day garbed in the livery of the King's Men, had to be aware of the political statement not only of the pageant itself but of the honored royal family as well. Because we are a family, parents and children, James's family seems to say, all is well in the kingdom, the golden age is now. The presence of the Stuart royal family solidifies James's claim to the crown; the pageant and the adoring crowds ratify that claim: public, political purpose is served. Domestic life transforms into political statement.

Offering a family portrait, the Venetian ambassadors, Francesco Contarini and Marc' Antonio Correr, reported on 18 February 1610, of an audience with James, accompanied by the rest of his family: "The Queen stood by him and with her the Princess, who, in common opinion, is held to be of a rare beauty; she is fourteen years old. On the King's right stood the Prince of Wales and hard by the Queen the Duke of York, his father's and mother's joy" (*CSP Venetian*, 11:423). Were there an actual picture of this gathering, it could join Ariès's study of family iconography.

The public had glimpses of the assembled family on many occasions; I cite but a few other examples. Activities associated with the investiture of Henry as Prince of Wales in 1610 put the royal family again in the public light. One report pictures the family waiting for the appearance of Henry during some of those ceremonies: "Approaching neere to Whitehall, the King and the Queene, with the young Duke of Yorke and Lady Elizabeth, stoode in the Privie Gallerie window to see the order of their comming" (Nichols, 2:326). Despite strife and tensions apparent by 1610, the family could rally together and meet public expectations, serving the political aim of securing Henry's favor with the people as the likely ultimate successor to James. Later that year various members of the royal family, separately or together, came to visit the great ship being built at Woolwich by Phineas Pett for Prince Henry. In September they all gathered for the launching of the ship upon the Thames; Pett reports: "There was a standing set up in the most convenient place in the Yard for his Majesty, the Queen, and their royal children."[17] Typical of many events during the Jacobean era, the ship stubbornly resisted all efforts to launch it. But the royal family had already been successfully launched into public focus for some time.

The births and subsequent deaths of the two daughters born during the first years of James's reign aroused considerable attention to the royal family. Samuel Calvert wrote to Ralph Winwood about the preparations for the birth of Mary in 1605: "The Queen expects her Delivery every Hour, and Prayers are dayly said every where for her Safety. There is great Preparation for the christening Chamber, and costly Furniture provided for Performance of other Ceremonies."[18] Finally the birth came: "The Lady Mary, borne at Greenewitch upon the eight of Aprill about 11 or 12 of the clock at night; for joy whereof, the next day after, the Cittizens of London made bonefiers throughout London, and the bells continued ringing all the whole day."[19] As Ethel Williams correctly notes: "Over eighty years had elapsed since Jane Seymour had given birth to a son, and owing to the passage of time and the reigns of two childless Queens, many of the customs attached to a royal birth had been forgotten."[20]

The christening of Mary took place on 5 May 1605, amid much pomp and display at Greenwich. Howes's description reveals the attention that focused on this, the first royal christening in England since 1537:

> First, the three Courts at Greenwich were rayled in and hung about with broad cloth, where the proceeding should passe. The Childe was brought from the Queene's lodgings through both the Great chambers, and through the Presence, and downe the winding stayres

into the Conduit-court. At the foote whereof attended a canapy borne by eight Barons, before which went the Officers of Armes, and divers Bishoppes, Barons, and Earles. (Nichols, 1:512)

One cushion held many jewels "of inestimable price." Arbella Stuart served as one of the godmothers, the Countess of Northumberland the other. In the chapel "stoode a very rich and stately font of silver and gilt, most curiously wrought with figures of beastes, serpents, and other antycke workes." For the first time in English history the christening ceremony for a royal child followed the rite of the firmly established Church of England. As P. M. Handover suggests: "A christening marked more comfortably than any other ceremony the security with which the family of James the First held the throne of England."[21] He now had a child born on English soil.

But not for long. In late summer 1607, Mary became ill; she had, according to a letter from Rowland Whyte to the earl of Shrewsbury, "a burning fever for 23 daies, and a continuall rhewme fell to her lunges, and putrified there, which she had not strength to voyd" (Nichols, 2:154). On 16 September the little princess died. Shortly before her death the Venetian ambassador reported: "The King is at Theobalds; the Queen at Hampton Court, very sorry about the indisposition of her daughter, to whom the King is devotedly attached, and it is thought he will give up the chace to go to her" (*CSP Venetian*, 11:39). We may detect an implication, perhaps unintended, in the diplomat's dispatch: neither parent was with the dying child. After Mary's death, James sent the earl of Salisbury to console the queen, as indicated in a letter from Sir Roger Aston to Salisbury 17 (?) September 1607: "[James] desires you to bend all your force to persuade her Majesty that this burial may not be a second grief: it is not for charge, but only for removing of the grievous present and the griefs to come. He is going this morning to Chesson [Cheshunt] Park to hunt."[22] Either an example of Stone's "psychic numbing" or of James's incapacity for confronting death, the episode rankles. Of course, Mary's death had been preceded by the birth of Sophia on 22 June 1606 and by her death less than twenty-four hours later. Both of James's English daughters lie buried in a tomb next to that of Queen Elizabeth. The union of James and Anne was to yield no more children.

As several historians have suggested, 1607 was a fateful year in the life of the royal family, as it was also in Shakespeare's because of the deaths of his brother, a niece, and a nephew, but the wedding of his daughter Susanna. Writing about James, McElwee observes: "The death of the infant Princess Sophia within twenty-four hours of her birth in June of 1606, followed the next year by that of the other baby daughter, Mary, seems to have damaged the relationship between James and Anne irreparably."[23] Anne had borne James seven children, only three of whom survived; and she had suffered several miscarriages, including one shortly after James ascended the English throne in 1603. McElwee also suggests that James had lost the affections of Henry and Elizabeth by 1607 and that Charles was still too young to fill James's need to spoil and pamper his children. With the members of his family in some state of disaffection, James's attentions turned in 1607 to a young Scot, Robert Carr; the results of this infatuation were not good either for James or for the kingdom. But though this seemingly irreparable turn occurred in the private life of the royal family in 1607, the political life of the family survived essentially intact. Therefore, the family came together for Henry's investiture, engaged in the negotiations for Elizabeth's marriage, suffered the death of Henry, and reveled in the wedding celebration of Elizabeth and Frederick in February 1613.

The royal family—any family—has many lives; despite changes, some elements of the public family life persist, a necessity recognized by all royal families. Part of their collective political function is to satisfy the public's expectations, whatever the personal, domestic reality of their relationships might be. All the world's a stage—a reality that James firmly understood. Having looked briefly at the public nature of this Stuart royal family, we turn now to a more expansive examination of their private lives, their personalities, and their relationships to one another. Out of the fabric of this family's life, with its bumpy seams and rough edges, we may perceive a prototype for the families of Shakespeare's Romances, in which the issues of politics and private life constitute a web of mingled yarn.

A roll call at James's baptism in December 1566 may epitomize much of his familial destiny: his mother, Mary Queen of Scots, was present and pregnant, though not by her husband; his father, Lord Darnley, was absent, being in the last stages of his battle with syphilis. Within two months, Darnley would die in a mysterious explosion on 10 February 1567; by May of that year, Mary would see James for the last time as she went off to marry the earl of Bothwell and, eventually, to forced exile. At the age of thirteen months, James was crowned king of Scotland, a troublesome political issue, since his mother was still alive, though imprisoned in England. Thus, as a child growing up in Scotland, James knew neither his father nor his mother. As Antonia Fraser comments: "Not only was he totally cut off from a mother's love in childhood, but he was also trained to regard his mother as the murderess of his father, an adulteress who had deserted him for her lover, and last of all, the protagonist of a wicked and heretical religion."[24] James's early years were spent in the household of the earl of Mar, as was the custom for Scottish royal heirs.[25] The wife of the earl was the mother substitute for James, but we have little basis for knowing what he thought of her.

His mother, however, retained intense, affectionate feelings for this son whom she did not truly know; her feelings were out of proportion to the truth. Indeed, by 1585, even she had to recognize that her son had betrayed her in his zeal to gain the English throne. He did nothing to prevent the execution of Mary on 8 February 1587, almost twenty years to the day after his father had died. James's response to the report of his mother's death was at best ambiguous, public mourning but no evidence of private grief. He had no familial feelings for her, nor can he rightly be expected to have had any; she had become for him merely a political obstacle. As Jonathan Goldberg rightly observes: "James had replaced his mother with Elizabeth; angling for her inheritance, he sacrificed his mother for it."[26]

In what must have been some kind of expiation, James, when he came to the English throne, dispatched a rich pall of velvet to hang over Mary's grave in Peterborough Cathedral (see Fraser, p. 552). Later he ordered a magnificent tomb to be built for his mother in Westminster Abbey, a monument, as Fraser observes, "to James's taste if not his filial piety" (p. 552). By 1612, her body was exhumed and moved to the abbey, where it rests in a tomb near to and rivaling that which James had erected for Queen Elizabeth. "The monument in Westminster Abbey," Goldberg writes, "effaces—erases—his part in Mary's death" (p. 17). A Victorian survey of the royal tombs in the abbey revealed that James shared the tomb of Henry VII, first Tudor monarch, while Mary's tomb was shared by many, including her grandchildren, Prince Henry and Princess Elizabeth (Fraser, p. 554). By accident or design, James, even in death, did not rest with his immediate family.

While a prisoner at Sheffield, Mary embroidered on the royal dais of state a motto, *"In my end is my Beginning"* (Fraser, p. 555). It might be truly said that in her end was James's beginning, his prospects for the English throne enhanced and his claim on the Scottish one uncontested by an imprisoned mother. Also, one might turn the motto around a bit and suggest that in James's beginning was his end. By this I mean that certain patterns of behavior, established early, remained with him throughout his life, dragging down his reputation. That curious scene at the baptismal font foretells a troubled future. Essentially an orphan all his life, James knew little of what a family is and how it functions, having not himself known the affectionate and emotional bonds that may exist between parents and child. It takes no great psychological insight to see here the seeds of the familial difficulty that he was to experience as a husband and a father.

Except for the wife of the earl of Mar, James's early life was spent surrounded by men, most of them either rude and uncouth or tyrannical, like his tutor, George Buchanan. As a teenager, James fell in love with his dashing older French cousin Esmé Stuart, who exhibited desirable qualities largely absent in the Scottish lords. James's sexual preference for men, first seen in the relationship with his cousin, is a predilection that he acted upon many times, as in the case of Carr and eventually in George Villiers, duke of Buckingham. Surely this pattern damaged the relationship with his family; it also distressed many courtiers who took it as yet another sign of the court's corruption.

Many contemporary accounts analyze James's virtues and vices both as king and as husband-father. William Sanderson, writing in the mid seventeenth century, paints a flattering portrait of the Jacobean court: "The splendor of the *King, Queen, Prince,* and *Princess* with the rest of the royall yssue, the concourse of strangers hither from forein Nations, the multitude of our own people from all parts of our three Kingdoms gave a wonderfull glory to the Court."[27] Beneath that outward glitter with the family at the political center lay many problems, beginning with James's ineptitude as a ruler. There is, after all, some truth in Anthony Weldon's claim, echoing Henry IV of France, that James was "the wisest foole in Christendome, . . . wise in small things, but a foole in weighty affaires."[28] Shortly after his marriage to Anne, two of James's trusted counselors, James and Robert Melville, wrote a letter advising James to avoid four things that wreck a monarch: "To be careless and slothful in his affairs; To forsake the counsel of his true servants; To give ear unto unthankful flatterers; and, To spend above his rents."[29] Perhaps James misunderstood the letter, believing it instead to be a program for a monarch; surely he was guilty of all four of these strictures. But even Weldon could manage some praise: "I wish this Kingdom have never any worse [king] . . .; for he lived in peace, dyed in peace, and left all his Kingdoms in a peaceable condition" (p. 175). Though the policy did not suit all Englishmen, James's peace treaty with Spain in 1604 was a wise move; he also peacefully united Scotland and England, though he never got his much-desired Act of Union from Parliament. Predictable grumbling accompanied his proclamation of himself as "King of Great Britain."

The Venetian ambassador, Nicolo Molin, offers a trenchant analysis of James in 1607:

> His Majesty is by nature placid, averse from cruelty, a lover of justice. . . . He loves quiet and repose, has no inclination to war, . . . a fact that little pleases many of his subjects, though it pleases them still less that he leaves all government to his Council and will think of nothing but the chase. He does not caress the people nor make them that good cheer the late Queen did. . . . this King manifests no taste for them [people] but rather contempt and dislike. The result is he is despised and almost hated. In fact his Majesty is more inclined to live retired with eight or ten of his favourites than openly, as is the custom of the country and the desire of the people. (*CSP Venetian*, 10:513)

Embedded in this perceptive insight are almost all of the strictures outlined to James by the Melville brothers. A French diplomat, Count Harley de Beaumont, had anticipated Molin as early as 1603: "It appears to them [the people] strange that this king should despise them and live in so complete retirement. They exclaim aloud, the residence at Theobald's will spoil him."[30] Beaumont elsewhere reports James's extreme anger when the public pressed in upon him while he was hunting: "he cursed every one he met, and swore that if they would not let him follow the chase at his pleasure, he would leave England" (Raumer, 2:202). Such outbursts, Beaumont suggests, "draw upon him great contempt and inextinguishable hate from the people."

Barely six months after James came to the throne, Beaumont's diplomatic report, dating from September 1603, demonstrates James's conflict with the public, a tension that persisted throughout the reign. The word "hatred" crops up with frightening regularity in numerous reports. James seems to have forgotten many of the precepts that permeate his *Basilicon Doron*, especially his observation "that a King is as one set on a stage, whose smallest action and gestures, all the people gazinglie doe beholde" (p. 163). To his great

43

To the High and mightie *I A M E S*, King of greate Britaine,

TWOO Lions ſtout the Diadem vphold,

Of famous Britaine, in their armed pawes:

Scilicet Anglicus
et Scoticus, The one is Red, the other is of Gold,

And one their Prince, their ſea, their land and lawes;

Their loue, their league: whereby they ſtill agree,

In concord firme, and friendly amitie.

BELLONA henceforth bounde in Iron bandes,

Shall kiſſe the foote of mild triumphant **PEACE**,

Nor Trumpets ſterne, be heard within their landes;

Envie ſhall pine, and all old grudges ceaſe:

Braue Lions, ſince, your quarrell's lai'd aſide,

On common foe, let now your force be tri'de.

Vnum ſuſtentant gemini diadema Leones,   **Fœdere iunguntur ſimili, cœloque, ſaloque,**
Concordes vno Principe, mente, fide.   **Nata quibus Pax hæc inuiolanda manet,**

C m.e

Emblem of King James, from Henry Peacham's *Minerva Britanna* (1612).

cost, James chose to play out in the theater of the state a role that ignored the people, often more content with hunting than responding to the needs of his own family. At moments he is in danger of becoming the "skipping king," referred to contemptuously by Henry IV in his interview with Prince Hal in *1 Henry IV*.

James was often whimsical and petty in dealing with his subjects. Gervase Holles recalls asking why the earl of Clare had never attained prominence in James's court; the answer came from Sir Francis Nedham: "'For (sayes he) two sorts of men K. James had never kindness for: those whose hawks and dogges flew and run as well as his owne, and those who were able to speake as much reason as himselfe.'"[31] The archbishop of York, old and sickly, wrote to Salisbury in 1604, complaining of James's gift giving: "His Majesty's subjects hear and fear that his excellent and heroical nature is too much inclined to giving, which in short time will exhaust the treasure of this kingdom and bring many inconveniences."[32] How right the archbishop's prediction was; one notes again how early in James's reign these accurate perceptions of him accumulate. James's prodigality finds a literary analogue in Shakespeare's *Timon of Athens*, where Timon believes, mistakenly, that his generosity buys friends. The empty coffers of James's treasury marred his reign throughout, culminating in the awful situation of not having enough money for Anne's funeral in 1619, a funeral that had to be postponed for several weeks as James scrounged for money. The land of milk and honey to which James came in 1603 from the bleak northern latitudes of Scotland did not have limitless resources for a squandering monarch.

To be fair, there were moments of giving that seemed altogether right and kindhearted. I think of the letter from Lord Harington, Princess Elizabeth's guardian, to Salisbury early in 1607, in which Harington reported a gift from father to daughter: "I have received your letter and therewith the jewel of a diamond, a ruby and a pendant pearl, the diamond set about with little diamonds; which was delivered to the Lady Elizabeth from the King, which she received with great joy as an assured testimony of his favour" (*Salisbury MSS*, 19:14). The extravagance of this gift aside, James had responded to his daughter in a way that he understood.

In an exceedingly rare display of courage and gallantry, James had sailed across stormy seas in 1589 to fetch his bride, Anne, who was stranded in Norway. By meditating on her picture, James had convinced himself that he was in love with her. Perhaps only playing the role, James wrote love poems and generally exhibited all the symptoms of a romantic lover. The marriage went reasonably well at first; but the early, relatively peaceful years of their marriage gave way to sometimes hysterical, acrimonious disputes. James, after all, made clear that he had married for political reasons, and the first blush of love for this woman lasted about as long as morning dew.

One of the battle grounds of their relationship was the children, especially Henry.[33] Upon receiving word of his proclamation as king of England, James decided to hurry south, leaving the family behind for a while. Anne, pregnant at the time, seized the opportunity to gain custody of Henry, who had long since been farmed out to the earl of Mar. With James out of the country, Anne struck, only to be rebuffed by the dowager mother of the earl of Mar, who had explicit instructions not to release Henry to anyone, including his mother. Anne's screams of protest traveled quickly to England, and James finally relented, but not before Anne had miscarried. Such battles were to be repeated many times.

What is one to make of the relationship of husband and wife, James and Anne? The "revisionist" writer William Sanderson comments in 1656: "A matchless pair, drawing evenly in all courses of honour, and both blessed with fair issue, because never loose from eithers Bed" (p. 474). Francis Osborne (1593–1659) reports an outward display of affection presumably shortly after the arrival in England: "He [James] that evening parted with his queene, and to show himself more uxorious before the people . . . than in private he was, he did at her coach side take his leave, by kissing her sufficiently to the middle of the shoulders."[34] A letter from Anne to James in the Harleian manuscript collection implies genuine concern (the letter would be more valuable if we knew its date). Anne writes:

> Sir, as nothing is more wellcom to me then your letters (for which I thank you) so can they bring me no better tidings then of your good health (of me much desired) for I cease not to praye for the encrease and continnance of your good both of mynd and bodie, and thereof rest assured, so kissing your handes I remaine she that will euer loue you best   Anna. R.[35]

Bishop Godfrey Goodman (1583–1655), writing about 1650 in reaction to Anthony Weldon's unfavorable account of James, tried to make the best possible case, observing that at least they did have children: "It is true that some years after they did not much keep company together. The King of himself was a very chaste man, and there was little in the Queen to make him uxorious; yet they did love as well as man and wife could do, not conversing together."[36] I wonder if by "not conversing together," the good bishop means not having sexual intercourse, a now obscure meaning of "converse." That is the clear implication of Edward Peyton's report: "Now King James, more addicted to love males then females, though for complement he visited Queen Anne, yet never lodged with her a night for many yeers."[37] Only a tortuous kind of logic could lead Sanderson to claim that they were never "loose from eithers Bed." Weldon notes that James "was ever best, when furthest from his Queene, and that was thought to be the first grounds of his often removes, which afterwards proved habituall" (p. 168). One can safely assume that after 1607 there was little left of a husband-wife relationship for James and Anne—only personal accommodation and separate little kingdoms within the kingdom. Only the rosiest-colored spectacles would allow one to see them as a "matchless pair." "I believe it is shameful," Lionardo Alberti said, "not to know how to gain the affections of one's family."

At the time of the coronation in 1603, the Venetian ambassador, Scaramelii, reported that despite the entreaties of James and the archbishops, Anne steadfastly refused to "*take the Sacrament along with him, after the Protestant rite*" (*CSP Venetian*, 10:81). Surely one of the most open secrets of the Jacobean era was Anne's Catholicism. So, in fact, she informed the French diplomat Beaumont: " 'I am at heart a Catholic, and have sought, though in vain, to convert my husband' " (Raumer, 2:200). The Venetian ambassador Molin is in apparent error when he reported in 1607 that she is "a Lutheran" (10:513). This open opposition to James's apparently deeply felt religious predilections is but another sign of strife between husband and wife, as it is also a sign of Anne's determined independence. Molin describes her in 1607: "The Queen is very gracious, moderately good looking. . . . She likes enjoyment and is very fond of dancing and of fêtes. She is intelligent and prudent; and knows the disorders of the government, in which she has no part" (10:513). Rather like James, Anne "is full of kindness for those who support her, but on the other hand she is terrible, proud, unendurable to those she dislikes." Probably the earl of Mar and others would concur with the ambassador's assessment.

Several historians have called Anne stupid and vacuous; hence, they argue, James could not possibly have loved her. That view is too harsh, I think. True, she gave herself over rather totally to pleasure— to dancing, to the court masques. But could not one argue that this

Queen Anne, based on Paul van Somer's painting; reproduced in Thomas Henderson, *James I and VI*. Courtesy of Folger Shakespeare Library.

preference was encouraged by her difficulties with James and her failure to share in the rearing of the children? Which is the more vacuous: dancing or hunting daily to the exclusion of tending to governmental duties? She may not have been James's intellectual equal, but recall how James sometimes used his intelligence. Anne was perceptive enough to see the dangers inherent in the style of James's rule; she remarked to Beaumont: " 'My husband ruins his affairs by excessive kindness and carelessness' " (Raumer, 2:199).

In addition to indulging herself frivolously and sometimes scandalously (by appearing in court masques), Anne also was a mother who had given birth to seven children, who had had miscarriages, who had suffered severe depression at the birth and death of Sophia and had been revived only by the appearance of her brother, Christian IV of Denmark, in 1606. Small wonder that much of her energy flowed in the direction of her children—sometimes, admittedly, in petty schemes to win them over. She was obviously capable of simple and spontaneous kindness to children—witness her action at the king's birthday celebration in 1603: the Queen "took Cecil's little son in her blessed arms and kissed him twice, and bestowed a jewel on him, tying it herself in his ear" (*Salisbury MSS.*, 15:143). She opposed James in domestic matters but seldom dabbled in the larger problems of the kingdom, though she did push the cause of amicable relations with Spain. One of her chief concerns, as already indicated, was Prince Henry.

Imprudently, Anne informed the French diplomat Beaumont in 1604: " 'It is time that I should have possession of the Prince and gain his affection, for the King drinks so much, and conducts himself so ill in every respect, that I expect an early and evil result' " (Raumer, 2:209-10). Beaumont captures the essence of Anne's strategy "to corrupt the spirit and disposition of the Prince . . . by flattering his little passions, by diverting him from his lessons and exercises, and (to the vexation of his father) representing the sciences to him as unworthy of a great commander and conqueror" (Raumer 2:209). On another occasion, she even told Beaumont, to his dismay, that she hoped "her son will one day overrun France as well as his ancestor Henry V" (Raumer 2:206). The Venetian ambassador reported in 1607 that Anne was devoted to Henry "and never lets him away from her side" (*CSP Venetian*, 11:10). That view seems at best exaggerated, for, in fact, neither parent exercised much authority over Henry. They were neither the first nor the last parents to use a child for their battle ground; and though James seems to have won the battle, he lost the war.

The choice of Frederick Elector Palatine as the future husband of Princess Elizabeth clearly annoyed Anne; perhaps she did not like the Protestant arrangement. In any event, the betrothal ceremony in late December 1612 took place without Anne. The Frenchman Spifame says: "The Queen was not present, either on account of an inflammation in her foot, as she pretended, or for another reason, as others believe" (Raumer, 2:227). Anne's action reminds one of the character Cousin in the medieval morality play *Everyman,* who breaks his promise to journey with Everyman to death because he has a cramp in his toe—or for some other reason. The inveterate letter writer John Chamberlain reported to Ralph Winwood on 9 January 1613: "The Quene is noted to have geven no great grace nor favor to this match, and there is doubt will do lesse hereafter."[38] For the sake of the young couple, however, Anne mellowed by the time of the actual wedding; she even abandoned her contempt for the choice of Frederick. Chamberlain wrote to Winwood on 23 February 1613: "The Quene that seemed not to taste yt so well at first, is since so come about that she doth all she can to grace yt, and takes speciall comfort in him [Frederick]" (1:427). In the long run, history has probably vindicated Anne's reservations about Elizabeth's husband.

Having lost Prince Henry finally through his death in 1612, and having lost Elizabeth, Anne turned her attention to Charles. The Venetian ambassador, Foscarini, noted in early January 1613: "The post of Governor to the Prince [Charles] is being eagerly sought by all the great nobles; but as the Queen has begged the King to leave that duty to her it is likely that he will not refuse to allow the mother to have the charge of her only son" (*CSP Venetian,* 12:472). There may be a touch of pathos here.

If Anne had any particular political ambitions, she failed, having had little impact on James's policies, having been incapable of shaping Henry's destiny, and having been unable to arrange a Catholic husband for Elizabeth. As a political force Anne was negligible. As a mother she was frequently shut off from the nurturing of her own children by tradition and by the dint of James's masculine will. As a wife Anne soon found that she was destined for a subordinate position, frequently second to James's infatuation with young and attractive men. Anne's pettiness and her self-indulgent pursuit of pleasure are probably compensations for an unfulfilled life as mother and wife. Small wonder that she set up a separate household. In many ways her case is not a little sad.

Writing in the late nineteenth century, the historian Samuel Gardiner offers this self-congratulatory glowing assessment of Prince

Henry: "In his bright face old men saw a prospect of a return to the Elizabethan glories of their youth. His mind was open to all noble influences, and, if he had lived, he would have been able to rule England, because he would have sympathised . . . with all that was good and great in the English character."[39] Gardiner further suggests that in time Henry would have acquired the qualities of prudence and circumspection that he lacked. Gardiner's Victorian excesses aside, this view of Henry squares with much that was said by contemporaries, especially after his death, where the elegiac outpouring rivaled anything that England had experienced. E. C. Wilson and, more recently, J. W. Williamson provide book-length studies that do much to put Henry in the proper perspective; Williamson punctures several of the myths that attended Henry.[40]

Despite the praise and adulation heaped on Henry then and later, an occasional voice spoke of the dangers inherent in the expectations. Francis Osborne, in his *Memoirs*, was one such later voice: Henry "whom they [people] ingaged by so much expectation, as it may be doubted, whether it ever lay in the power of any prince meerly humane, to bring so much felicity into a nation" (1:259–60). Those disgruntled with James, those yearning for a Protestant union of Europe, those itching for war—all rallied to the cause and hope of Henry. Surely some who looked on him with adulation did so through nostalgic eyes. But death dashed all those expectations. The great white hope of England and Protestantism became instead but a shooting star, an actor who strutted and fretted his hour upon the stage but then was heard no more. Historians have been left with a favorite parlor game: speculating on what might have happened had Henry lived. As a growing political force, Henry stood out among the royal children. Assessing his own designs is difficult, but we know that he did little to dissuade those who wanted to use him for a political cause. The crucial years from his arrival in England to his death marked an ever-enlarging role for Henry in the political arena. We turn now to examine some of the qualities of this eldest child of James and Anne.

Unfortunately for the sake of those trying to write about this Stuart royal family, there was no one at James's court, either in Scotland or in England, to compare with the French doctor Heroard at the court of Henry IV, who kept meticulous details about the infancy and childhood of the young dauphin, later Louis XIII. The pattern in that household resembles what we know of aristocratic families throughout western Europe. As indicated above, Henry was sent away from home as a child, according to his father's will to be brought up in the earl of Mar's household in Scotland, just as James had been, thus carrying on the Scottish tradition. Whether James had any personal feelings on this subject or was merely following convention, we do not know. The writings of Charles Cornwallis, who eventually would be Henry's treasurer, contain the fullest account of Henry's youth. Yet these are but snippets of information, pale by comparison with Heroard's account of the dauphin; they do provide, however, a general outline of the pattern of Henry's upbringing.

Cornwallis records, for example, that after Henry's baptism "he was resigned to the custody and keeping of the earle of Marre, assisted also by the continuall and vigilant care of the venerable and noble matron his mother."[41] Henry remained there until he was five or six years old, according to Cornwallis, when James decided that Henry needed a tutor. "A little after," Cornwallis writes, "the women being put from about his highnesse, divers of good sort were appointed to attend upon his person" (2:227); and "in the 7. 8. and 9. yeares of his age, leaving those childish and idle toyes, . . . he began to delight in more active and manly exercises" (2:227). William Sanderson, in his *Compleat History*, offers a physical description, indebted to Cornwallis: "Hee was comely tall, five foot eight Inches high, strong and well made, broad shouldred, a small wast, amiable with Majesty, Aborn Hair, long-faced, broad forehead, a peircing grave Eye, a gracious smile, but with a frown, daunting" (pp. 379–80). This description corresponds with the pictures of Henry, such as the militant one in Michael Drayton's *Poly-Olbion*.

The reliable Nicolo Molin offers this assessment of Henry in 1607: Henry "is about twelve years old, of a noble wit and great promise. His every action is marked by a gravity most certainly beyond his years. He studies, but not with much delight, and chiefly under his father's spur, not of his own desire" (*CSP Venetian*, 10:513). James, Molin reports, admonished Henry for not studying more, threatening that the crown would be left to his brother Charles, "who was far quicker at learning and studied more earnestly." Henry held his tongue until later, when his tutor carried on in the same vein; then he snapped: " 'I know what becomes a Prince. It is not necessary for me to be a professor, but a soldier and a man of the world. If my brother is as learned as they say, we'll make him Archbishop of Canterbury' "—a witty if insolent response.

Praise of Henry as a warrior governs a number of contemporary accounts of him. George Marcelline, for example, in *The Triumphs of*

Prince Henry, from Michael Drayton's *Poly-Olbion* (1612). Courtesy of
Folger Shakespeare Library.

King James (1610), writes boldly: "This young Prince is a warrior alreadie, both in gesture and countenance, so that in looking on him, he seemeth vnto vs, that in him we do yet see *Aiax* before *Troy*, crowding among the armed Troops, calling vnto them, that he may ioyne body to body with *Hector*, who standes trembling with chill-cold feare" (p. 66). Marcelline hints darkly of Henry's waiting for the right opportunity to spring into action: "Yet let it not be immagined, that the execution of great desseignes, are vtterly lost by deferrence and delay" (p. 67). Portraying his ultimate image of Henry, Marcelline offers a veritable emblem of him: "as one figured Caesar, aloft, deposing or treading a Globe vnder him, holding a book in one hand, and a sword in the other: so that it may be saide of you, *That for the one & other you are a* Caesar" (p. 73). The implications are a little frightening. Interestingly, two years later, in 1612, Henry Peacham presents an emblem of Henry, depicted in full armor astride a rearing horse, suggesting in the verses that whatever enemy confronts Henry, his "Trophees may be more, / Then all the HENRIES ever liu'd before."[42] Unintentionally, this view echoes Anne's imprudent threat to the French diplomat. Clearly, some who rallied about Henry did so precisely because of his militaristic tendencies, which stand in great contrast to his father's pacifist policies.

But this same Peacham saw another side of the prince: his generous interest in the arts. Peacham, in fact, dedicated his emblem book to Henry, making him titular patron of the volume. Peacham writes in the Dedication: "Hauing by more then ordinarie signes, tasted heeretofore of your gratious favour . . . I am emboldened once againe, to offer vp at the Altar of your gratious acceptance these mine *Emblemes*" (sig. A2). In addition to Peacham, Henry served as patron for George Chapman, Jonson, Drayton, and Inigo Jones. Henry began also to build an impressive collection of paintings that eventually passed to Prince Charles.[43] Henry's interests extended to architecture and music. Of course, he also served as patron for one of the London adult acting companies; but a contemporary account by a certain "W. H." says that he was not carried "away with any affection to stage-playes."[44]

Demonstrating a gentle spirit, the prince treated Phineas Pett with much kindness. As the designer and builder of the royal ship, Pett had many accusations made against him, culminating in a "trial" of him in 1609 with James and Henry present. Henry had great faith in Pett and made a public display of it; as Pett reports, Henry summoned him to St. James, "where his Highness vouchsafing to

Hopefull , HENRIE Prince of VVALES, &c.

Anagramma Authoris.

Βϵσπαρτίϵὖ τὶ χαρϵί.

HENRICVS Walliæ Princeps.

Par Achillis, Puer vne vinces .

T HVS, thus young HENRY, like Macedo's fonne,
 Ought' ft thou in armes before thy people fhine .
A prodigie for foes to gaze vpon,
But ftill a glorious Load-ftarre vnto thine:
 Or fecond PHOEBVS whofe all piercing ray,
 Shall cheare our heartes, and chafe our feares away .

That (once as *PHILLIP) IAMES may fay of thee,
Thy BRITAINE fcarcely fhall thy courage hold,
That whether TVRKE, SPAINE, FRAVNCE, orITALIE,
The RED-SHANKE, or the IRISH Rebell bold,
 Shall rouze thee vp, thy Trophees may be more,
 Then all the HENRIES ever liu'd before .

* Plutarch in A-lexandro .

Made tua virtute decus, fpes alma BRITANNVM Provocet Hifp̄ anus, feu Turea, rebellis Hibernus
Alter ALEXANDER confp̄ciende tuis: Herulus a tergo five laceffat inepts .

Rafil : Doror.

E corpore.

Emblem of Prince Henry, from Peacham's *Minerva Britanna* (1612).

lead me in his hand through the park to Whitehall, in the public view and hearing of many people there attending to see him pass to the King, . . . did in such loving manner counsel me with such comfortable, wise, and grave advice touching my carriage and resolution in my trial" (*Autobiography*, p. 50). Exonerated in the trial, Pett went on to complete the ship. Pett recalls the last meeting with Henry in August 1612: Henry "gave me a farewell in these words 'Go on cheerfully' saith he 'in that which I entrust you with, and let not the care for your posterity incumber you any ways, for you shall leave the care both of yourself and others to me' " (p. 98). Moved to tears, Pett parted from Henry, "though I little thought . . . that had been the last time I should have seen him alive" (p. 98). What strikes one in reading Pett's account is the unaffected, sincere, and generous nature of Henry, for all his militaristic image. One could easily multiply such examples of Henry's kind relationship to an extended family.

Gentle patron of the arts and would-be warrior—what about this young man's relationship to his parents, his sister, and brother? Much has already been said about Henry and Anne, especially her ongoing campaign to control him in some way. In his account, W. H. says that Henry went often to visit his mother; sometimes she would not receive him, and though Henry "inwardly with himselfe" might be displeased, "yet in show did he never seeme to be any wayes discontented therewith, but returned alwayes to his lodging with great patience" (p. 4).

With James, Henry could be both dutiful and obstinate. Isaac Casaubon, writing to friends, says that Henry was remarkable "for his piety and unaffected reverence for his Royal Father and Mother."[45] Thomas Birch notes that Henry sometimes opposed his father but that "filial piety" mainly governed Henry's actions (pp. 380–81). One must take with suitable caution James Maxwell's enthusiastic verse about Henry "That from his Cradle to his mournfull end, / He neuer did his father once offend."[46] Small wonder that this stanza closes by referring to Henry as a "Saint"; one could easily write Henry's hagiography, given such effusive praise. In a letter accompanying his New Year's gift to his father in 1608, Henry explained that for seven years now he had paid his duty to James by presenting some "literary offering," typically a Latin thesis of some kind. Though the accomplishment was modest, Henry did "not despair of having it received as a testimony of his piety and obedience, especially by a most loving and most benign Father" (Nichols, *Progresses*, 2:162).

Striking indeed was Henry's occasional function as intermediary between his father and mother. In a puzzling letter of December 1609, Henry was obviously trying to mediate between quarreling parents. He wrote at one point to James: "I durst not reply, that your Majesty was afraid, lest she [Anne] should return to her old biass; for fear that such a word might have set her in the way, and made me a peace-breaker, which I would eschew" (Nichols, 2:265–66). Probably because he was the eldest child, it fell Henry's lot to be caught in the middle between his parents—sometimes the cause of their battle, at times the mediator or arbiter. One of W. H.'s anecdotes captures a fusion of Henry's concern for James as father with a political concern for him as king. Coming out of his house at St. James to walk in the park, Henry was accompanied by a large number of people. But seeing James approaching "with a verie small companie, he was ashamed, and looking about him commanded his followers to depart and goe no further with him" (p. 3). Thus Henry was able to meet his father "not hauing past three or foure to attend and waite on him." The modesty and sensitivity reflected in this episode are refreshing. In another example that W. H. gives, Henry displayed his acute political awareness of the matter of rightful succession (p. 14); obviously he was a young man attuned to his political function.

One area of parental conflict was the selection of a suitable wife for Henry, about which, according to Cornwallis, Henry "shewed no vehement desire, yet he demonstrated a good inclination"[47]—like his father, Henry saw marriage as his duty. W. H. reports that Henry, in response to the marriages of some of his young gentlemen, said: "I would not be so soone maried, and yet I wish to see my Father a grandfather" (p. 24). As a royal child, Henry deferred to James's judgment on the issue of marriage. In a letter to James written from Richmond, 5 October 1612, just a month before his death, Henry wished his father to resolve the issue, to determine "my part to play, wch is to be in loue wth any of them."[48] Here is a son who has heeded the father's advice (and example) in *Basilicon Doron:* he is willing to marry for the sake of the kingdom.

On the other hand, considerable evidence demonstrates that father and son often annoyed each other: Henry by poking into things his father deemed not his business, and James by presiding over a profligate and corrupt court. (Henry's household of counselors and servants, by contrast, was a model of circumspection, financial frugality, and efficiency.) Even Bishop Goodman has to admit: "I confess that the prince did sometimes pry into the King's actions and a little dislike them" (*Court of King James*, 1:250). One word that crops up with some regularity to describe James's attitude toward his son is "jealousy." Molin noted in 1607 that James was not "overpleased to see his son so beloved and of such promise that his subjects place all their hopes in him; and it would almost seem, to speak quite frankly, that the King was growing jealous" (*CSP Venetian*, 10:513–14). Surely James was intelligent enough to be aware of some of the problems in his court; and if indeed Henry did set up a rival household, then it became the foil to James's decadence. Even in the elaborate festivities for Henry's investiture as Prince of Wales in 1610, James tried to manipulate the public's perception of his son. The Venetian ambassador, Correr, reported: "The King would not allow him [Henry] on this occasion, nor yet on his going to Parliament, to be seen on horseback. *The reason is the question of expense or, as some say, because they did not desire to exalt him too high*" (*CSP Venetian*, 11:507). A week later, on 23 June, Correr wrote: "*It seems that the King has some reasonable jealousy of the rising sun; and indeed the vivacity of this Prince grows apace, and every day he gives proof of wisdom and lofty thoughts far in advance of his years*" (11:516).

Henry was, however, very close to his sister Elizabeth, bearing out Stone's observation that brother-sister relationships in this period were often stronger than brother-brother ones, primarily because they were devoid of any inherent rivalry. Cornwallis writes that Henry did "entirely" love Elizabeth and Charles; W. H. notes that Henry "did send often to inquire of her [Elizabeth's] health, with diuers unfallible signes and tokens of his great loue & affection towards them both" (p. 4). But the expected childlike struggles were evident, too. Cornwallis says: "Yet must I confesse that sometimes by a kind of rough play and dalliance with the one, and a semblance of contradicting the other, in what he discerned her to desire, he tooke a pleasure in giving both to the one and to the other, some cause in those their so tender yeares to make proofe of their patiences."[49] More of Elizabeth and Charles in a moment.

In what was to be the last time, Henry entertained his family in late August 1612 at Woodstock; it was a most pleasant occasion for this royal family. So impressed was James with how excellent and orderly everything was at this feast, "that he was forced to say, that he had neuer seen the like before all his lifetime, and that he could neuer doe so much in his owne house."[50] On the latter point, James is surely right. Soon, however, illness, possibly typhoid fever, afflicted Henry; and despite the best, and often gruesome, efforts of the physicians, he died on 6 November, at the age of eighteen. Cornwallis in his *Life and Death of Prince Henry* offers day-to-day accounts of the last two weeks of Henry's life.

When death came, neither parent was present: Anne was at Somerset House, and James at Theobalds, according to Cornwallis "not willing nor being able to stay so neere the gates of so extreame sorrow" (Somers, *Tracts*, 2:241). The reaction of the country was shock, dismay, and a profound sense of loss. The Venetian ambassador, Foscarini, sums up the grief of the royal family:

> The King received the news of the Prince's death at Theobalds; it affected him greatly and made of the happiest the saddest father in the world. . . . The Queen's life has been in the greatest danger owing to her grief. She will receive no visits nor allow anyone in her room, from which she does not stir, nor does she cease crying. The Princess has gone two days without food and cries incessantly. . . . The Duke of York . . . shows a grief beyond his years. (12:449)

The ambassador adds poignantly that the "Elector Palatine does not know what to do," having arrived for his betrothal and wedding to Elizabeth and now having to face loss in the family. Foscarini concludes his dispatch: "And so the nuptial festivities of this house are turned to mournful trappings."

Henry's death had to be a great shock to his family; though there were other royal children, the seemingly inevitable process of Henry's rise to the throne had been blocked: uncertainty clouded the future. John Chamberlain wrote to Dudley Carleton about the loss that Elizabeth felt: "The Lady Elizabeth is much afflicted with this losse, and not without goode cause, for he did extraordinarilie affect her, and during his sicknes inquired still after her, and the last wordes he spake in good sense, (they say) were, Where is my deare sister?"[51] One could cite dozens of texts that responded to Henry's death with fervent and apparently genuine sorrow.

The dashed hope that Henry represented for so many people permeates Anthony Weldon's comment: "He was only shewed to this Nation, as the Land of *Canaan* was to *Moses*, to look on, not to enjoy: wee did indeed joy in that happinesse we expected in him."[52] Messianic hopes have fallen prey to death's sting; Prince Henry is not the Promised Land. The central fact of death, to which Stone has given great emphasis in his history of the English family, also touches the royal family: two infant daughters and now the teenage son—all dead within six years. Mystery surrounds Henry's death because we cannot be certain of the precise nature of his illness. Without wishing to enter the thicket of speculation about the cause of Henry's death, one can note that several contemporaries thought he had been poisoned—a view apparently shared by Anne.[53]

To turn from things dying to things new-born, we shift our attention to Elizabeth, whose greatest public moment in England will be her wedding in February 1613. She had, of course, already attracted much attention as the only surviving royal daughter. She had been placed in the care of Lord and Lady Harington at Combe Abbey in Warwickshire, where she remained until 1608, when she arrived at court, though still under the care of the Haringtons. Early in her experience in England she toured nearby Coventry on an official visit, where, in April 1604, the mayor and alderman, in their scarlet gowns, met her outside the city: "The Mayor alighted from his horse, kissed her hand, and then rode before her into the City with the Aldermen, &c" (Nichols, *Progresses*, 1:429). She moved through the streets of the city, attended a banquet in her honor, and received a silver cup. Though merely eight years old, she was beginning to enter the public political sphere. A thread of unstinted praise of her runs through the accounts.[54]

Lord Harington speaks of Elizabeth in glowing terms, referring to her in May 1604 as the King's "jewel": "Her Grace is very healthful and every way a child of such hope that when the King shall be an eye-witness it will be much to his comfort" (*Salisbury MSS.*, 16:111). James Maxwell in his *Laudable Life*, proclaiming Henry's love for his sister, says that she is one of the Graces, "whose happie breeding, worthy inclination, / Makes her admir'd, desir'd of euery Nation" (sig. B3). Thomas Ross, in a Latin tribute to Elizabeth, describes her thus:

> A princess of lovely beauty, in whom, at the first glance, majesty shines out, though hidden by courtesy. Although she has not yet passed her 12th year, yet all behold in her lively proofs of most excellent and noble disposition. . . . her manners are most gentle; and she shows no common skill in those liberal exercises of mind and body which become a royal maiden. In fine, whatever was excellent or lofty in Queen Elizabeth, is all compressed in the tender age of this virgin princess, and if God spare her to us, will be found there accumulated.[55]

Few could resist linking the princess to her namesake. Ross's assessment epitomizes the general view of Elizabeth when she arrived at court in 1608.

Crispin van de Passe, *Princess Elizabeth* (1613). Courtesy of
Folger Shakespeare Library.

One of the designs of the conspirators in the Gunpowder Plot
was to capture Elizabeth and set her up as queen. But Harington
reports her reaction to that scheme: ''Her Highness doth often say,
What a Queen should I have been by this means? I had rather have
been with my royal father in the Parliament-House, than wear this
crown on such condition.''[56] Responding to the awesome nature of
his task, Harington writes in January 1606: ''With Gods assistance we

hope to do our Lady Elizabeth such service as is due to her princely endowments and natural abilities; both which appear the sweet dawning of future comfort to her royal father" (*Nugae Antiquae*, 2:237).

Elizabeth and Henry would meet from time to time, particularly on special occasions, such as the Christmas season. Through these encounters and their exchange of letters a strong bond developed, confirmed when Elizabeth finally came to court in 1608. Harington, writing to Henry's tutor, encourages the deepening of the brother-sister relationship: "For my part, I wish with all my heart his highness might see her grace every day, to increase the comfort they receive in each other's company. I will be ready to further all occasions that may draw them together."[57] To cite a typical example of Elizabeth's letters to Henry, I quote from an undated one, probably written before 1608 and addressed "To my most dear brother ye Prince":

> I will euer endeavo^r to equall you, esteeming that time happiest when
> I enioyed your company, and desiring nothing more then the fruition
> of it again: that as nature hath made us neerest in our loue together,
> so accident might not separate us from liuing together: Neither do I
> account yt ye leste part of my present comfort that though I am
> depriued of your happy presence yet I can make these lines deliuer
> this true message that I will euer bee during my lyfe
>
> Yo^r most kinde and
louing syster
Elizabeth.[58]

Several such letters in the manuscript collection reveal a deep love. Brother and sister must on occasion have taken refuge in one another from the disagreements of their parents and the corruption of the court about them. Not surprisingly, these two royal children loomed large in the public imagination and hopes, constituting a diamond in the midst of much that was jaded.

The princess, whom Peacham in *Minerva Britanna* describes in an emblem as "great, religious, modest, wise, / By birth, by zeale, behauiour, iudgment sound" (p. 14), was the focus of news by the summer of 1612 when the marriage negotiations entered the final phase. Henry, supporting his father, favored Frederick; thus, as early as September 1611, John Holles could write to Sir John Digby: "Yet have I good grounds to believe that the Palsgrave will get the golden fleece."[59] Elizabeth would be a fortunate match for any eligible suitor by reason of both personality and politics. As the Venetian ambassador, Foscarini, noted on 9 August 1612: "If the King of Spain is to marry, he could find no better match, as the Princess is eligible for the succession to these realms if her two brothers died childless; besides which she is very beautiful, of the noblest blood, gentle manners, speaking several languages and of singular goodness" (*CSP Venetian,* 12:405–6). Despite Anne's unpleasant behavior, the teenage Elizabeth seems truly to have fallen in love with Frederick, transferring to her husband the great affection that she had felt for Henry. Shortly before the wedding in February 1613, John Chamberlain wrote to Alice Carleton:

> On Tewsday I tooke occasion to go to court because I had never seen the Palsgrave, nor the Lady Elizabeth (neere hand) of a long time: I had my full view of them both, but will not tell you all I thincke, but only this, that he owes his mistres nothing yf he were a Kings sonne as she is a Kings daughter. The worst is mee thincks he is much too young and small timbred to undertake such a taske. (*Letters,* 1:416)

The glittering festivities of the wedding hid any doubts that others may have had about the match; even Anne had been brought round to participate and to give the couple her sanction. The life so beautiful and new that loomed before the elegant couple turned to dismay and despair as they were left alone and isolated on the darkling plain of Europe. As Parry reminds us, Elizabeth wrote a letter of fond farewell to her father from Dover in 1613, "in which she lamented that they would probably never see each other again."[60] Caught in the Thirty Years' War and cut off from her parents and remaining brother in England, Elizabeth became the ill-fated Queen of Bohemia, the "Winter Queen." Francis Osborne, in his seventeenth-century *Memoirs,* notes that all that Elizabeth has received is a "multitude of children," and she has been cast "into an ocean of calamities, in which she still remaines a floting example to other princes of the instability of fortune, as she did in her prosperity for civility and goodnesse" (1:283). If 1607 constitutes a watershed year for James's royal family, certainly the winter of 1612-13 forms another one: Henry dies in November, Elizabeth marries in the following February. Two great hopes for the kingdom are in a way lost, one by death, the other by a marriage which, though desired, nevertheless separates parents from child. The royal family becomes a paradigm of tragicomedy, as it also risks dissolution. Prince Charles alone gathers the remnants of public expectation in the royal issue.

When the royal family had moved to England in 1603, Charles, born in 1600, was left behind in Scotland because he was in unstable health. Illness marred his first few years, and he did not come to England until late in 1604. Assessing Charles's condition, Dr. Atkins, who attended him, wrote in a letter to the queen on 3 June 1604: "His Highness now walketh many times in a day all the length of the great chamber at Damfermelinge like a gallant soldier all alone. He often talketh of going to London and desireth to see his gracious Queen mother" (*Salisbury MSS.*, 16:163). Atkins promised the queen that when next she saw Charles, she would "behold a most sweet picture and 'vive' image of his most royal father. Then shall you behold wit and beauty striving for superiority, his body and mind contending which of the two nature hath most adorned."

The doctor's enthusiasm may be a bit ahead of the facts, at least regarding Charles's health. Anne, apparently exercising her own will, chose the family of Sir Robert Carey in which to place Charles, already in his fourth year. Robert Carey's *Memoirs* contains information about the care of the young prince. Carey notes, rather bluntly, the risk involved in taking care of a sick royal child: "Those who wished me no good were glad of it [the choice of his family], thinking that if the Duke should die in our charge (his weakness being such as gave them great cause to suspect it) then it would not be thought fit that we should remain in court after."[61] When Charles moved to their household at some time in 1604, he was, according to Carey, "not able to go, nor scant to stand alone, he was so weak in his joints, and especially his ankles, insomuch as many feared they were out of joint" (p. 68). Fortunately, for the sake of the Careys and Charles, he got better.

But King James occasionally attempted to interfere in Charles's care; for example: "The King was desirous that the string under his tongue should be cut, for he was so long beginning to speak as he thought he would never have spoken" (p. 69). James also suggested that iron boots should be put on Charles's feet in order to strengthen them. Lady Carey, however, won the battle on both of these issues. Carey points out: "My wife had charge of him from a little past four, till he was almost eleven years old" (p. 69). When Charles left their household, Lady Carey "with great grief took leave of her dear master, the Duke." Charles had reached the stage at which he was to be turned over to the administration of men, "the Duke to have none but men to attend upon him." The schedule of Charles's nurturing runs several years behind that of Henry's, probably because of his

Prince Charles, from Robert Dallington's *Aphorismes Civill and Militarie* (1613). Courtesy of Folger Shakespeare Library.

illness. Henry had moved into the male world at about six years of age.

Because Charles was still a child at the time when prospective marriages were being talked about for his brother and sister, we do not find as much information about him as about the other two. The studious, intellectual quality of the young prince, probably the result of his illness and enforced inactivity, attracted James to him. The Venetian ambassador reveals something of James's delight in Charles; Giustinian reports in February 1608: "While talking on this point the young Duke of York, the King's second son, came in;

65

he is the joy of the King, the Queen and all the Court. His Majesty began to laugh and play with him. In the course of his jokes he took up the Duke and said, 'My Lord Ambassador, you must make my son a Patrician of Venice' " (*CSP Venetian*, 11:95). Bishop Goodman insists that "the Queen did ever love Charles better than Prince Henry" (1:251). But I think we need not put great credence in that judgment. Insofar as it might be true, it could be the result of her awareness of the loss of Henry to his own ideas and plans and of the simple delight of a young child in the family and at court. Charles's innocent letters to Henry contain sweetness, but it is difficult to know the depth of any feeling that might have existed. Charles, for example, concludes one letter: "Good Brother looue me and I shall euer looue and serue you."[62] As indicated earlier in this chapter, Henry was perfectly capable of taunting his weaker brother.

Brave are Marcelline's words in 1610 that God "will very quickly raise and exalt Great *Brittain*, in the *Apogaeum* of his [Charles's] Greatnesse" (*Triumphs of King James*, p. 67). Further, Marcelline compares the ten-year-old Charles to other famous rulers also named Charles. In keeping with the militaristic image that Marcelline has painted of Henry, he says of Charles: "Methinkes I see a Sword in your hand, and you vpon the walles of *Nicomedia, Nicea, Antiocke,* and *Tripoli*, ayming at the fairest through all perilles . . ." (p. 73). Hard pressed in his emblem of Charles, Peacham emphasizes that Charles "bear'st thy Fathers Image right / Aswell in bodie, as thy towardly mind" (p. 18). In Charles's cheeks the red and white roses "yet againe conioind." His virtues "shall make vs loue thee more, / Then all thy state we outwardly adore." Literary license operates here. Lamenting the death of Henry and indulging in some wishful thinking, James Maxwell, in his *Laudable Life*, suggests that Charles is "another / Great-hearted HENRY, borne by starrie fate, / This Ilands honour to perpetuate" (sig. B3).

With irony produced by historical events, one looks at the emblem dedicated to Anne in Peacham's *Minerva Britanna*; depicted here, a genealogical tree of sorts symbolizes the three royal children on the branches. Peacham writes:

> Fairest of Queenes, thou art thy selfe the Tree,
> The fruite thy children, hopefull Princes three.
> Which thus I ghesse, shall with their outstretcht armes,
> In time o'respread Europa's continent,
> To shield and shade, the innocent from harmes,
> But overtop the proud and insolent:
>> Remaining, raigning, in their glories greene,
>> While man on earth, or Moone in heauen is seene. (P. 13)

Anagramma D:
Gul : Fouleri.

In ANNA regnantium arbor.

ANNA *Britannorum Regina.*

A N Oliue lo, with braunches faire difpred;
Whofe top doth reach vnto the azure skie,
Much feeming to difdaine, with loftie head
The Cedar, and thofe Pines of THESSALIE,
Faireft of Queenes, thou art thy felfe the Tree;
The fruite * thy children, hopefull Princes three.

* Non claffes,
non Legiones,
ſ eri :de fiːma im-
perii munimenta
quam numerum
liberorum. Ta-
citus. 4 . Hiſt :

* parcere fubiec-
tis. &c.

Which thus I gheffe, fhall with their outftretcht armes,
In time o'refpread Europa's continent,
* To fhield and fhade, the innocent from harmes;
But overtop the proud and infolent :
Remaining, raigning, in their glories greene,
While man on earth, or Moone in heauen is feene.

Fatum

Emblem of Queen Anne, from Peacham's *Minerva Britanna.*

The tree bore good fruit; but the winds of change and death spoiled the potential, because none of the children achieve the full fruition that seemed so promising and inevitable in the halcyon days of the first decade of James's English rule.

It remains to speak of Arbella Stuart, James's cousin. We may recall that Arbella rode with other members of the royal family in the 1604 royal entry into London—full public and political recognition that she was to be esteemed a member of James's family. Queen Anne and Arbella were the same age, and as G. P. V. Akrigg points out, Anne took her up with enthusiasm.[63] The royal children delighted in her, practicing their penmanship by writing letters to Arbella. She was godmother to James's daughter Mary. Brought out of languishing obscurity, Arbella gained a place in Whitehall. Being incorporated into the royal family, Arbella was for a while very happy indeed. The Venetian ambassador Molin, who in 1607 described and analyzed the royal family, also includes Arbella. He writes of her: "She is twenty-eight; not very beautiful, but highly accomplished, for besides being of most refined manners she speaks fluently Latin, Italian, French, Spanish, reads Greek and Hebrew, and is always studying" (*CSP Venetian*, 10:514). Her studious quality itself should have endeared her to James, though I doubt that he paid much attention to it. Molin adds: "The King professes to love her and to hold her in high esteem. She is allowed to come to Court, and the King promised, when he ascended the throne, that he would restore her property, but he has not done so yet." James put her off, saying that she would receive her property when she married. But as Molin observes, nothing has happened yet on that score: "She remains without a mate and without estate."

James's benign neglect of Arbella turned to sharper confrontation when Arbella, increasingly desperate for marriage and her property, fell in love with and attempted to marry William Seymour, the future earl of Hertford. The first big crisis came in 1610; Venetian diplomatic dispatches record the events, as the ambassadors report: "*After examination separately they* [Arbella and Seymour] *were both summoned before the King, the Prince and the Council and ordered to give up all negotiations for marriage*" (*CSP Venetian*, 11:439). Despite Arbella's impassioned plea, James was adamant.[64] This bad situation worsened the following year when Arbella and Seymour defied James by getting married. James's objection rested on a narrow and jealous understanding about his control of kingship and the likely heirs to the throne. Bishop Goodman explains the point: "She did match with one of the blood royal who was descended from Henry the Seventh, so that by this match there was a combination of titles, which princes have ever been jealous of" (*Court of King James*, 1:210). Why James should have taken this view in 1611 is puzzling; after all, he had three healthy children who could presumably succeed to the throne. Poor Arbella had no designs on the crown at all; she simply wanted to be married. Even Bishop Goodman, prone to think highly of James, blames James for his perverse behavior; and he observes that in "every way [the marriage was] a fit and a convenient match" (1:209).

James was insistent: he had the couple imprisoned. Eventually Arbella and Seymour escaped through sympathetic help from their jailers. Possibly Arbella's learning came in handy, as she seems to have taken as her plan an episode from some romance or Elizabethan comedy: she disguised herself as a man and rode in man's attire to Greenwich. But the attempt to sail to France ran into problems, and James sent word to have the lovers apprehended. Captured and brought to the Tower, Arbella was to spend the remainder of her life there. As Handover says: "Indifferent to his cousin's suffering, absorbed in his hunting and favourites, James was well content to let her pay the penalties of disobedience" (*Arbella Stuart*, p. 288). The public, apparently moved by the romance of Arbella's escape, took a dim view of James's action.

Arbella persisted in believing that James would relent and release her. One particularly poignant action during her final years was her purchase of four new and expensive gowns for Princess Elizabeth's wedding, which, of course, James did not let her attend. Arbella's mind increasingly filled with illusions, she went mad in the Tower and died there in 1615. The peacemaker James had not been able to reconcile himself with his cousin. In this case, family feeling and ties counted for little. James's treatment of Arbella illustrates his increasing lack of sensitivity in responding to the needs of his family.

What I have described in the preceding pages sounds like the dissolution of the royal family because that is partly what goes on during the period 1603–13 in James's family. But such a disintegration of the family should not be altogether surprising. Claude Lévi-Strauss, in an essay on the family, observes:

> The primary social concern regarding the family is not to protect or enhance it: it is rather an attitude of diffidence, a denial of its right to exist either in isolation or permanently; restricted families are only permitted to live for a limited period of time, either long or short

according to case, but under the strict condition that their component parts be ceaselessly displaced, loaned, borrowed, given away, or returned, so that new restricted families may be endlessly created or made to vanish.[65]

Within the forming of James's family lies its potential undoing, a natural process of new families to be established—as in the case of Elizabeth. The children who survive move out to create their own restricted families. The process is ongoing. The present ruling family in England is, after all, a direct descendant of James's family.

From the perspective of the kingdom, several ideas run through the experience of this Stuart family. First, great joy initially greeted this family, a mixture of relief at a peaceful succession to the throne and fascination with having a family to surround the English monarch again. Allowing for some exaggeration, there is nevertheless much truth in what Sir Thomas Wentworth said in Parliament in 1614, in behalf of yet another request by James for money. Wentworth urged his fellow members of Parliament to recall their fear at the death of Elizabeth and how that was overcome by James and his family:

> I speake not unknowen things whear now we see by the bright arriual of his Maiesty to this Crowne, all thos mists happily dispersed and ourselfs in a fare and glorious sunshine. O let us neuer be unthankfull to God for soe great a blessing, . . . or ingratefull to soe good a Prince that hath ruled euer since by our owne lawes with iustice, clemency, fatherly care and in peace.[66]

Tragedies have surely invaded the domestic life of the family, but the kingdom has survived.

One of the near-tragedies was, of course, the Gunpowder Plot. James and others seized on the fortunate outcome to speak of God's deliverance. The Venetian ambassador, Molin, reported an encounter with James and the young Prince Charles just a few weeks after the plot was exposed: "His Majesty turned to him [Charles] and said, 'This poor boy's innocence and that of the Prince and of others has had more power with God than the perfidious malignity of men.' I said that was very true, and that his Majesty must feel a singular satisfaction from the very evident protection of God" (*CSP Venetian,* 10:296–97). It is not merely that God has chosen to deliver them, but that He has done so in part because of the innocence of James's family, a clear case of the intermingling of the domestic and public life of the royal family. George Marcelline, in *The Triumphs of King James,* referred to the "wonderfull deliuerance" that God had provided because God "will haue his Maiesty to liue and flourish more then euer heeretofore" (p. 51). In a sermon commemorating the event, preached at Whitehall before the king on 5 November 1606, Lancelot Andrewes suggested that it was no particular miracle for a king to be delivered: "But, to see King, Queen, their seed, all their estates delivered, that is *mirabile*, that is 'a new thing created on the earth.' I conclude: as that was the devil's doing, and was monstrous in our eyes; so, 'This is God's doing,' and it is 'marvellous in our eyes.' "[67] Sparing the family—that is the miracle.

Unmistakable throughout the evidence that I have offered is the great hope and expectation that rested with James's children, especially with Henry and Elizabeth. How early in James's reign public affection shifted to the children, not just because they were children and fascinating but also because they came to represent a way out of the increasing corruption of James's court. The people looked for another kind of deliverance; on this, of course, they were frustrated by the death of Henry and the marriage of Elizabeth. Because James was soon sized up for what he was, focus naturally moved to the children, who offered hope of political and moral renewal.

From March 1603, when word reached James that Elizabeth had died and that he would be King of England, to February 1613, when Princess Elizabeth married Frederick, the Stuart royal family learned much of joy and sorrow, of hopes raised and expectations dashed, of life and death. In these experiences this family does not greatly differ from other families of its own time or later. But because this is a royal family, the consequences of its life are always political. If what I have suggested is valid—namely, that 1607 is a watershed year for the Jacobean royal family and so is the winter of 1612–13—then Shakespeare's Romances appear in this important interval. Shakespeare steps into this wide gap of time: the Romances are the artistic result.

Fires of passion, enthusiasm, hope, and anger burn brightly in this Stuart family; the ice of isolation, loneliness, despair, and unconcern banks and sometimes extinguishes the flame. When husband and wife become that in name only, when children are disaffected from parents, when the father presides over an increasingly corrupt court, then the family sustains only a tenuous bond. Physical separation and fragmentation characterize much of the private domestic life of James's family. Without wanting to exaggerate, it is nevertheless difficult to shake the image of parents who are absent from the bedside of their dying child—with one parent going off to hunt. Despite what seems like an impossibly fractured family, it can, however, still experience moments of spontaneous and shared joy in the routine of daily living.

Especially can it respond to public demands and expectations. Thus James's family comes together in the 1607–13 period at the great moments of public celebration: Christmas, an investiture, a royal birth, a royal wedding. The text that this family presents on such occasions for all to read is that of a family united and inviolate against any political attack. The politics of the family is intact despite personal conflicts. Citizens behold the family as if it were on a stage, as indeed it was, and enjoy the performance. Jonathan Goldberg remarks: "Unlike modern families, Renaissance families need to be read from the outside in: from the state to the family; from the spiritual to the material" (*James I*, p. 89). One of the reasons for focusing on the Jacobean royal family is to accomplish precisely the activity of reading from the outside in; such a method is also important for understanding Shakespeare's royal families. The intermingling of private and public life, so evident in this historical family, finds its counterpart in Shakespeare's families of art.

James's family becomes a prototext for the Romances where the reunions of royal families signal feasts, marriages, and other public displays. Shakespeare, standing in London's streets for James's royal entry in March 1604, must have been impressed with the royal family as family and with its concomitant political expression of the language of power. With his own power of language he creates royal families in the Romances, families susceptible to suffering and separation yet ultimately able to triumph in ways possible in fiction but sometimes alien to actual experience.

The tapestry of the Stuart royal family, its mingled yarn, thus contains many colors and themes—bright and shiny, dark and shadowy. I argue, in the analysis of the Romances, that Shakespeare gazed on this tapestry, or—to come back to my earlier metaphor—that he read the text of the family and re-presented the royal family in his late plays. Having examined James's family in the preceding pages, we have the advantage of understanding this particular context for the Romances by getting to know the personalities, conflicts, events, and themes that characterize the royal family that Shakespeare knew.

3

Family, Sex, and Marriage in Jacobean Comedy

> More belongs to marriage than four bare legs under a blanket.
> —A seventeenth-century proverb

If we may regard the Stuart royal family as a text known to Shakespeare and important for the Romances, then I think we also need to examine comic dramatic texts of the first decade of James's reign. Critics have often sought a courtly aesthetic, particularly the influence of the court masque, in order to provide the context of Shakespeare's last plays. Without ruling out a connection of the masque to the Romances but believing that this subject has already been rather thoroughly discussed, I choose to focus on the comic drama performed in public and private theaters and on occasion at court. The Romances are not court masques, whatever features they may share; they are part of the tradition of Jacobean comedy. More than fifty plays make up the canon of Jacobean comedy from 1603 to 1613. Given the limitations of space, I cannot discuss all of them, but I have selected ones that I think illuminate some features of family life. Having read the royal family from outside in, we can now read the families of Jacobean comedy in a similar manner.

The character Rhodoricke in Chapman's *Monsieur D'Olive* says: ". . . the Court's as t'were the stage . . ." (I.ii.120).[1] Certainly the evidence of the preceding chapter confirms this assessment, because James and his family were conscious of their public role, their performance. But if all the world's a stage, as Jaques and modern interpreters such as Stephen Greenblatt and Jonathan Goldberg assert, then awareness of performance permeates all of life. Signior Antifront in Edward Sharpham's *The Fleire* (1607) observes: "The Cittie is like a Commodie, both in parts and in apparell, and your Gallants are the Actors: for hee that yesterday played the Gentleman, nowe playes the Beggar; shee that played the Wayting-woman, nowe playes the Queane; hee that played the married-man, nowe playes the Cuckolde; and shee that played the Ladie, now playes the Painter."[2] Life imitates the stage, as the stage imitates life. In the theater, then, one may obviously expect to find some reflection of society's habits and customs. Certainly the theater of Jacobean comedy fastens onto the family as one of its principal subjects. Trying to establish the context of the family for Shakespeare's Romances, I think it necessary to look not only at the Stuart royal family but also at families represented on the stage by Shakespeare's contemporaries.

Satire dominates comic form in the Jacobean period. This period is, after all, the heyday of "city" or "citizen" comedy. This drama, mainly satiric, reflects many of the qualities of the family as documented in Lawrence Stone's historical study: psychic numbing, insensitivity, lack of affect, and breaking of the child's will. In its nature, satiric drama is subversive and heretical, inveighing against society's institutions; thus when dramatists examine the family, they depict it as fragmented and in disarray, consumed by its aspiring Faustian greed. Indeed, satiric dramatists seldom present a whole family, healthy or unhealthy; instead they explore parts of a family. In that artistic choice lies a statement about the perspective on the family: this unit of society lacks cohesion and sometimes coherence; its bonds are inadequate to counter the transient quality of the family.

Why this outbreak of satiric drama in the early years of James's reign? The harsh verse satires of the late Elizabethan period had been suppressed; but satire gained new life in the Jacobean theater, casting its wary eye on such social institutions as the family, religion, and the legal system.[3] I believe that the family was becoming especially vulnerable for two reasons: children were attaining greater prominence in the family structure, and the sense of family was undergoing a transition from its extended to its nuclear state. Questions of inheritance were becoming more significant for many families as the wealth of different classes increased, a situation thus inviting prospects of greed. I think it also possible that the advent of the Stuart royal family and the political and social stability that it offered the kingdom made more likely the luxury of satire. The Stuart royal family therefore provokes a paradox: some writers, like Shakespeare, idealize the family in partial response to James's family; others, under similar circumstances, launch an attack on the family, although they never, it is important to observe, attack *royal* families. One response leads to pastoral or romance; the other, to satire.

The anthropologist Clifford Geertz writes: "A world wholly demystified is a world wholly depoliticized."[4] Though Geertz is not writing about satiric drama, I think his observation fits quite well the pattern that one finds in Jacobean drama. It is my contention, therefore, that satiric drama demystifies, demythologizes, the family by focusing on its follies, liabilities, and fragmentation. Such drama thereby creates a depoliticized world. Shakespeare and a few of his contemporaries do quite the opposite, embracing a mythos of the family that centers on the center, the royal family. The world of Shakespeare's Romances, I argue, is highly political and inextricably linked to the family. The politics of the family, so crucial in James's own family, as I demonstrated in the previous chapter, and so vital in Shakespeare's Romances, as I will argue in the next chapter, has little relevance for Jacobean satiric comedy.

Because I want to establish the dramatic context for Shakespeare's last plays, I find that a study of his contemporaries' comic drama is essential. Even though Shakespeare may not seem to agree with most of his fellow playwrights on the subject of the family, his drama comes into clearer focus as we understand what surrounds it. His image of the family defines itself in part by contrast to the demystifying process that others engage in. Pastoral and satire, typically so different from one another, are nevertheless two forms written exclusively from the viewpoint of city dwellers. In Jacobean England urban dramatists saw the family from at least two different angles. In this chapter, I will trace the demystified and depoliticized world of satire, and then its opposite in the few plays by Shakespeare's contemporaries which create a mythos of the family. Family, sex, and marriage constitute the center. We confront Maynard Mack's question, cited in chapter 1 above: "At what points in which plays may one reasonably suppose that a contemporary spectator sensed cross-currents between the conflicts and configurations before him in the playhouse and those known from family life around him, or possibly from his own?" (*Rescuing Shakespeare*, p. 6).

Francis Bacon writes in his essay "Of Love": "The stage is more beholding to Love, than the life of man. For as to the stage, love is ever matter of comedies, and now and then of tragedies; but in life it doth much mischiefe; sometimes like a syren, sometimes like a fury."[5] In the comedies, one finds plenty of evidence both of the alluring and of the destructive nature of love. A few comments, excerpted from the drama, reveal much of the mood that presides over comedy in the early Jacobean period. Cloe, for example, in John

Fletcher's *The Faithful Shepherdess* observes: "It is impossible to Ravish mee, / I am soe willing" (III.i.212–13). Sex is bought and given away freely in the drama; it is a readily available commodity. Adultery and cuckoldry are commonplace; men and women risk their marriages to satisfy their lust. The cynicism that permeates many marriages is perhaps epitomized by Matheo's answer to the question posed in Thomas Dekker's *2 The Honest Whore:* "Is this thy wife?"; and he responds: "A poore Gentlewoman, sir, whom I make vse of a nights" (III.ii.85). Marriages are often a means of settling a score, gaining an inheritance, or triumphing over a kinsman; and only occasionally are they a product of love. The fusion (or perhaps confusion) of economics and marriage determines a response made in Fletcher's *The Night-Walker*. When the Nurse complains that the Mother might have chosen a better, more handsome man to be the daughter's husband, the Mother replies: "Peace, he is rich Nurse, / He is rich, and that's beauty" (I.i). That money complicates and often obscures the issue of love is apparent in most of the marriages that parents arrange for their children. The drama reflects economic concern, primarily in aristocratic marriages, for gaining estates and dowries as the basis for marrying. Small wonder that Moll, in Dekker and Middleton's *The Roaring Girl*, describes impossible terms under which she might consider marriage. To such terms, Lord Noland says: "This sounds like domes-day"; and Moll responds: "Then were marriages best, / For if I should repent, I were soone at rest" (V.ii.221–22). In short, we are a long way from the spirit of *A Midsummer Night's Dream*.[6]

Family struggles are both the cause and the effect of sexual and marital difficulties. Parent is set against child, child against parent: the natural bond cracks. Sir Alexander, in *The Roaring Girl*, complains that his son should be "The columne and maine arch vnto my house, / The crutch vnto my age"; instead, he has become a "whirlewind / Shaking the firm foundation" (I.ii.117–19). Disinheritance is the threat that looms large in the plays. Also we may find a son or a nephew trying to gain an inheritance from a reluctant father or uncle—witness Middleton's *A Trick to Catch the Old One* or Jonson's *Epicoene*, to cite obvious examples. Children flee from parents in order to pursue love or some other quest. From whatever perspective one views the comic drama, one thing is clear: many tempests beat against the validity and permanence of the family. To recall the close of Bacon's essay: "Nuptial love maketh mankind; friendly love perfecteth it; but wanton love corrupteth and embasseth it" (6:398).

In many of these plays, familial and marital corruption refracts through the prism of a satiric vision.

These comments from the plays provide a foretaste of some of the principal issues in Jacobean comedy. As we look at family problems in the satiric drama, several points emerge. First, as mentioned above, the family seldom appears whole in these plays; instead, we find fragments or fractions. In this case the total is less than the sum of its parts. To focus on the part and not the whole assures a demystified view of family life. Reconciliations of family members, when they do occur, are often of a dubious sort: one is not always sure what has been gained by the truce. Questions of inheritance and succession, so politically important in Shakespeare's Romances, are depoliticized in the satiric drama, becoming there largely economic games rather than a search for a family and for assurance of political stability in the kingdom. To generalize, sex in satiric comedy falls in the category of recreation; in the Romances it is more a matter of procreation. In most Jacobean comedy, marriages are made in the marketplace, not in heaven. Economics, not politics and certainly not love, determines the selection of marriage partners. Children are of little consequence; mainly they are to be avoided, or they become mere pawns in some economic scheme. The healing potential of children that we generally find in the Romances and the loving, nurturing attitude toward such children are alien to the drama epitomized by Jonson and Middleton. Most of Shakespeare's contemporaries in the early Jacobean period view the family as the lowest common denominator, stripped of its mythos and its political consequences for the state. Shakespeare and a few other dramatists, to be discussed at the end of this chapter, see the family whole with its political implications. Both perspectives constitute early Jacobean comedy; we understand each viewpoint better by understanding its opposite.

This examination of unequal parts begins with those plays, mainly satiric in tone, that focus on ordinary families. The study will conclude by analyzing those few comedies, outside of Shakespeare, that center on royal families. I begin with a play about ordinary domestic life that was nevertheless performed before the royal court: Beaumont and Fletcher's *The Coxcomb* (1609). Although certainly not the finest Jacobean comedy, this play nevertheless creates special interest because of one of its performances, as well as its insight into marriage. Virtually inexplicable is a performance of this play at court on 2 or 3 November 1612, a mere three or four days before Prince

Henry died. As indicated in the previous chapter, Henry's condition had been deteriorating for several weeks; certainly by this point in early November, everyone knew that he was gravely ill. How does one reconcile that somber fact with a court-sponsored performance of this facile and bawdy play? If we could answer such a question, we might truly have insight into the "courtly aesthetic." The court, after all, saw more performances of conventional plays than it did of masques. Did someone at court somehow think *The Coxcomb* an appropriate play amidst the anxiety about Henry's impending death? Did any member of the royal family actually see the performance? Beyond these fascinating but unanswerable questions lie the family issues in the play itself, with primary focus on marriage.

Two distinct plots, which I will examine separately, constitute *The Coxcomb:* the Viola/Richardo love story and the curious Antonio/Maria/Mercury love triangle. Spied upon and kept virtually a prisoner by her father, Viola nevertheless responds to Richardo's offer of love by making plans to escape and to rendezvous with him. By I.iv she does escape, hoping that the household gods will "hold my Father in" (27).[7] Presumably, her father wants to select a husband for her. In a cruel twist the drunken Richardo rebuffs Viola, and she is left desperate in the night to fend for herself. From that moment in the play until Act V she endures a series of episodic adventures; the dramatists' task is somehow to bring Viola and Richardo together.

Viola's adventures include capture by a Tinker and his trull and eventual rescue by Valerio, who, though married, becomes attracted to her. Valerio punctures the fairly conventional romantic love story by offering quite a different perspective on love and marriage. He and Viola have a long discussion in Act III on this topic, she but sixteen years old and he worldly wise. To her question of what is love, Valerio responds: "Why, love faire maid is an extream desire, / That's not to be examin'd but fulfil'd . . ." (III.iii.14–15). Cynical and opportunistic, Valerio wants Viola to submit to his sexual desires. She refuses and finally asks about his wife:

> *Viola.* How fell you in love with such a creature?
> *Valerio.* I never lov'd her.
> *Viola.* And yet married her?
> *Valerio.* Shee was a rich one. (III.iii.49–52)

There, in a nutshell, is the heart of the satiric perspective on marriage: marriages occur for economic advantages; love is irrelevant.

Released unharmed by Valerio, Viola eventually meets Richardo; they are reconciled as she offers him all her jewels and, more precious, her forgiveness (V.ii.143–47). She seems a bit wiser now, remarking that she will have a story for the winter's fire: "When we are old; I'le tell my daughters then, / The miseryes their Mother had in love: / And say my girles bee wiser . . ." (V.ii.158–60). The meeting and reunion of father and daughter in the play's final scene (V.iii) fall particularly flat; obviously Beaumont and Fletcher are not especially interested in the parent/child relationship.

The marriage of Antonio and Maria is at best perverse. Antonio creates a love triangle, including his friend Mercury. For what are simultaneously and paradoxically perverse and magnanimous reasons, Antonio wants to share Maria with his friend, thereby, he thinks, ranking their friendship with that of Damon and Pithias (II.i.153). Antonio will not be a cuckold so much as a wittol, the coxcomb of the play's title. Mercury, for his part, weary of traveling with Antonio for three years and puzzled by the offer of Maria, nevertheless admits that he finds her attractive. Antonio's strategies culminate in his sending out word that he is dead, thereby freeing Maria to do as she will.

As irony will have it, however, Mercury, by IV.vii, has grown weary of his sexual involvement with Maria. Nagged by guilt, Mercury also gets a reminder from her: "Then remember your promise you made to marry mee" (IV.viii.31). She had not agreed to marriage earlier, she says, because such haste after her husband's death might be unseemly (one can count on moral values being a little askew in satiric drama). When a bungling Justice (in V.iii) accuses Maria and Mercury of murdering Antonio, then turns to the disguised Antonio and also accuses him, Antonio decides to unmask. Curiously, he praises his wife and friend and says: "ah good wife, love my friend, friend love my wife, harke friend" (V.iii.221–22). Mercury confesses that he has lost his passion for Maria. Beaumont and Fletcher stand the institution of marriage on its head. The love story of Viola and Richardo counters the perverse and ironic marriage of Antonio and Maria, but the two plots do not cohere well. It is difficult to determine the dramatists' judgment on the story that they have created. The audience seems to be offered a choice between naïve and perverse love. *The Coxcomb* does, however, hint at marital problems that will occupy many other dramatists as they demystify the family.

Marriage, King James had written to Prince Henry in *Basilicon Doron*, is the greatest earthly felicity or misery that can come to a man. Most Jacobean dramatists accent the misery, including Ben Jonson, to whose drama I turn. In his major satiric comedies, Jonson includes no love story comparable to the Viola/Richardo one in *The Coxcomb*, but he portrays marital problems that rival anything that Beaumont and Fletcher could devise. In *Volpone* and *Epicoene*, the two plays that I will concentrate on, Jonson explores three major questions of family life: marriage, children, and economics, chiefly the question of inheritance. Marital relationships are all flawed, parent/child relationships are contentious, and the economics of greed drives the plots. One can rightly talk about the cash nexus of the family. Jonson points the direction for much Jacobean comedy by not presenting complete families: in their fragmentation lies their lack of mythos. The limited yet crowded world of Jonson's satire provides no place for healthy families, nor is there any extended concern about politics, only Sir Politic's benighted view of statecraft. I should add that I am not saying anything about Jonson's personal attitude in regard to family life; indeed, recalling a few of Jonson's poems on the deaths of his children and the boy actor Salomon Pavy should clarify Jonson's emotional response to children. We separate the satirist from the satire.

"Has he children?" Corvino asks about Volpone (I.v.43).[8] Mosca answers: "Bastards, / Some dozen, or more, that he begot on beggars, / Gypsies, and Jews, and black-moors when he was drunk" (43–45). Further, it is common knowledge that "The dwarf, the fool, the eunuch are all his; / He's the true father of his family . . ." (47–48)—the unnatural father of an unnatural family. In another sense, Volpone has children within the play: the legacy hunters who are would-be surrogate children, anxious to gain their father's inheritance. If together they constitute a kind of family, then it is a family devoid of love and motivated only by greed. Volpone himself says: "I have no wife, no parent, child, ally, / To give my substance to; but whom I make / Must be my heir" (I.i.73–75). He establishes the dominant tone in his opening hymn in praise of gold when he praises it as "being the best of things, and far transcending / All style of joy in children, parents, friends, / Or any other waking dream on earth" (I.i.16–18). As each of the legacy hunters enters in Act I, the issue of family relationship arises. Assuring Voltore that he will be named heir, Mosca makes a request: "I do beseech you, sir, you will vouchsafe / To write me i' your family" (I.iii.34–35). Mosca, of course, tells Corbaccio to disinherit his son (I.iv. 95–97). Corbaccio warms to the possibility, assuring Mosca: "I do not doubt to be a father to thee" (127). But we also hear Mosca's aside: "Nor I to gull my brother of his blessing" (128)—a comment reminiscent of Jacob and Esau. We see what value Mosca places on family; he is totally cynical about such an institution. Voltore and Corbaccio are thus ready themselves to be unnatural fathers, thereby paralleling Volpone.

One of the terrible things that a parent could do was to disinherit a child—witness Lear's treatment of Cordelia—and yet Corbaccio would do that to Bonario and adopt Mosca into his family. Bonario learns, thanks to Mosca, of his father's intention and waits to confront him, only to be interrupted by the cries of Celia, whom he rescues. Mosca compounds the difficulty of this father/son relationship by telling Corbaccio that Bonario had appeared with the intent of killing him—a situation that finds its tragic counterpart in Edmund's accusation about Edgar to Gloucester in *Lear*. The presumed threat of murder now joins the matter of disinheritance in destroying this family. In the trial scene in Act IV Corbaccio denies his son totally: "He is an utter stranger to my loins" (IV.v.110); and he turns to Bonario: "Monster of men, swine, goat, wolf, parricide! / Speak not, thou viper" (111–12). Lear has his pelican daughters; and Corbaccio, his viperous son. But judgment falls heavily on Corbaccio; Mosca scolds him and urges: "Go home, and die, and stink" (V.iii.74). The final trial scene concludes that Bonario shall be given all the properties, and Corbaccio is to be confined to a monastery (V.xii). The father loses his son; the son, his father—all the result of Corbaccio's insatiable thirst for Volpone's treasure. The economics of greed sullies and destroys the family.

The same could be said of the marriage of Corvino and Celia. The issue for Corvino is not his child but his wife and how she might assist his quest for Volpone's inheritance. Corvino is the typical jealous husband; but he changes to potential wittol, reminiscent of Antonio in *The Coxcomb*, when Mosca suggests that if Celia would lie with Volpone, Corvino would become heir. With breathtaking irony, Corvino now insists that if Celia does not surrender herself to Volpone, he will drag her by the hair through the streets of Venice, shouting that she is a strumpet (III.vii.96–97). In the inventory scene, in which Mosca lists his new treasure, he also renders judgment on the legacy hunters, saying to Corvino: ". . . do not you know I know you an ass, / And that you would most fain have been a wittol / If fortune would have let you?" (V.iii.50–52). It was, we recall, the disinherited son, Bonario, who rescued the abandoned wife, Celia, both victims of families that are torn apart by greed. In the second trial, V.xii, Corvino receives his formal punishment: he is to row about the canals of Venice, "Wearing a cap with fair long ass's ears / Instead of horns . . ." (137–38). Further, to expiate the harm done his wife, he is "to send her / Home to her father, with her dowry trebled" (143–44)—end of marriage, with economic loss instead of anticipated gain.

The other married couple in the play, Sir Politic and Lady Would-be, do not exactly offer a model, a pattern from above, from which future lovers may draw inspiration. Theirs is a flawed marriage also, primarily because each partner really has little to do with the other; they truly inhabit their own separate worlds, Lady Would-be caught up in the legacy hunters' sweepstakes and Sir Pol trapped in his own imagination of great issues of statecraft and secrecy. The only model that Lady Would-be offers is for the Collegiate Ladies in *Epicoene*. Volpone renders judgment on this married couple without having met them: "I wonder at the desperate valour / Of the bold English, that they dare let loose / Their wives to all encounters!" (I.v.100–102). What an apt description of Lady Would-be: loose to all encounters! She is thoroughly caught up in her search for fashion, whether in clothes or literary tastes, while her husband goes his own bungling, dim-witted way. Her only thoughts of him come when Mosca intimates that Sir Pol has been seen "Rowing upon the water in a gondole, / With the most cunning courtesan of Venice" (III.v.19–20). The only meeting in the play between this husband and wife occurs in IV.ii, when Lady Would-be arrives in a jealous rage, condemns Sir Pol, thinks Peregrine a courtesan in disguise, realizes her mistake, goes to join in the trial against Bonario and Celia, and makes suggestive comments to Mosca, urging him to "use me." Through all this sound and fury, Sir Pol quietly slips away. His departure seems an appropriate emblem for their relationship; that is, there is no real marriage apparent in this couple. It is significant that Jonson has them meet but once in the play and that briefly. Mosca's judgment on Lady Would-be seems the play's judgment: "Go home and use the poor Sir Pol, your knight, well . . ." (V.iii.44).

As the play comes to an end, there is a potential marriage in the making—a minor matter, I admit, but indicative of Jonson's brilliance. Despite all the hubbub of the final trial scene, there is at least one person present who marches to a different drummer. I refer to the Fourth Avocatore, who delights in the presence of Mosca and thinks him a possibility for his daughter: "A proper man and, were Volpone dead, / A fit match for my daughter" (V.xii.50–51). This reminds us that parents often exercised their prerogative to select marriage partners for their children, which is a bone of contention between Viola and her father in *The Coxcomb;* and the Avocatore's remarks underscore the economic consideration in determining such partners. Mosca is attractive in part because he may be wealthy. A few lines later, in an aside, the Avocatore says: "It is a match, my daughter is bestowed" (62). Who knows what the daughter may think? Emboldened, the Avocatore finally asks Mosca: "Sir, are you married?" (84). Before Mosca can answer, Volpone removes his disguise. The Fourth Avocatore has nothing further to say, though his fellow judges have much to say. Is he so dashed by the loss of marriage prospects for his daughter that he is speechless? In light of what Jonson shows of married life in this play, the Avocatore and his daughter are better off without an impending marriage to Mosca. Children, this satiric play suggests, are merely impediments that must be overcome or set aside if the parent is to pursue his own desires: there is nothing here of love or nurturing. Jonson diminishes the matter of family succession or inheritance to a simple, greedy economic game—a game that overwhelms and distorts ordinary family values.

One of Jonson's most extensive explorations of the problems of marriage in a major play is in *Epicoene,* where the center of the play, unlike *Volpone,* is the prospect of marriage for Morose, the hater of noise. In fact, Jonson views marriage from three different but related perspectives in this play: the Morose/Epicoene marriage, the Otters, and the Collegiate Ladies. The Otters are in a state of constant warfare; and the Collegiate Ladies, drawing inspiration from Lady Would-be, live away from their husbands. In each case, Jonson parodies the traditional expectation of marriage—namely, that the husband should dominate. He turns this part of family life upside down. Morose, it could be argued, is a hater of women; in this sense he has something of a counterpart in Gondarino, the title character in Beaumont and Fletcher's *The Woman Hater,* who, after having committed several destructive actions, is sentenced to stay away from women. Morose receives no such judgment, though it would be appropriate. Morose's only reason for wanting to marry is to outfox his nephew Dauphine and to disinherit him. Blood ties obviously count for little. To Truewit's question "Art not thou next of blood, and his sister's son?" Dauphine answers: "Ay, but he will thrust me out of it, he vows, and marry" (I.ii.16–18).[9] As evidence from *Volpone* confirms, sons and nephews in Jacobean comedy live under constant threat of disinheritance. Dauphine, of course, seeks to outwit his uncle by setting up Epicoene and making her the obvious choice to be the wife of Morose. Though Jonson's focus is on marriage, we find here also the family issues of children and economics.

It is impossible to improve on the description of the Collegiate Ladies given by Truewit in the play's opening scene:

> A new foundation . . . of ladies . . . that live from their husbands and give entertainment to all the Wits and Braveries o'the time, as they call 'em, cry down or up what they like or dislike in a brain or a fashion with most masculine or rather hermaphroditical authority, and every day gain to their college some new probationer. (I.i.70–77)

Epicoene will eventually come under their tuition as they function with an open-admissions policy. In a word, they are unnatural—to match the unnaturalness of Morose's aversion to noise. They do not live like wives to their husbands; they are truly free-spirited and noisy—to Morose's chagrin. We learn of them early in the play; but Jonson delays their appearance until III.vi, when they swarm into Morose's house, headed by Lady Haughty with Centaur and Mavis in tow. Their plan is simple: "We'll make her [Epicoene] a collegiate" (50). By IV.iii Epicoene indeed receives instructions from them. Their views of marriage and family travesty conventional ideas. Centaur, for example, "has immortaliz'd herself with taming of her wild male" (25–26). Epicoene's question about their promiscuity receives questions from Haughty: "Why not? Why should women deny their favors to men?" (30). Epicoene's final question and the answer have chilling implications for family life: "And have you those excellent receipts, madam, to keep yourselves from bearing of children?" (50–52). Haughty replies: "Oh yes, Morose. How should we maintain our youth and beauty else? Many births of a woman make her old. . . ." (53–54). So goes the instruction from the Collegiate Ladies. Their self-centeredness rivals that of Morose. Failure to procreate obviously leads to the eventual destruction of the family. What one sees in the Jacobean satiric comedies is that there is little place in the scheme of things for childbearing and nurturing.

It seems that Mistress Otter has been to school to the Collegiate Ladies; at least she puts into practice several of their dubious principles. An amusing dispute breaks out when she asserts: "Why, I am a collegiate" (III.vii.34), to which Mavis says: "But not in ordinary" (35). Mrs. Otter insists: "But I am"; and Mavis responds:

"We'll dispute that within" (36–37). Perhaps there are degrees or rites of passage that Mrs. Otter has not fulfilled. Maybe the shortcoming is that Mrs. Otter lives with her husband; but what a relationship it is: "She commands all at home" (I.iv.26), as La Foole, her kinsman, notes. The domination by Mrs. Otter mirrors what Morose hopes to establish in his marriage. Her control operates fully in III.i, where she gives Tom Otter a verbal thrashing. The string of questions that she asks him is incriminating (26–45). She has tired of all the nonsense about his cups: "Is this according to the instrument, when I married you? That I would be princess and reign in mine own house, and you would be my subject and obey me?" (28–30). Apparently there has been a formal agreement before marriage, outlining the rights and prerogatives of marriage, all clearly in Mrs. Otter's favor. As Clerimont rightly observes: "Alas, what a tyranny is this poor fellow married to" (III.ii.10).

Only in his cups in IV.ii does Tom Otter express his biting contempt for his wife, she not initially being present. Dauphine ignites his railing by saying to Otter: "Captain he-Otter, your she-Otter is coming, your wife" (42). The word "wife" sets him off: "I have a cook, a laundress, a house-drudge, that serves my necessary turns and goes under that title [of wife]" (44–46)—brave words in the night among the boys. To the inevitable question of why he married her, Otter replies: "A pox—I married with six thousand pound, ay. I was in love with that. I ha' not kiss'd my fury these forty weeks" (69–71)—an answer that echoes later in *The Coxcomb*. One marries for money, not love. Stripped of its thematically amusing quality, the Otter relationship disturbs us. How many marriages in Jacobean England begot in economic considerations ended in such a miscarriage of what love might be?

The Collegiate Ladies live away from their husbands, and Mrs. Otter dominates her husband; there is one final perspective on marriage: Morose's attempt to find and marry a silent woman whom he can control. Truewit provides an early image of Morose: ". . . a huge turbant of nightcaps on his head, buckled over his ears" (I.i.136–37). As with the Ladies, Jonson delays Morose's actual appearance until Act II. Noise is only part of the problem for Morose; indeed, noise becomes a metaphor to suggest the unnatural quality of his character. Morose underscores his self-centeredness when he comments that he likes only the sound of his own voice; all other sounds "seem harsh, impertinent, and irksome" (II.i.5). Truewit, believing that he does Dauphine a favor, tries to dissuade Morose from marrying by carefully anatomizing the problems that wives produce. Morose, Job-like, interrupts the extensive catalogue: "Oh, what is my sin! What is my sin?" (II.ii.85). Ironically, many of the things that Truewit says materialize in the person of Epicoene. But for the moment, Morose does not give in to the rope halter that Truewit leaves behind; instead, he moves with alacrity in the marriage plans.

Like the Collegiate Ladies with their admission standards, Morose tests Epicoene to see whether she is worthy (that is, quiet enough) to be his wife (II.v). Her silence and submissiveness delight Morose. Not only may this be a desirable marriage but also it will provide the means for overcoming the nephew. Morose boasts: "This night I will get an heir and thrust him out of my blood like a stranger . . ." (97–99). If one marries for economic reasons, then one may beget children for similar purposes. No sooner does the wedding conclude, however, than Epicoene finds her voice and begins to speak and rule, even before she comes under the sway of the Collegiate Ladies. Epicoene makes her position clear: "I'll have none of this coacted, unnatural dumbness in my house, in a family where I govern" (III.iv.48–50). Like Mrs. Otter and the Collegiate Ladies, Epicoene will govern in her household, again upsetting any possibility of equality in marriage.

From this moment Morose seeks an escape from his lawful marriage. He worries that he "might die intestate" (IV.iv.47) and leave Epicoene possessed of all, the ultimate ironic twist on his plans. After the wonderful exploration of the legal bases for divorce, Morose accepts the plea of *"frigiditatis causa"* (V.iii.210). Thus in V.iv he tells the assembled ladies: "I am no man, ladies"; "Utterly unabled in nature, by reason of frigidity, to perform the duties or any the least office of a husband" (V.iv.40, 42–43). In a society in which the main function of marriage was procreation, we understand this basis for divorce.

To Morose's chagrin, however, Epicoene vows to "take him with all his faults" (V.iv.56–57), which for a fleeting moment may seem noble. Dauphine (and Jonson) finally plays the trump card; by getting Morose to assure the inheritance, Dauphine then reveals what no one knows (including us), namely that Epicoene is no woman. Morose is speechless and soon exits. Has this close brush with marriage affected Morose's view of marriage or women at all? Jonson does not say; the rest is silence: silent woman, silent man. But the play is not silent about the perversity of these marriages. Whether early audiences left the theater in their own silence, chastened by what they had seen, is, of course, impossible to know. Jonson's satiric vision exhibits the failings of families, obsessed with power, with greed, and with contempt for children. Mosca at one point refers to himself as a divider of families; may that not be an apt description of Jonson and his fellow satiric dramatists as they analyze families and portray the attributes that lead to dissolution of families? As Jonson observed or imagined family life, he found it difficult not to write satire.

The economic issue of family life that Jonson touches on— namely, inheritance—receives full treatment in *Fortune by Land and Sea*, written by Thomas Heywood with help from William Rowley, a play from about the time of *Epicoene*. Heywood, in his own earnest manner, offers what may be a fairly realistic perspective on the issue of inheritance. We know from Louis Montrose's study of *As You Like It*[10] and from those of historians of the family that the plight of younger brothers, typically shut out of any significant inheritance, was often desperate indeed. The eldest brother enjoyed most of the benefits of inheritance. One has little trouble imagining the strife that this predicament caused in many families. Heywood makes this conflict the central focus for one of the families in his play.

The situation in the Harding family is that the father has recently remarried, to the dismay of his younger sons, William and John, who complain that their stepmother Anne has come "almost dowerless" into the marriage (I.ii, p. 371).[11] Anne, contrary to many traditions about stepmothers, is one of the most sensitive and compassionate members of the family. The eldest son, Philip, has decided, against his father's wishes, to marry the attractive but poor Susan Forrest. Indeed, the father determines to disinherit the eldest son and divide the estate between the younger sons (II.i), which suits their purposes well. Despite Philip's plea that he at least retain the love if not the land of his father, Old Harding says: "My love goes with my land, and in this marriage / Thou hast lost both" (II.i, p. 380). The father's clear but misguided idea about the relationship of love and money places him in that increasing list of characters who become caricatures of what a loving parent ought to be. Bearing in mind the importance of inheritance, we can understand what Philip is willing to surrender for his love of Susan.

Not only does Philip lose the land and his father's love, but he also loses the title of son and brother. Indeed, he and Susan, in a curious twist of family life, become servants in the Harding household. When Philip reminds his brothers, "I had then priority of birth," William points out: "But now it seems we have got the start of you, for being but a servant you are taken a buttonhole lower'' (II.ii, p. 387). After several attempts the younger brothers finally get their father to agree to make his will, officially disinheriting Philip. But the old man is a procrastinator; and when word comes of a major loss at sea of one of his economic ventures, Old Harding suddenly dies. We hear William's frantic cry that his father at least make the will before he dies—so much for childlike love! Because the father has died intestate, the thing that Morose had feared, all the lands fall to the elder brother; for such is the normal pattern of inheritance.

Philip is both forgiving and generous toward his brothers, giving them their patrimony, which they immediately go away to squander. When these prodigal brothers return, Philip accepts them: ''. . . you are my brothers / (A name you once disdained to call me by) . . .'' (V.i, p. 435). Heywood's dramatic solution to the problem of inheritance is probably too pat, but the problem is obviously central in many family relationships. Knowing Heywood's play, we comprehend the magnitude of what Corbaccio would do to his son Bonario in *Volpone*. To disinherit also clearly carries the implication of the loss of all recognition of the child as son, thereby striking another blow against the sanctity of the family. The threat of disinheritance carries with it potent seeds of distrust and destruction. It, of course, may have tragic consequences, as in the case of *King Lear*. Economic concerns may determine the make-up of a marriage, and they may cause the destruction of that marriage and family. There could not have been many in Jacobean theater audiences impervious to what the dramatists were portraying. Though Heywood presents a complete family, parents and children, he depicts this family in disarray, governed, as in Jonson's comedy, primarily by greed. The question of succession in the family produces not stability but war.

Three other marital problems, common to much literature, predictably pervade Jacobean comedy: the shrewish wife, the jealous husband, and the plight of the widow. The portrait of the shrew has been around in English literature at least as long as the character of Noah's wife in the medieval cycle drama. The Wife of Bath knows a thing or two about female domination of husbands. Jealousy has been a given in literature since ancient times. Death that dissolves marriages causes practical and sometimes moral problems for the surviving spouse. Though the Jacobean dramatists in one sense merely echo what writers have said for centuries about such problems, they do nevertheless cause us to confront anew the more serious question of the precise relationship of husband and wife in marriage. In the process of raising such questions, the dramatists demythologize presumed marital bliss and family harmony.

Candido in Dekker and Middleton's *1 The Honest Whore* (1604) triumphs over his shrewish wife Viola by his unswerving and undaunted patience. He kills her with kindness. In his final rousing hymn in behalf of patience—with perhaps faint echoes of Portia's speech on mercy—Candido insists that patience "is the hunny gainst a waspish wife" (V.ii.509).[12] No such honey, however, exists in Fletcher's *The Woman's Prize, or The Tamer Tamed* (c. 1611), a barely veiled re-creation of *The Taming of the Shrew*, complete with such characters as Petruchio, Tranio, and Biancha. But there is a radical difference: this time the wife, Maria, sets out to tame her new husband, Petruchio; she does so by being a shrew. The paramount marital issue is the relative position of the spouses: will there be submission, domination, or equality? Fletcher's play, which I see as his interpretation of Shakespeare's earlier one, argues for equality in marriage, a condition scarcely the norm in Jacobean England.

An old father, Petronius, has two daughters, Maria and Livia, who are accompanied by their cousin Biancha, referred to in the dramatis personae as "Commander in chief." These three constitute a formidable trio of self-assured women, inspired by the instructions of Biancha. Maria has recently married Petruchio; this is his second marriage, and one imagines that his first wife must have been named Katherine. To her female companions Maria asserts her independence: "I am no more the gentle tame *Maria*; / Mistake me not; I have a new soule in me / Made of a North-wind, nothing but tempest . . ." (I.ii.71–72).[13] Secluded in her chambers with Biancha, Maria holds out against Petruchio on their wedding night; she has laid in provisions and will resist whatever siege he may try. She even rebuffs her father, who orders her to come out as an act of obedience to him. Maria makes clear to Petruchio her purpose:

> Ile make ye know, and feare a wife *Petruchio*,
> There my cause lies.
> You have been famous for a woman tamer, . . .
> A woman now shall take those honours off,
> And tame you. . . . (I.iii.266–71)

Revealing how little he understands the nature of the battle, Petruchio says, "Ile humor her awhile" (II.vi.148), as he readies to give in to her lengthy list of conditions (II.vi.136ff.). He confirms his incomprehension when he reminds Maria of her "due obedience" to him. She lashes back: "Tell me of due obedience? what's a husband? / What are we married for, to carry sumpters?" (III.iii.97–98). What, to put it another way, is the purpose of marriage? That, I take it, is Fletcher's serious question amidst all of the good-natured but seemingly cruel behavior. Giving up all hope of gaining Maria, Petruchio decides to flee the country; but on second thought, he decides to pretend that he has died. He is brought in in a coffin in V.iv, but Maria sees through the ruse.

Therefore her speech has no lamentation, only regret for his foolishness: "He had a happy turn he dyed . . ." (V.iv.27). This speech gets a rise out of Petruchio, literally. He comes out of the coffin, saying, "O *Maria,* / Oh my unhappinesse, my misery" (40–41). She has won: "I have done my worst, and have my end, forgive me; / From this houre make me what you please: I have tam'd ye . . ." (44–45). Her shrewish nature has been but a pose to gain victory and equality with her husband. Petruchio now understands the nature of the struggle; his former boastful, swaggering nature has been exorcised. Fletcher's Epilogue makes clear the play's purpose: "*They* [men] *should not raign as Tyrants o'r their wives*" (4); "*it* [this play] *being aptly meant,* / *To teach both Sexes due equality . . .*" (6–7). Only marital warfare and Maria's pose as a shrew bring refreshing honesty at the end of the play. Out of the demystifying nature of the struggle we at least catch a glimpse of an ideal. But for some, Maria's final statement of triumph may be too submissive to imply actual equality in the marriage. What is fascinating in Fletcher's drama is his taking Shakespeare's earlier play on this subject and turning it upside down. The question remains: What is the role of a husband and a wife in a patriarchal society?

Jealousy is a powerfully destructive force in marriages; we need look no farther than *Othello* or *The Winter's Tale.* Some Jacobean dramatists, however, view it in a somewhat more amusing light, less ultimately threatening or damaging. Don Zuccone in Marston's *The Fawn* is a jealous husband who believes that many men have sexual affairs with his wife Zoya. He even says: "I hear there's one jealous that I lie with my own wife . . ." (II.i.202–3);[14] but he denies it vehemently: "I lay not with her this four year, this four year" (205–6). Family, sex, and marriage all come into sharp focus. Though the couple reconciles at the end, one cannot be certain of the lasting effect of the triumph over jealousy. More unsettling is the treatment of jealousy in Edward Sharpham's *Cupids Whirligig* (1607), the only Jacobean play that I know of in which jealousy is the subject from the opening line to the conclusion.

Edward Sharpham in his limited dramatic canon must have known his Marston rather well, especially *The Fawn*, for both *The Fleire* and *Cupids Whirligig* show an indebtedness to that Marston play. Sharpham offers another version of Marston's examination of the jealous husband and the effects on marriage. *Cupids Whirligig* must have been a popular play, judging by its four quarto editions. The primary action involves Sir Timothy Troublesome's jealousy of his wife. Though the tone of the play is light, the attitude toward love and marriage is somewhat cynical. Sharpham's dramatic problem is to see how many changes he can ring on the same basic situation of Sir Timothy's jealousy, as we witness his several reversals, first distrusting then trusting his wife, only to start over.

Our first view of Troublesome suggests that his jealousy is truly an illness, so obsessed is he. His imagination works overtime: the mere mention of another man's name sets him off with the assumption that this person is having an affair with his wife. He hits on a new strategy, and Sharpham gives the ancient issue of jealousy a new twist, if I may put it that way. Sir Timothy says: "I haue now found out a tricke to know if my wife make me Cuckold, I will gelde my selfe, and then if my wife be with child, I shalbe sure I am a Cuckold . . ." (Act I, sig. A4ᵛ).[15] That, it is safe to say, is going to extremes, an idea seized upon but not pursued by Morose in order to get out of his marriage to Epicoene. By the opening of Act III Troublesome has followed through on his intention; he tells Wages: "Then I am lighter by sixteene pound now then I was, I may now lie with any Lady in Europe, for any hurt I can doe her" (sig. E1). He boasts: "I can Cuckold no man." His action cuts several ways: he is now less than a man, and he can no longer function sexually with his wife. To boast that he cannot cuckold any man is, to say the obvious, to lose sight of the imagined problem—namely, all the ones who are presumably cuckolding him. After a particularly acrimonious encounter with his wife, Troublesome sets out to get a new wife. When confronted with the problem of his having been gelded, the knight says to "tell her [prospective wife] I did it onely to preserue my voyce" (Act V, sig. H4ᵛ).

The status of husband and wife vacillates. Small wonder that the Lady takes a dim view of marriage, observing at one point that husbands "are but like to painted fruite, which promise much, but still deceiues vs when we come to touch" (Act I, B3ᵛ). She concludes that ". . . shee's married best, that's wedded to her will." In Act V the conversation among the ladies on the subject of marriage (sigs.

K2–K2ᵛ) might well have been taken from a page in the Collegiate Ladies' textbook. As Lady Troublesome notes: "Why, thou knowest t'is not the fashion in all places to lie with ones owne Husband euery night" (K2).

Sir Timothy eventually desires reconciliation. Forgiveness abounds, jealousy abates, and the couple reunites. But harmony never lasts. In a final episode a group of women put on masks and exchange the love tokens that the men have sent so that each can pair off with the right man, regardless of what the men intend. (This situation recalls the Masque of the Muscovites in V.ii of *Love's Labour's Lost*.) It is by such a strategy that Lady Troublesome, earlier divorced, has the dubious success of remarrying her husband. When they discover the trick of their remarriage, only Sir Timothy speaks: "What now, remaried?" (Act V, sig. K3ᵛ). Small wonder that the Lady has nothing to say. Sharpham never adequately confronts the ramifications of Troublesome's obsessive jealousy. Unlike the situation in *The Fawn*, where there is a more satisfactory solution, here not much has changed. To have Sir Timothy and his Lady remarry scarcely solves the problems of their marriage. Throughout the play, however, Sharpham has been exploring the absurdity of jealousy; perhaps this ending is but one more example, an ironic change of a sort quite different from Marston. On the surface the marriage has been preserved, but serious questions remain unanswered. One could hardly argue that this couple is better off at the end.

Jealousy is also an issue in George Chapman's *The Widow's Tears*, but I want to focus on the plight of the widow. Given the mortality rate in Jacobean England, widows were commonplace. Often they were left in desperate financial straits, necessitating that they quickly find another marriage partner. We see in Heywood's *Fortune by Land and Sea* how, without wasting much time, Anne married Young Forrest after her husband had suddenly died. The Countess of Shrewsbury consolidated her financial strength and political power by her several marriages, ending with a wealth that rivaled that of Queen Elizabeth. Hamlet's mother has engaged, by her own description, in an "o'er hasty marriage." The Wife of Bath is on a pilgrimage for husband number six; through funeral tears she is always on the lookout for another eligible husband. Nan in *Cupids Whirligig* has a different perspective: "For I long to bee a Widdowe, that I might haue a newe Husband" (Act V, sig. K2), an argument in favor of variety. The plight of the widow (or widower) raises the question of the continuity of the family: is it dissolved, or does it re-form in some new structure? Death, as Lawrence Stone has amply demonstrated, was the great disrupter of marriages and families.

The dramatic problem that Chapman explores is the faithfulness of the spouse to the memory of her dead husband. He tells the story of two widows, Eudora and Cynthia, each dominating one half of the play. By Act III Eudora has married Tharsalio. Cynthia is both a widow and no widow; that is, her husband only pretends to be dead: he uses the experience to test her love and faithfulness. This is Chapman's retelling of the story of the Widow of Ephesus, told by Eumolpus in Petronius's *Satyricon*. The common denominator in the case of Eudora and Cynthia is the heartfelt pledge not to remarry, a vow that ultimately they break. We recall the Player Queen in *Hamlet*, who says to her husband: ''A second time I kill my husband dead / When second husband kisses me in bed'' (III.ii.176–77). But the Player King has a perspective that turns out to be valid: ''I do believe you think what now you speak, / But what we do determine oft we break'' (177–78).

In Chapman's opening scene, Tharsalio announces his intention to woo Eudora, the widow; but Cynthia reminds him of Eudora's ''vowes . . . to preserue till death, the vnstain'd honour of a Widdowes bed'' (I.i.79–81).[16] But Tharsalio turns the issue back on Cynthia and her husband Lysander (Tharsalio's brother), asking her whether if she were to become a widow, she would remain faithful. Lysander is confident that she would. Here is the essential dramatic problem of the play: Tharsalio will test Eudora's vow, and Lysander will challenge his wife's. Can widows remain faithful to the memory of their husbands? the play asks. Tharsalio wastes little time in beginning his attack on Eudora's fidelity. She points out that she does not lack worthy suitors ''That may aduance mine honour; aduance my estate; / Strengthen my alliance (if I list to wed) . . .'' (II.iv.150–51), a catalogue of practical reasons for widows' remarrying. By III.i Tharsalio is able to announce to his somewhat startled brother and sister-in-law that ''the great Countesse is mine . . .'' (79). Cynthia is incredulous and ashamed. Perhaps she also dimly perceives, even now, the possibility of her own fall. Certainly in the drama Eudora's ''fall'' foreshadows Cynthia's.

Cynthia reacts to the presumed death of her husband by descending with Ero, her maid, into the family tomb. All is well at first. Cynthia's suffering and abstinence reassure Lysander, who has returned disguised as a soldier. But Ero gives in to his offer of food, and in her we see the hint of Cynthia's eventual capitulation. Indeed, by the next scene (IV.iii) Lysander senses that the somber clouds have dispersed; Cynthia confirms this view by letting him kiss her. In V.ii we hear his bitter soliloquy on how this "mirrour of Nuptiall chastitie; this Votresse of widdow-constancie" has changed (36–37). What he never confronts is his own responsibility in the whole matter; after all, it is his jealousy that has led to this situation. The issue is not, then, simply Cynthia's change but also Lysander's. Chapman brings the two together at the end of the play, but their union is strained, leaving important issues unresolved. Eudora and Cynthia demonstrate the vulnerability of widows and the infirmity of human purpose. But they also illustrate that sometimes one must lose one's oath in order to find life. Cynthia's fugitive and cloistered virtue gives way to the natural demands of life. Berowne reminds us in *Love's Labour's Lost* that we have no right to expect a rose at Christmas or snow in summer: that is unnatural. Chapman vividly illustrates that the vow of the widow may also be unnatural. In art, as in life, many choose to remarry, thereby reconstituting a family. The simple financial need for this in Jacobean life was intense.

If one wanted to go to a London theater in the Jacobean era and see a handful of plays that would recapitulate and epitomize the demystified, depoliticized view of the family overlaid with a satiric tone, one could accomplish that task easily by seeing Thomas Middleton's drama. His plays resonate with most of the family problems that we have examined here: struggles over inheritance, jealous husbands, shrewish wives, temporary widows, disregarded children, and plentiful sexual activity. I will focus on *The Family of Love, Michaelmas Term,* and *A Chaste Maid in Cheapside*—the last being an inevitable choice for any discussion of fictional Jacobean family life. I suggested earlier that Jonson's major family issues were marriage, children, and economics. Middleton shares these problems, with some differences, however. He, for example, explores more thoroughly than Jonson the situation of children and the parent/child relationship. He provides examples of procreation, which are, however, strikingly devoid of ordinary joy: children born within Middleton's comedy are economic pawns. In two of the plays, Middleton links religion and family, raising the possibility of a mythos of family, only to have that prospect completely shattered. He also presents another marital triangle in *Chaste Maid*, reminding us of *The Coxcomb*, with which this discussion began. If we have not exactly come full circle, we can at least recognize Middleton as offering a convenient summary of domestic problems in ordinary families.

One of the mottoes that pervades Middleton's drama comes from Glister in *The Family of Love:* ". . . wealth commands all . . ." (III.ii.108-9),[17] a variation of the Faustian Sir Epicure Mammon's gospel in *The Alchemist:* "Be rich." The desire for wealth naturally governs all marital arrangements: it threatens and overshadows natural impulses toward love. Middleton gives in the words of Lipsalve in *The Family of Love* a striking emblem of a lover, tormented by love; such an emblem may be said to inform much of Jacobean comedy. Lipsalve offers this image as a "true picture of a lover":

> . . . a man standing naked, a wench tickling him on the left side with a feather, and pricking him under the right side with a needle. The allegory, as I take, is this: that at the first we are so overjoyed with obtaining a wife, that we conceit no heaven like to the first night's lodging; . . . but, sir, now come to the needle on the right side,— that's the day-time, wherein she commands; then, sir she has a certain thing called tongue, ten times more sharp than a needle, and that, at the least displeasure, a man must have shot quite through him. (I.ii.19-30)

This needle that rankles so is the badge of satire; the sweet darts of Cupid, the hallmark of romance.[18]

Knowing only the title of Middleton's *Family of Love*, one might be inclined to breathe a sigh of relief that at last we have a decent, happy exploration of a family bound together in love. Even a cursory perusal of the play, however, will soon disabuse us of such a notion. But Middleton does offer in Gerardine and Maria the typical lovers of romantic comedy, deterred from their love by Maria's uncle Glister. Glister's view of love has no room for romantic illusions: "Tut, love is an idle fantasy, bred by desire, nursed by delight . . ." (I.i.23-24). He incarcerates Maria in her room, but Gerardine shrewdly gains access to her by hiding in a trunk brought into her chamber, as Iachimo will do in *Cymbeline*. The lovers are successsful. Gerardine, triumphant at the end, offers reconciliation and recognition of what has happened: "Now join with me / For approbation of our Family" (V.iii.454-55). Glister, unable to defend himself against the false charge of having practiced incest with his niece, signs documents granting Gerardine £1,000, plus her father's portion, if Gerardine will marry her. Though it is but a trick, the uncle has been eager to marry off the niece, lest the hint of scandal make her undesirable marriage material.

I suppose that one could argue that the "Family" that Gerardine refers to is in a way a "family of love," but it is surely not *the* "family of love." The family that the play's title refers to is a religious sect, Puritan in some of its ideas, at least as Middleton portrays it. In fact, it is a thinly disguised family of lust, which chooses to meet in the dark, clearly for carnal rather than spiritual reasons. Inherently, then, this family of love is a debasement of ideas both of love and of family. "Collegiate Lusters" might be a better term for them. Mistress Purge, beset with a jealous husband, is the principal follower of the sect. Club points out that the Familists "love their neighbours better than themselves" because "they love them better than their husbands, and husband and wife are all one; therefore, better than themselves" (II.iv.73–78). If the Collegiate Ladies of *Epicoene* may represent something of a perversion of learning, then the Family of Love illustrates a perversion of religion. Mistress Purge, explaining why the group meets at night, offers a telling revelation: "O Lord, ay, sir, with the candles out too: we fructify best i'th' dark: the glance of the eye is a great matter; it leads us to other objects besides the right" (III. iii.21–24). It is better to embrace the darkness than to light a candle. Religion stands on its head. Gerardine wittily says that he has endorsed most of the group's principles; for instance, "I never make my neighbour a cuckold for any hate or malice I bear him, but in love and charity to his wife" (IV.ii.74–75).

Engaged in such practices, the traditional family cannot survive. Having secretly attended a meeting of the Family and there having obtained his wife's wedding ring, Purge believes himself a cuckold and so files charges against her. But she disposes of him in the "trial" scene at the end, by first insisting brazenly that she gave the ring "to the relief of the distressed Geneva" (V.iii.278), however her husband may have come by it. Then she argues that of course she recognized him in the dark, "e'en by very instinct" (298) and therefore gave him the ring. She is generous in the dark by instinct, if not by religious principle. In the judgment of the trial he extracts from her the promise that she will "come no more at the Family" (423); she yields to the authority of her husband, but one wonders for how long.

In many ways *Michaelmas Term* is about disowning one's family bond. Middleton comes at this problem from three related angles through three families: the Country Wench and her father; Mother Gruel and her son, Andrew Lethe; and the Quomodo-Thomasine family. Hellgill, a pander, has brought the Country Wench to the city to make her fortune, having enticed her away from her father. The father comes in search of his daughter: "She was my joy, / And all content that I receiv'd from life, / My dear and only daughter"

(II.ii.4–6).[19] He worries about the temptation that she will perhaps taste in the city, as he has done in his youth; so he decides to put on a disguise until he finds her "to fright her from base evils . . ." (37). Tricked out in new garments, the Country Wench goes unrecognized by her father when they meet in III.i, as he is brought in to be her servant. But there is further irony in that she does not recognize him because he is disguised. In fact, he finds the Wench quite beautiful and wishes that his daughter might have such fortune. By the end of the scene he realizes that bawdry is afoot, and he ponders the discrepancy between the beautiful outside of the Wench and her black soul (III.i.259–71). His moral instructions in IV.ii fall on deaf ears, and he departs from the play. She eventually marries Lethe. The daughter has disowned her father by chasing after life in the city. The family bond severs. Given Middleton's satiric vision, the moral voice of the father fades in the din of voices clamoring for wealth and lust.

The relationship of Andrew Lethe and his mother mirrors the Country Wench and her father. Lethe has changed his name in order to forget his father, Walter Gruel, and he tries not to recognize his mother, who does not know him because he dresses in a totally different and elegant manner. Lethe's question to himself, when he spots his mother, probably tells us all that we need to know about his character: "Does she come up to shame me, to betray my birth, and cast soil upon my new suit?" (I.i.236–37). Mother Gruel reveals that her husband has recently died "and left me a lone woman" (255); therefore, she has come as a widow seeking relief. She also says, much later in the play, that she has had four husbands (IV.iv.65). Just as the Country Wench's father becomes her servant, so Mother Gruel becomes a "drudge" for Lethe, carrying his scandalous messages to Thomasine, mother of the girl Susan, whom he hopes to marry. As with most marriages that we have examined, economic considerations predominate. Here Lethe desires Susan for her wealth (III.i.203–4). But forced into marrying the Country Wench, Lethe decides finally to acknowledge his mother: "Let the world know you are my mother" (V.iii.148). And she says to him: ". . . when thou hadst scarce a shirt, thou hadst / More truth about thee" (162–63). In the Lethe/Mother Gruel relationship the family bond holds, whatever that may mean for the likes of a Lethe, a child who attempts to disown his parents.

Economics governs Quomodo's approach to marriage and life. By Act IV he has achieved his major goal, the acquisition of Richard Easy's lands, but he is not satisfied. He decides to pretend to die in order to see how his family will respond, thereby resembling Volpone and Lysander. But Quomodo thinks also of the land: ". . . I am as jealous of this land as of my wife, to know what would become of it after my decease" (IV.i.110–11). Thomasine, his wife, shedding no widow's tears, moves with alacrity to marry Easy. As Quomodo's coffin goes by, Thomasine remarks: "The worst is past, I hope" (IV.iv.67)—so much for her marriage to Quomodo. In disguise, Quomodo hears his son's unflattering comments about him, and Quomodo decides to disinherit the son (IV.iv.40). The whole tangled mess, after Quomodo reveals that he is alive, ends up in court. When the judge rules that Thomasine is still married to Quomodo, she cries out: "Oh, heaven!" (V.iii.56)—her last words in the play. Her words carry all the resonance of one who does not face the future of this family with eagerness. Quomodo has disowned the family by his pretended death, and Thomasine has disowned their marriage. The Country Wench, Andrew Lethe, and Quomodo parallel one another in economic quests at the expense of sustaining family bonds.

Coming at the end of the historical period that I concentrate on, *A Chaste Maid*, in addition to being Middleton's finest comedy, has the advantage of embodying most of the matters of family and marriage that I have discussed. George Hibbard suggests that an appropriate subtitle for the play would be *The Anatomy of Matrimony*.[20] More than elsewhere in the satiric plays, Middleton pays particular attention to the plight of children. There is also no clearer example of the economic nexus for marriage. Yellowhammer's question in his Goldsmith's shop is a veritable motto for the play: "What's your price, sir?" (I.i.108).[21] Knowing the price, knowing the dowry, knowing the likely inheritance are the stuff of which marriages are made in virtually all of the Jacobean satiric comedies. Middleton exploits the ironic distance between the attitude epitomized in Yellowhammer's question and the season of Lent, which is part of the play's setting. Not only are family relationships perverted but so is the holy time that requires sacrifice and abstinence—two qualities in short supply in this play. Four families compose *A Chaste Maid*, all touched in some way by the character Sir Walter Whorehound, who is concerned with solidifying his position by an appropriate (read "wealthy") marriage and a future heir.

The first three scenes of the play introduce the four families; I will consider the lesser ones first. Fecundity plagues the family of Touchwood Senior and his wife. "Our desires," Touchwood says, "Are both too fruitful for our barren fortunes" (II.i.8–9). Burdened with many children, the couple reluctantly agree to live apart, a necessity, Mrs. Touchwood says, that "must be obeyed" (2). Touchwood praises her as "a matchless wife" (37), assures her that he will visit her and do "Anything, wench, but what may beget beggars . . ." (40). Like their counterparts in actual Jacobean life without modern contraceptive devices, this couple lives cursed with more children than they can sustain economically. Every year, Touchwood observes, "a child, and some years two . . ." (15). This potentially destructive element in family life has not been seen in the drama elsewhere. Middleton gives no hint as to how this couple actually feel about their children or why they continue to propagate with such regularity. We also learn that Touchwood is by nature not only fecund but promiscuous. He admits to seven births for which he is responsible (62) during the last progress, and a Country Wench appears with evidence of his handiwork. He dismisses her with a meager amount of money, pleading, "I am a younger brother and have nothing" (88), a family problem evident in several plays.

Contrasting the Touchwoods' productivity is the Kixes' sterility. Sir Oliver and Lady Kix have no children after seven years of marriage. They have apparently tried everything; Sir Oliver says, "I'd give a thousand pound to purchase fruitfulness" (II.i.141). Lest we get caught up in some sentimental view of this couple's touching desire for a child, Lady Kix puts things in focus: " 'Tis our dry barrenness puffs up Sir Walter . . ." (153); that is, they need an heir to thwart Sir Walter's inheritance. In this they resemble Morose of *Epicoene*, whose only desire for marriage is so that he may get an heir and thus disinherit Dauphine. Children, then, are but pawns in an economic game of inheritance. Sir Oliver and his Lady spend much of their time arguing about who is to blame for their childlessness. Sir Oliver threatens to divorce her, set up another house, and "keep some fruitful whore . . ." (III.iii.59).

To their rescue comes Touchwood Senior with the ultimate remedy. He and Sir Oliver strike a bargain: "Four hundred pounds of me [Oliver] at four several payments" (125). Touchwood sends Sir Oliver on a little trip so that Touchwood can properly administer the potion to Lady Kix, for the medicine "must be taken lying" (141)—in bed. The Lady does not resist. We eventually hear Oliver's misguided ecstasy when his wife becomes pregnant; he boasts: "The child is coming and the land comes after; / The news of this will make a poor Sir Walter" (V.iii.14–15)—always the economic concern. In a final gesture of generosity, Sir Oliver promises to take care of Touchwood

Senior and his wife and urges them to have more children. The joy that attends childbirth in the Kix household is the joy of economic advantage: first the child, then the land.

The Yellowhammers differ from these couples by having marriageable children, Moll and Tim. The business of the play's first scene—and I think that is the right term—is to arrange marriages for their daughter and son. As George Hibbard points out, the Yellowhammers plan a double contract by marrying Moll to Sir Walter Whorehound and Tim to his "landed niece brought out of Wales . . ." (I.i.42)—actually Sir Walter's discarded whore. Money motivates both proposed marriages. Maudline Yellowhammer, the mother, sets the tone of sexual relationships when she chides her daughter for not being married yet, observing: "When I was of your youth, I was lightsome / And quick two years before I was married" (10–11). Later, when Tim meets the Welsh Gentlewoman, his mother hopes to speed things along: "I'll put together both / And lock the door" (IV.i.73–74). The parent seeks to make sex serve the purpose of commerce. Allwit attempts to prevent the marriage of Moll and Sir Walter in order to protect his own investment. In disguise he goes to Yellowhammer and reveals the scandalous truth about Walter. Yellowhammer hesitates but finally shows that where his treasure is, there will be his heart also: "The knight is rich, he shall be my son-in-law; / No matter, so the whore he keeps be wholesome . . ." (IV.i.247–48).

Moll, in fact, loves Touchwood Junior, brother to Touchwood Senior. Trying to avoid the marriage that her parents intend, Moll escapes from the house only to be captured and brought back by her mother: "*Enter* Maudline *drawing* Moll *by the hair* . . ." (IV.iv.18 S.D.). Maudline threatens: "I'll make thee an example / For all the neighbours' daughters" (21–22). This may qualify as an example of what Lawrence Stone refers to as the deliberate attempt to break the child's will. Yellowhammer decides that it is time to accelerate the wedding process; he promises a wedding the next morning to Sir Walter, who relishes the prospect: ". . . ere tomorrow noon / I shall receive two thousand pound in gold / And a sweet maidenhead worth forty" (48–50). But Moll and Touchwood Junior are quite resourceful and eventually triumph over the parents' will. The Yellowhammers' marriage plans receive one final blow: Tim does marry the Welsh Gentlewoman, who is, of course, penniless—she is not the heir to nineteen Welsh mountains nor a scholar, as the dim-witted, Cambridge-educated Tim had thought. If the point of having children is to pair them off in good (i.e., profitable) marriages, then the Yellowhammers have failed miserably.

The ultimate debasement of family and marriage is the Allwit/ Mrs. Allwit relationship, one of the strangest in Jacobean comedy, a clear case of psychic numbing. Like Antonio in *The Coxcomb*, Allwit shares his wife with Sir Walter, not out of misguided generosity and friendship, as in Antonio's case, but because it relieves him of the responsibilities of being husband and father. Allwit has not literally gelded himself, as Sir Timothy Troublesome had in *Cupids Whirligig*, but in a sense he has. Allwit is a wittol; therefore, he delights in Sir Walter's use of his wife. In a great speech Allwit characterizes his situation: "The happiest state that ever man was born to!" (I.ii.21); "I have the name [of father], and in his [Walter's] gold I shine . . ." (40). He knows no fear of being a cuckold because he encourages Walter to beget his children. It is Walter, in fact, who experiences jealousy; he chides Allwit: ". . . I heard you were once off'ring / To go to bed to her"; "No, I protest, sir!" is Allwit's response (94–95)—reminding us of Don Zuccone in *The Fawn*, who discards the issue of jealousy by swearing that he has not gone near his wife in four years. The unnatural relationship of the Allwits and Sir Walter has been going on for seven years, the amount of time that the Kixes have been childless. There is also sterility in the Allwit household, metaphorical rather than literal. Allwit pretends to be the true father of his family, to borrow Mosca's phrase, but he is not. In yet another outrage of family convention, Walter decides to be godfather to his own latest child born of Mrs. Allwit; it "prevents suspicion," he suggests (II.ii.32). Middleton provides a celebration of the christening (III.ii), a scene fraught with irony.

This strange "venture tripartite" (to use Jonson's term in *The Alchemist*) comes to an end when Sir Walter, wounded and growing increasingly moral, seeks refuge with the Allwits, who turn on him and send him packing. A child causes the undoing of their relationship; the Kixes's child will bar Sir Walter from an inheritance. He is now therefore worthless, in more ways than one. Several ironies operate: one is that a child born only out of economic desire destroys the unwholesome Allwit/Sir Walter arrangement. Children are mere objects to be manipulated. In a speech that rivals any in Jacobean drama for both its audacity and its understatement, Allwit says to Sir Walter: ". . . I tell you truly / I thought you had been familiar with my wife once" (V.i.144–45). The Allwits merely move off to set up shop in a different location and will presumably continue to exploit their

101

curious and perverse marriage. Part of their baggage will be a group of adulterine children. The play makes no clear moral judgment about the Allwits because they are beyond the reaches of moral strictures: they are amoral.

A final word about children in this play—two brief episodes call attention to the plight of children: the "Promoters' scene" (II.ii) and the postchristening scene (III.ii). Promoters stand about on street corners to catch those who violate Lent by carrying meat. Of course, as we would expect, there are ways to get around promoters in Cheapside: one purchases Lent as Master Beggarland has done; then anything goes. What is the price of Lent? The absurdity of the question points to the deeply satiric spirit in the play. As the Promoters stand guard, the Country Wench appears, the one we last saw in II.i, who confronted Touchwood Senior with another one of his products. She carries a basket, which contains mutton and her child. They gladly confiscate her basket, but instead of finding more meat in the heavy basket, they find the infant. They regret not only being tricked but also having to do something with the child. One of the Promoters complains: "Half our gettings / Must run in sugar-sops and nurses' wages now . . ." (II.ii.161–62). Eventually they will "send the child to Brainford" (174), a place where children were put out to nurse (according to Parker's note). Children are commodities to be disposed of.

The celebration of the christening of the latest Allwit child underscores the enormous gap that exists between what is said and the truth of the Allwit household. In simple fact another adulterine child has been christened with no less than Sir Walter as godfather. One can only imagine the scene at the baptismal font, a moment that would have reinforced the discrepancy between what seems to be and what is: a religious ceremony that focuses on the child and heightens family bonds contrasts with the actuality of adulterous parents and a lecherous godparent, all giving the lie to the usual understanding of family. At the feast, one of the Gossips comments that the child is "So like the father" (III.ii.9); another suggests that Sir Walter cuts a much more impressive figure than does Allwit. A Puritan says: "Children are blessings, / If they be got with zeal by the brethren . . ." (33–34). In this play, only the Kixes think that children are desirable, and this is because a child gains for them an inheritance. Lurking on the outer edges of this gathering is Allwit, the pseudofather, whose comments focus on his relief that he is not paying for the celebration.

Reviewing these plays that address the domestic problems of ordinary families, we hear several voices: we hear a character assert that "wealth commands all"; another asks, "what's your price?"; and others instruct on how to prevent pregnancy or sing the virtues of having no children. In these plays, often satiric in intention, families are threatened or destroyed not by tragedy but by greed, jealousy, perverse behavior, sexual infidelity, and struggles over inheritance. The few love stories that seem true and wholesome are always subordinate. Children have no function in these plays as a potential healing force; instead, children are to be avoided or, on the other hand, used in some economic game, usually to gain an inheritance. Children are contingent—to be welcomed if they serve some purpose. The accident of history puts *A Chaste Maid* at the end of the period I am studying; but design could not improve on this happy arrangement, for this play epitomizes the topsy-turvy world of family, sex, and marriage. It presents a world in which almost everything and everybody has its price, and children become mere instruments in the grasping for wealth. Such a world demystifies the family as it also fragments it. To generalize, the dramatists studied here depict, not a golden, but a brazen world of family relationships.

Poets are capable, Sidney reminds us, of providing a golden world. Something like a golden world, at least in contrast to the one studied in the preceding pages, exists in comedies about royal families; such plays I now examine. These plays, few in number, are romantic and sometimes pastoral; they center on royal or noble families. Family problems do not evaporate, for that would be totally unrealistic; but the attitude toward the family changes. It is possible in these plays to refer to a mythos of the family, an idealizing of the family. Two attributes of these Jacobean comedies highlight the change: the place of children and the politics of the family. Children are important, their position not governed by economics; they sometimes serve as a healing, reconciling force. Procreation itself has political consequences, because royal children affect the destiny of kingdoms. Plant and growth images pervade these plays, replacing images of decay and dissolution in the satires. The fate of the family intertwines with the future of the political state. Though separation may occur, royal families ultimately reunite—gone is the fragmentation of the satiric comedies. The comedies of royal families, several of them paralleling the time of Shakespeare's Romances, reveal a different strain of comedy, one that takes the family seriously.

I begin with the work of John Day because he forms a convenient bridge. Not without satire, his plays explore political implications of the family. His three plays of this early Jacobean period, *Law-Tricks* (1604), *The Isle of Guls* (1606), and *Humour out of Breath* (1608), all contain romance, including matters of wonder, love, and reconciliation. In *Humour out of Breath*, for example, warring political houses are reconciled through the love and marriages of their children. Thus Octavio, Duke of Venice, can rightly pronounce at the end of the play that "all hate is banisht, and reuenge lies dead."[22] I will concentrate on *Law-Tricks* as illustrative of two different approaches to family life; this play functions well as a transition between the satiric and the romantic plays. Two families, related by marriage, constitute the main action of the play: Duke Ferneze of Genoa, his son Polymetes, and his daughter Emilia; and the Count Lurdo and his Countess, the Duke's sister.

Count Lurdo and the Countess recall several of the married couples that we examined in the satiric plays. The Count announces in the opening scene that despite the Countess's kinship with the Duke, he has secured a divorce. He has accused his wife of being a harlot; but he suggests to Horatio, a young count who secretly desires the Countess, a different reason for divorce: ". . . my Auarice thought she liu'd too long / I know one man that coffind vp sixe wiues / Since she was mine . . ." (I.i.245–47).[23] Such an attitude toward marriage coincides with the spirit of Cheapside. Lurdo also claims that he never did love his wife (III.i.872), and he moves to drastic measures when he gets Horatio to agree to poison the Countess. Horatio carries out the request, and the Countess ostensibly dies. Horatio's page, however, has seen to it that the Countess has been given a sleeping potion, not poison; she eventually awakens in the tomb. Both Lurdo and Horatio, contrite about their actions, go to the tomb and find the Countess alive. Chastened by the sentence that the Duke has placed on him, Lurdo says: "And wronged Countesse though I hated thee, / I come to take my latest sleepe with thee" (V.ii.2276–78). She accepts his apology and forgives him. In this play the grave's a fine and private place where some do there embrace.

Reunion and reconciliation also govern the destiny of the other family. Two major problems confront Duke Ferneze's family: the return of the lost daughter and the testing of the son. Polymetes reports, early in the play, about Emilia's disappearance. Gathered in another city in Italy with "all the choycest virgins of the Land" (I.i.198), Emilia and the others were attacked while at their orisons by a band of "faithlesse Turkes"—one can always count on the Turks! The attackers profaned the temple, sacrificed the priests, ravished maidens, and carted some off to their boats. The fate of Emilia is unknown; therefore, the father goes in quest of her, leaving Poly-metes in charge of the kingdom. Day's somewhat unsure grasp of his material reveals itself in the Duke's disappearance from the play until Act IV, where we do not learn what he has been up to. Emilia, it turns out, is very much alive; she appears in the second scene of the play but is not recognized by her brother, who tries to seduce her.

The politics of the family receives severe testing by Polymetes, who, left in charge of the kingdom, becomes a thoroughgoing prodigal, failing every moral and political test. His new behavior shocks the Duke when he returns in Act IV: "It is not possible, is this my sonne?" (1334). Ironically, the Duke also does not recognize his own daughter when she first appears to him in V.ii.1930ff. He denies this impertinent girl: "Out of my sight, thou art no childe of myne" (1946). Finally Emilia establishes her identity, and her father welcomes her:

> *Duke.* Art thou Emilia?
> *Emilia.* Emelia, your Daughter, once a Turkish prisoner
> *Duke.* Receiue a ioyfull blessing rise and say,
>   What wit or power freed thee. (2169–72)

She promises to relate at some more convenient time how she escaped. Perhaps because he is so shallow, Polymetes has no serious reunion with either his father or his sister. But in the reunion of the long-lost daughter with the father, we find the skeletal event that Shakespeare will explore fully. The family is whole again, and the political state is secure.

Two royal families, a royal marriage, and the birth of a royal child form the center of William Rowley's *A Merrie and Pleasant Comedy: called A Shoemaker a Gentleman* (c. 1607–9). Inspired by Thomas Deloney's *The Gentle Craft*, Rowley overlays the plot of great adventure and sometimes tragic events with the genial, humorous life in a shoemaker's shop; this part of the play has clear affinities with Dekker's earlier play on this subject. The subplot is one of tragic martyrdom as Winifred, Sir Hugh, and others go to their deaths resolute in their Christian faith, unyielding to Roman oppression and torture. In a word, the play is a curious mixture of things, and it is not always successful. But the story of the royal families has considerable power and charm, reflecting sincere love among members of the family. The dramatist takes marriage and family seriously. Were we more certain of the date of this play, we could possibly know something about influence or indebtedness. Suffice it to say that Rowley's drama seems to have been written at about the time of Shakespeare's Romances. Its setting in a Britain overrun by the Romans reminds one of *Cymbeline*. The serious loving response to the birth of a child clearly sets this play apart from Jacobean satiric comedy.

As the play opens, the king of Britain, Allured, has received fatal wounds from the invading Romans. As he dies, he urges the Queen and his two sons, Offa and Elred, to flee the advancing Romans. The brothers change into the garb of some slain soldiers, receive their mother's blessing, and escape. The Queen, however, steadfastly refuses to leave, choosing to stay with her dead husband. The conquering Roman emperors, Maximinus and Dioclesian, who are busy making "the world our owne" (Act I, sig. B3),[24] take the Queen prisoner. The sons, somewhat improbably, have taken refuge in a shoemaker's shop, where they become known as Crispinus (Offa) and Crispianus (Elred). They have barely accepted the shoemaker's terms when they see their mother being carted away to prison. The brief encounter between mother and sons, all having to hide their emotions, demonstrates a strong bond of familial love (sigs. C1v–C2).

The British royal family and the Roman royal family intersect in Act II, when Leodice, daughter of Emperor Maximinus, and Offa (Crispinus) meet and fall in love. He has visited her in his function as shoemaker. Giving Crispinus a mirror in which by her "speculatory magick" (sig. E2) she will show him his future wife, Leodice reveals her love for him: ". . . introth I love thee; nay, doe not feare—Ile / Share all dangers with thee" (sig. E2). In the flush of such avowals of love, Crispinus reveals his identity to her as a royal son, of "Royalst Blood in *Britany*" (sig. E2v). They secretly marry; the opening stage direction in Act IV shows how their relationship has flourished: "*Enter* Crispinus *and* Leodice *with childe.*" Such a stage direction is out of place in the satiric comedies that we have examined, in which procreation is abhorred by many of the women.

Escaping from the court and taking refuge in the shoemaker's house, Leodice eventually gives birth to a royal son (Act V, sig. K2). The Shoemaker and his wife, Sisly, for all their agitated verbal exchanges, come to function as surrogate parents for both Offa and Elred, who acknowledge this parentlike affection. Offa, in fact, takes them into his confidence and reveals his identity. His brother, Elred, who has been conscripted to fight with the Romans in France and who has twice saved the life of Emperor Dioclesian, returns in time to greet this new birth. Elred offers a benediction and hope for the new royal child: "The eye of Heaven looke on thee, / And maist thou spread like to the / Bay Tree, . . . / And through this land plant a whole race of Kings" (Act V, sig. K2ᵛ). The image may have been suggested by the Queen's earlier reference to her sons as "My Royall Plants" (sig. B3ᵛ). Royal issue assures heritage and family continuity, and it potentially offers political stability to the state.

One major political problem still hangs over the state, namely the Roman occupation. Rowley solves this by revealing the marriage between Leodice and Offa, who themselves represent a union of the kingdoms. Maximinus, alarmed at the disappearance of his daughter, issues a proclamation that is eventually fulfilled: ". . . whosoever brings me / Her alive, goes laden with rewards; / If nobly borne, we give her him to wife" (sig. K1). Two major events occur at the close of the play: the redemption of the Queen from prison and the return of Leodice. At one point, Maximinus, impressed by the reports of Elred's valor in battle and of his affection for his mother whose release he begs for, offers Leodice to him, should she be found. The irony is that she is already married, but to Elred's brother. Eventually the shoemakers, Crispinus, Leodice, and child enter to the accompaniment of music. The simple stage direction captures the reunion of father and daughter: "Leodice *kneeles and* Maximinus *embraceth her*" (sig. K4). After momentary confusion, Maximinus accepts Crispinus as his son-in-law and the child as his grandchild.

Amidst such celebration the freed Queen enters. Maximinus points out to her that they are now kin because of the royal marriage of their children. In a last gesture of reconciliation Maximinus returns the British crown to Offa and Elred: "Be true to *Rome,* none shall disturb your peace" (sig. L2). "Kinship," "bond," "parent," "child": such words recur in this play, resonant with serious, not mocking, significance. The private lives of the families have been sorted out; but equally important, the state gains peace because the royal families are reconciled. For the first time in the plays that we have examined, a child makes possible such healing, carrying with him the hopes of years to come.

This chapter began with a consideration of Beaumont and Fletcher's *The Coxcomb;* it now closes with an examination of two other plays by them of a quite different kind: *A King and No King* (1611) and *Philaster* (1608–9). (I omit *The Faithful Shepherdess* because family relationships are insignificant in it.) These two plays contain royal families, reconciliation, and reunion. *A King and No King* explores a family problem that we have not seen elsewhere, even in the bitterest satiric comedy: incest, a problem full of tragic potential, as we see later in the century in John Ford's *'Tis Pity She's a Whore.* Beaumont and Fletcher's play calls for a redefinition of the family bonds that at first seem apparent; such a process also redefines the political state. Arbaces, king of Iberia, has been away at battle for some time and has succeeded in capturing Tigranes, king of Armenia. Initially, as a sign of his conquest, Arbaces insists that Tigranes should marry Panthaea, whom Arbaces himself has not seen in years: ''. . . shee but nine yeere old, / I left her, and nere saw her since'' (I.i.103–4).[25] For reasons that remain unexplained for some time in the play, Arbaces' mother has been trying to destroy him ever since his father died. The solution to this mystery must await the final revelations in the play. The play will therefore have to clarify Arbaces' relationship to his sister Panthaea and to his mother.

In the initial meeting of brother and sister, Arbaces is almost immediately aware of strange feelings of passion for Panthaea. He perplexes the onlookers because he seems to be distracted and irrational, even pretending at one point that she is no kin to him. By the end of the scene he names his feelings: ''Incest is in me / Dwelling alreadie . . .'' (III.i.330–31). Trying to enlist the help of his friend Mardonius, Arbaces reveals his passion, saying that he desires Panthaea ''Lasciviouslie, leudlie, incestuouslie . . .'' (III.iii.77). Quite apart from its being taboo or its sinful nature, incest paradoxically destroys traditional family bonds by the intimate uniting of members of a family.

Understanding the danger of the course that he has chosen and trying to protect himself, Arbaces places Panthaea in prison. They meet nevertheless in IV.iv, and Arbaces confesses his longing for her. He knows that to destroy the sacred family bond will only produce another kind of bondage. Arbaces tells her bluntly: ''I have beheld thee with a lustfull eye . . .'' (IV.iv.71). She resists, preferring to die in her innocence. Frustrated and tormented, Arbaces lashes out at the stumbling block of the terms ''brother'' and ''sister,'' something that he would like to obliterate. To quench the flames, they quickly depart. But the fire still burns in Arbaces' breast as we hear at the opening of V.iv, when Arbaces says:

> I must beginne
> With murder of my friend, and so goe on

To an incestuous ravishing, and end
My life and sinnes with a forbidden blow
Upon my selfe. (7–11)

Sin will compound with sin, bringing tragic destruction.

Fortunately, a series of revelations begun by Gobrius, Arbaces'
counselor, makes these tragic acts unnecessary. Gobrius startles
Arbaces by admitting, ''. . . I am thy Father . . .'' (V.iv.123), a fact
confirmed by Arane, Arbaces' supposed mother. Arbaces kneels and
''with the obedience of a childe'' (183) urges his new-found father to
speak. What he discovers also is that Arane is not his mother; and
because Panthaea is her natural child, Arbaces and Panthaea are not
in fact brother and sister. Being the mere son of Gobrius, Arbaces is
no king; instead, Panthaea is the legitimate Queen of Iberia. Arbaces
quickly asks her to marry him, and she agrees. He asks everyone to
join in praise for what has happened: ''Loude thankes for me, that I
am prov'd no King'' (353).

Whatever one may think of the dramatists' sleight-of-hand
resolution of the essential dramatic problem, family bonds have been
restored by clarification. Arbaces loses a mother and a sister, but he
gains a father and a wife. Skirting perilously close to tragedy,
Beaumont and Fletcher preserve the comic form by the im-
probabilities of romance. One should add that Arbaces has lost a
kingdom as well, though his marriage to Panthaea overcomes that
loss. But the proof that he is not a royal child redefines the political
realities of the kingdom. The politics of this family changes drastically
when the family takes a different shape. The dramatists hint at the
final political truth by their choice of a title, though they could have
titled the play ''a brother and no brother.''

Political succession, family relationship, the nature of kingship,
and love conflict are the major issues that make up *Philaster*. Given
these matters and the presumed date of the play, critics earlier in this
century argued for the connection with or influence on Shakespeare's
Romances, some suggesting that Beaumont and Fletcher set the style
for Shakespeare's last plays, especially *Cymbeline*.[26] The safer critical
position is, I think, that Beaumont and Fletcher and Shakespeare
were moving along parallel courses, the issue of possible influence
being indeterminate. The opening scene of *Philaster* establishes most
of the principal conflicts of the play: the basic situation is that the
King of Sicily and Calabria has decided that Pharamond, prince of
Spain, is a worthy suitor for his daughter, Arathusa. From this

proposed marriage come most of the other problems: Philaster's struggle for the kingdom and for Arathusa and the King's relationship to him. Three fathers in the play help give a structure to family concerns: the King, who would determine the destiny of his daughter through marriage; Dion, who has lost his daughter, Euphrasia; and Philaster's father, who, though dead and therefore not in the play, nevertheless has a compelling influence on him.

The politics of royal marriage is much in evidence as the play opens. Dion, Cleremont, and Trasiline are discussing the proposed marriage of Arathusa to Pharamond and the overthrow of Philaster's rightful claim to the kingdom of Sicily. Pharamond, in their view, compares unfavorably with Philaster, who is much admired by the people and whose father "was by our late King of *Calabria*, unrighteously deposed from his fruitfull *Cicilie*" (I.i.23–24).[27] The politics of marriage—a subject of current interest in the Jacobean court—is the topic of the King's first speech (I.i.78–110); he intends not only to give Arathusa to Pharamond but also "To plant you [Pharamond] deeply, our immediate Heire, / Both to our Blood and kingdomes" (85–86). In one sense this is merely the pattern followed by many parents who arrange marriages for their children, but the stakes are much higher, since the kingdom itself and its future are the issue. Royal children inevitably find their private lives and desires subject to a broader political determination. Philaster challenges the proposed marriage and the destiny of the kingdom, claiming his legitimate rights from his father. This earth, which "My fathers friends made fertile with their faiths" (189), shall never be Pharamond's, Philaster says. When the King and others assert that Philaster must be possessed, he replies: "Yes, with my fathers spirit" (268). One father, the King, tries to shape the future, while another father, Philaster's, a voice from the past, contravenes the plans. The essential dramatic problem thus involves love and politics: namely, how to prevent the marriage of Pharamond and Arathusa and how to restore Philaster's rightful political claim.

The love pursuit in the play takes several turns. Pharamond's attitude toward love is a means of defining his unworthiness to be Arathusa's husband. He suggests to Arathusa, for example, that they not wait for marriage "but take a little stolne / Delights, and so prevent our joyes to come" (I.ii.196–97). She refuses and exits; but Pharamond says: "The constitution of my body will never hold out till the wedding: I must seeke else-where" (200–201). Seek he does, and he finds a willing Megra. Meanwhile, Philaster has given his page, Bellario, to Arathusa as a means of smoothing the path of their love. But in that doing is the potential undoing of their love, for much of the remainder of the play focuses on accusations made about the presumed illicit relationship between Arathusa and Bellario. These charges greatly disturb the King, leading him to believe that he is being punished through his royal child for the usurpation that was done by his father.

Out of the confusion that occurs in the woods in Act IV, Philaster wounds Arathusa, then stabs Bellario, believing that Bellario can be blamed for Arathusa's injury. But eventually conscience triumphs, and Philaster emerges from hiding to admit his guilt: "Philaster *creepes out of a Bush*" (IV.vi.82 S.D.). Though thrown into prison, Philaster nevertheless manages to become reconciled to Arathusa and to marry her, to the dismay of the King, who cries out: "Heare you Gods: / From this time do I shake all title off, / Of father to this woman, this base woman . . ." (V.iii.61–63). One reconciliation begets an attempt by a father to disown his child. Philaster persuades the King to abandon his anger by offering forgiveness to the King for the usurpation. Soon the King relents: ". . . take your love, / And with her my repentance, all my wishes, / And all my prayers" (174–76). By V.v the King has not only regained his daughter but also has acknowledged Philaster as his son: "My sonne, / . . . now thou art in mine armes, / Me thinkes I have a salve unto my brest . . ." (8–11). And Philaster addresses the King as "my royall Father . . ." (198). Marriage has enlarged this royal family, by having the King gain a son, and Philaster gain a father to replace his dead father.

One family relationship remains to be straightened out: Dion finds his daughter, Euphrasia, known to everyone (including us) up to this point as Bellario. Echoing *Epicoene*, Beaumont and Fletcher destroy the last vestige of false accusations about Arathusa and her page by revealing that Bellario is in fact a woman. Fathers have found daughters, and a son has acquired a new father. The King's last speech grows naturally out of such joy:

> Last joine your hands in one: enjoy *Philaster*
> This Kingdome which is yours, and after me
> What ever I call mine; my blessing on you,
> All happy howres be at your marriage joyes,
> That you may grow your selves over all lands,
> And live to see your plenteous Branches spring
> Where ever there is Sunne. (210–16)

Families have been reunited, but the emphasis is on the future. The royal family will by its private life assure political stability by procreation—planting a tree is the King's image, recalling a similar image in Rowley's play. These royal children provide for political succession. *Philaster* thus offers quite a contrast to *The Coxcomb* and to the satiric drama; it illustrates another vein of drama in the early Jacobean period, flowing counter to the dominant mood.

Jacobean comedy offers a bifurcated view of the family: the dominant perspective focuses on its fragmentation and strife; the other view centers on a center that holds—a royal family—which is not devoid of problems but is capable of rising above them. The first attribute demystifies and therefore depoliticizes the play world; the second attribute underscores the vitality of the family and its crucial political function. All the early Jacobean comedies constitute the dramatic contexts for Shakespeare and his Romances—those plays that he was likely to have known in his everyday life in the theater. In the final plays that I examined here—those by Day, Rowley, and Beaumont and Fletcher—we catch glimpses, or hints, of an approach to the family that Shakespeare adopts and adapts in the Romances. Royal families, most often the subject of tragedy, now invade the comic mode with a peculiar force and growing strength coincident with the establishment of the Stuart royal family on the English throne. By speculating on Jacobean comedy, we prepare ourselves to be spectators in the theater of Shakespeare's Romances. As we sometimes understand one dramatic genre by understanding its opposite, so I think in the case of Shakespeare's last plays we gain a rich preparation for them by learning how they differ from the dominant dramatic texts that surround them. Clearly Shakespeare does not echo contemporary dramatic fashion; he heeds another text that will be incorporated into his own texts: the Stuart royal family— the radical and predicate of the Romances.

4

Shakespeare's Romances

> And, favorites or no favorites, he [James] has married a royal
> princess of Denmark and has produced heirs. If he should come to
> the English throne there need never be such an urgently confusing
> time as this again. He brings his own Succession with him.
> —George Garrett, *The Succession*

An appropriate and descriptive subtitle for this chapter might be
"oblique light," alluding to Maynard Mack's statement that the
family of history may throw at least an oblique light on Shakespeare's
family of art. No blinding road-to-Damascus light here, as that would
be unfair to expect. Awareness of James and his family will not
miraculously provide the "key" to understanding the Romances, nor
will such knowledge overcome or supplant all other critical interpretations. Just as the plays themselves contain, I think, an overlay of
several different traditions and influences, so there is space for varied
approaches to the Romances. Criticism is, after all, a house of many
rooms. We must not embrace any strategy of interpretation that
diminishes the undeniable richness of these plays. I believe that
knowing the context of the Stuart royal family and the other comic
drama of the period enables us to open a door of interpretation that
leads to many rooms largely unexplored.

In the following pages I will demonstrate that knowledge of the
Jacobean royal family sharpens our understanding of the intermingling of family and political matters in the Romances. Simply stated,
the royal family, whether of art or of history, cannot be separated
from politics; indeed, the family's very attitudes and actions translate
into political statements. Even though in most of the Romances,
Shakespeare chose old-fashioned romance for his subject matter, he
in fact re-presents the royal family known to Jacobean theater
audiences. I will argue that he found this particular historical royal

113

family a convenient and worthwhile text, one that engaged his imagination as did the texts that we commonly refer to as Shakespeare's sources. Part of our critical task is to determine, in John Donne's verb, what "elemented" the plays, those mixtures in which several parts are held in solution.

The centrality of the family in Jacobean drama has been remarked by Stephen Greenblatt, who offers several illuminating observations. Though writing about *King Lear,* Greenblatt provides an analysis of the theater's connection to society that is also pertinent to the late plays:

> We tend to assume . . . that Shakespearean self-consciousness and irony lead to a radical transcendence of the network of social conditions, paradigms, and practices in the plays. I would argue, by contrast, that Renaissance theatrical representation itself is fully implicated in this network and that Shakespeare's self-consciousness is in significant ways bound up with the institutions and the symbology of power it anatomizes.[1]

The theater was not "merely the passive reflector of social forms that lay entirely outside of it; rather, like all forms of art, indeed like all utterances, the theater was itself a *social event*" (p.103). Greenblatt even suggests that the drama contained many of the qualities and activities that families used in observing and training their children. He captures the predominance of the family when he comments: "Thus the Renaissance theater does not by virtue of the content of a particular play reach across a void to touch the Renaissance family; rather the theater is itself already saturated with social significance and hence with the family as the period's central social institution" (p. 104). In such a theater, it is relatively easy for a dramatist to represent the Stuart royal family.

We saw in the previous chapter, however, how most Jacobean comic dramatists chose to demystify and therefore to depoliticize their fictional worlds. The family as an institution frequently came under attack, its problems and conflicts being emphasized. Shakespeare, on the other hand, provides in his last plays a mythos, an idealization of the family; and because his subject is royal families, political issues are paramount. He invests these Romances with political issues, the likes of which we do not find in his earlier comedies. C. L. Barber notes a change from the early to the late plays:

> The festive comedies move out to the creation of new families; *Pericles* and *The Winter's Tale* move through experiences of loss back to the

114

recovery of family relations in and through the next generation. In the comedies of youth, the perverse and repressive are laughed out of court while release leads to the embrace of passion, sanctioned by clarification as to its place as part of the natural cycle. In the romances, however, fulfilment for the principal figure requires a transformation of love, not simply liberation of it.[2]

In a word, the emphasis shifts to family relationships, not simply the pursuit of love and marriage. Families in the Romances have a history and lineage that are crucial.

Matters of birth, marriage, and death of children, so prominent in the actual life of James and his family during their first decade in England, are also apparent in Shakespeare's Romances. There is a family iconography in these plays, portraits that help define the nature of the families, as Phillipe Ariès has discussed. And of course, the families in the late plays are inseparable from some idea of children and childhood. Shakespeare's attention focuses on both the public (political) and private (domestic) life of his royal families. Themes of peaceful succession, deliverance, and hopes for the royal children echo through the plays as they do in the life of the Stuart royal family. Some of the action and some of the themes may, of course, derive from the romance material Shakespeare presumably used; I freely admit that. But it will be instructive to note how Shakespeare departs and differs from those same materials; at such moments in particular it is obvious, at least to me, that another text looms in Shakespeare's artistic consciousness: I think it is the royal family that he knew.

Genealogy is destiny, Jonathan Goldberg reminds us,[3] a point that Shakespeare concentrates on in the Romances and a further way in which they differ both from his earlier comedies and from most Jacobean comedy. In the latter the issue is more a petty squabble over inheritance. Knowing one's heritage is vital also for the matter of political succession—which is true for both actual and fictional royal families. As the epigraph to this chapter observes, King James brought his own succession with him—part of his initial attractiveness to the English public, as I noted in chapter 2. The question of succession constitutes the dominant political issue in Shakespeare's last plays. I think that such an artistic preoccupation, much greater than in Shakespeare's acknowledged sources, grows out of the presence of James and his family, a presence that constantly calls attention to the issue.

115

In most of the Romances, succession depends on the female line. On this point D. W. Harding observes: ''In the historical context, the stress on royal succession through the female line may be viewed as flattery of James I, a foretaste of Cranmer's prophetic speech in *Henry VIII*.''[4] Without insisting on flattery, I nevertheless see the focus on royal succession in the Romances as a re-presentation of James and his family. James's claim to the Scottish and to the English thrones came, of course, through the female line. In March 1603, as James left Scotland to come to England to accept the prize that he had so assiduously wanted and worked for, he simply reversed what had happened exactly one hundred years earlier. In March 1503, Princess Margaret began her progress north to marry James IV of Scotland, thereby establishing the royal familial link that would eventually make James's succession possible. Because of her movement north, James is able to come south. I suggest that that road from London to Edinburgh and back is a road that Shakespeare travels in the last plays whether the setting is Tyre, Pentapolis, Sicily, or a magical island. The anxiety about succession that gripped England, especially in Elizabeth's last years, has been overcome by James and his family. Shakespeare resolves the issue in the Romances primarily by a royal daughter.

As we move from *Pericles* to *Henry VIII*, we will not discern some evolution of Shakespeare's concept of the royal family; we will see him doing things differently, placing emphasis in one place and not another. This, I suppose, is another way of saying that all the Romances, though similar, also differ from one another. With *Henry VIII*, for me not the greatest of these plays, we have the culmination of concern for a royal family. Abandoning romance or early history materials, Shakespeare goes to English history of only a century earlier to dramatize events from the reign of Henry VIII. Paradoxically, in dramatizing the last Tudor royal family, Shakespeare most self-consciously re-presents the Stuart royal family. Given the likelihood that *Henry VIII* was associated with the wedding festivities for Princess Elizabeth in 1613, the connection between the two families becomes explicit. In the gap between the reigns of Henry VIII and James I, England is a land of no royal children, no complete royal families. To use the text of Henry's reign selectively, with its final emphasis on the birth of Elizabeth, is to join the text of James's family, James being Elizabeth's successor, who is hinted at in the play, and royal heir. These are matters to be explored fully in what follows.

We turn now to hear the old songs that Shakespeare sings in the last plays, fully aware, I hope, that topical realities may lurk in those old melodies. As I see it, Shakespeare reads the text of the Stuart royal family, interprets it, using the eye of judgment that Gower refers to, and re-presents that family in the Romances. Louis Mac-Neice writes in his poem "Autolycus" that Shakespeare turned away

> From his taut plots and complex characters
> To tapestried romances, conjuring
> With rainbow names and handfuls of sea-spray
> And from them turned out happy Ever-afters.

Those tapestried romances contain for Shakespeare the possibility of reflecting current realities. Insofar as these last plays can be characterized as "happy Ever-afters," they are so because political and family problems resolve fortunately. What Shakespeare pursues through these plays is not the love of power but the power of love. Shakespeare discredits those, such as Dionyza and Cymbeline's Queen, who nakedly seek political power; he celebrates the transforming quality of love that reconciles and renews royal families.

PERICLES

Omitted from the first Folio and deemed not to be entirely Shakespeare's work, *Pericles* must seem at times a poor, unwanted child. On the question of authorship, I will assume that the play is wholly by Shakespeare, since the arguments for collaboration do not in fact prove collaboration. In some ways the issue becomes one of faith. The play does cohere whether some critics can always hear Shakespeare's voice in it or not. Part of the problem is the ancient one of Shakespearean criticism: when encountering poorly written passages or ones that offend morally, always postulate the possibility of another writer clandestinely at work. Even the editor of the Arden edition of *Pericles* can refer to passages as being either "worthy" or "unworthy" of Shakespeare. I have no new evidence or arguments to offer for or against Shakespeare's authorship. That problem will not affect the interpretation of the play as we find it, with all of its textual corruption and roughness.

Critical prejudice against *Pericles* has existed at least as far back as Jonson's contemptuous reference to it as a "mouldy play." Such sentiment persists. Schmidgall can suggest in 1981 that as we move

117

from *Pericles* to *The Tempest*, we move from "romance chaos" to "classical unity." He adds: "To judge from its crude characterization and often poor poetry, *Pericles* must have been intended for the delight of what Jonson called 'grounded judgments.' "[5] Obviously, in Schmidgall's view, "classical unity" is always to be preferred over "romance chaos." Such a characterization of *Pericles* is loaded and begs the critical question. *Pericles* is simply something to be discarded, a mere pothole along the path to Shakespeare's crowning achievement in *The Tempest*. I suppose I have one of those "grounded judgments" that Jonson refers to, for I find much delight and charm in *Pericles*. One of the problems with the "courtly aesthetic" approach is that some things, such as *Pericles*, do not readily fit, so the critic disposes of them. *The Tempest*, I believe, can easily stand on its own considerable merits without sniping at *Pericles* or any other play. I also do not think that "romance chaos" accurately describes what takes place in *Pericles*.

Several statements in the play call attention to the double nature of *Pericles*, by which I mean its ancient story and its current reality. The simple presence of Gower as the Chorus alerts us to an archaic tradition and specifically to his *Confessio Amantis*, part of which Shakespeare has used as a text for his play. Partly this is the tradition of Greek romance, a subject ably discussed by Carol Gesner.[6] Gower says in the opening Chorus: "I tell you what mine authors say" (20).[7] Later, in IV.iv, he implores: "I do beseech you / To learn of me, who stand i'th' gaps to teach you / The stages of our story" (7–9). What Gower says not only accurately describes his narrative function; it also nicely epitomizes Shakespeare's position with regard to the texts that he has inherited. He does tell us what his authors, such as Gower, have told him, and he stands in the gaps to reveal the inherited story. But like the fictional Gower, the dramatist does not passively rehearse the ancient story: he ignores some of it, changes parts of it, adds to it. Shakespeare re-presents the ancient tale; he differs from his text. Perhaps those "gaps" that Gower refers to may be precisely those points at which the dramatist differs from the old song.

Evidence that another kind of text is functioning in *Pericles* occurs in the simple exchange of Boult and the Bawd with regard to Marina in IV.ii. Boult reports that throughout the market at Mytilene he cried the enticing beauty of Marina. The crowd was attentive; in fact, "There was a Spaniard's mouth water'd and he went to bed to her very description" (97–99). The Bawd responds: "We shall have him here to-morrow with his best ruff on'' (100–101). Monsieur Verolles, the French knight, has had a similar reaction. Do not such comments put us squarely in the world of Jacobean topicality? Spaniards with their ruffs were frequent targets of ridicule in literature and life. Certainly such references are alien to the usual known sources for *Pericles*. It may seem a small matter, but I cite it here only as being indicative of another overlay of text in the play. I do not refer to the supposed Ur-*Pericles*; I mean the living world of Jacobean activity and royal family.

Howard Felperin suggests that the play changes in Act III; there is ''a shift in the play's center of gravity and interest from Pericles as prince to Pericles as man, husband and father. By the end of the second act the public plot has run its course.''[8] Felperin's idea has its genesis in an earlier essay by Gerard A. Barker, who argues that the theme of kingship, prominent in the first two acts, gives way to other interests in the remainder of the play.[9] What Felperin and Barker observe is valid, but it is also incomplete. Though the final three acts focus on Pericles as husband and father, we can never forget that he is a royal father of a royal child, with all the implications that this fact conveys. I will suggest that his relationship to his kingdom of Tyre is a current that runs through the whole play. Like James, Pericles is never merely a husband or a father; he is always a ruler. Political issues are never far from the surface of the play.

As we turn to the play, I will trace the inextricably linked issues of royal family and politics. In part, I will do this by noting Shakespeare's use and ''misuse'' of his sources, his texts. One might argue that one of the sources that Shakespeare incorporates is his own *Comedy of Errors*. I refer to the frame story of Egeon, which ultimately derives from the story of Apollonius of Tyre, as told by Gower in *Confessio Amantis*. To put *Comedy of Errors* alongside *Pericles* is to sharpen the distinction between this early comedy and the later Romances. The heart of *Errors* is, of course, the confusion of the two sets of twins, a retelling and refurbishing of a Plautine comedy. The romance story of Egeon is the focus only of the opening and last scenes of the play. Egeon offers a long—no one would wish it any longer—narrative account of the separation by shipwreck of the family. But the brief afternoon in Ephesus, the time of the play, offers little scope for expansion. At the end, we recall, the family reunites, including the added bonus of the Abbess, who turns out to be Egeon's wife and the mother of his twins. The day in Ephesus contrasts with the decade and a half that *Pericles* encompasses. The simple sorting out of correct physical identity in *Errors* contrasts with the process of transformation in *Pericles*.

Families are recovered in both plays, but in the later one we also have the begetting of a family, the birth of Marina. Indeed, this is the only time when we actually witness a birth in all of Shakespeare. When the Abbess in *Errors*, in a state of great joy, cries out, "After so long grief such Nativity!" (V.i.408), she uses a metaphor; but in *Pericles* that nativity is a reality. The procreative and nurturing qualities of women receive much emphasis in the late Romance, but they are of no significance in *Errors*.

Why, one wonders, did Shakespeare return to this old story first used in such an abbreviated form early in his career? Did that ancient story somehow linger in his consciousness? Why, roughly in 1608, did it seem appropriate to revisit and retell, with a difference, that story? Such teasing questions do not easily surrender to proof. Certainly the play itself suggests that Shakespeare might have developed it differently; by this I mean that *Pericles* contains ingredients that we see in other Jacobean comedy. I refer, for example, to the problem of incest that one finds in *A King and No King* and here in Antiochus and his daughter. The shrewish wife, as in Fletcher's *The Woman's Prize*, appears in Dionyza, who also possesses considerable jealousy in regard, not to her husband, but to her daughter. The sexual climate, including prostitution, that prevails in Mytilene we find repeatedly in comedies by Jonson and especially Middleton—in *The Family of Love* and *A Chaste Maid*, for example. In one sense, these dramatic contexts exist in *Pericles*; but clearly Shakespeare's emphasis and interest are elsewhere, for he abandons this demystified, de-politicized world in order to pursue the issue of the royal family. I find it plausible that the presence of the Stuart royal family may have urged Shakespeare to think afresh about fictional royal families, that their very existence led him to resurrect the old romances and to avoid the comic world of most of his contemporaries.

In the standard study of sources, Geoffrey Bullough claims two sources for *Pericles:* Gower's *Confessio Amantis* and Laurence Twine's *The Patterne of Painefull Adventures;*[10] both retell the old story of Apollonius of Tyre, probably a Greek romance originally. Shake-speare follows quite closely the general outline and details of this romance. What is striking is how often he seems virtually to have these texts at his elbow as he writes. Two examples will suffice to make the point. Marina in IV.i innocently asks Leonine from what direction the wind blows; he says from the southwest, and she responds: "When I was born, the wind was north" (51). Back in the storm scene itself (III.i), none of the characters comment on the direction of the wind, though Gower in the Chorus refers to it in passing. The detail about the wind comes from *Confessio Amantis:* "Out of the north thei see a cloude, / The storm arose . . ." (1047–48). Marina's knowledge of her birth and parentage have come from the nurse Lychorida, whose death Marina mourns in IV.i as she enters with a basket of flowers. *Confessio Amantis* does not have such a scene of mourning, nor does it indicate that the nurse has been the source of Marina's knowledge. Instead, such details apparently derive from Twine's *Patterne of Painefull Adventures,* chapters 10 and 11.

Recognizing the apparent care with which Shakespeare attended these texts, we are in a better position to wonder at, if not always to understand, the changes that Shakespeare makes. Indeed, source studies are particularly valuable, I think, insofar as they acknowledge what the artist does differently. My task is not to point out all such differences, because that subject has already been surveyed by Bullough and others; rather, I intend to call attention to those moments when some other source, specifically the Jacobean royal family, seems to be affecting Shakespeare's text.

What some may see as the "romance chaos" of *Pericles,* I see as its diffuse quality, an attribute characteristic of both Greek and chivalric romance. One could refer to the action as the "peregrinations of Pericles." In contrast to the other late plays, *Pericles* has many shifting geographical centers: Pericles himself visits six different Mediterranean cities and also spends considerable time at sea. The episodic nature of the drama reflects such movement—a comparable motion occurs in *Antony and Cleopatra.* The shifting centers are not merely geographical; they are also political and familial. Unlike the other Romances, the scope of *Pericles* involves three generations of one royal family, as well as several royal families. Shakespeare gains coherence by the focus on Pericles, his role as prince of Tyre and his function as royal husband-father. His fortunes and that of the play itself constitute an undulating pattern, like the waves of the sea, "Each changing place with that which goes before, / In sequent toil all forwards do contend" (Sonnet 60). Part of what gives shape to Pericles' adventures is his quest for a wife and a father, a quest fraught with political as well as familial significance. I think that the ultimate goal for Pericles is to resemble Simonides as king-father.

With the several generations of royal families presented here Shakespeare invites us to consider the importance of genealogy, the legitimacy that it may grant and the destiny that it may assure. Obviously James's claim to the English throne rests on his heritage; with wife and royal children he also embodies a destiny for England. In his first speech to Parliament in March 1604, James reminded the hearers several times of his lineal descent "out of the loynes of *Henry the seuenth*. . . ."[11] By such descent, James can claim both kingdoms. As in the Stuart royal family, so in the play: the matter of succession pervades all political considerations. Like James a ruler by virtue of the female line, Thaisa and then Marina, as only daughters of royal fathers, each in turn secures the future of Pentapolis and of Tyre. I am not concerned with identifying characters in Shakespeare's fiction with James or members of his family, though there may be some analogies; instead, I argue that Shakespeare re-presents this Stuart family in the play through the intermingling of family and politics. We will keep our eyes on the resolution of familial and political problems by examining the politics of the family and the family of politics in each of the cities that Pericles visits. Tyre is always the point of reference; experiences in Antioch, Tharsus, and Mytilene threaten family and kingdom; Pentapolis, Ephesus, and part of the Mytilene experience bring political and personal good fortune. The mythos of the royal family confirms the political nature of the play world.

Surviving personal danger at Antioch, Pericles, a troubled prince, returns in I.ii to his native Tyre, over which he rules. What he has experienced at Antioch disturbs him greatly, and what the future holds seems threatening. Two political and personal issues dominate the scene: the nature of his journey to Antioch and the action that must be taken so as to reduce the threat of Antioch's possible retaliation. Shakespeare presents a prince struggling with these problems in terms not included in the usual sources of the play. Pericles seeks the sage counsel of the noble Helicanus, part of whose value comes from his being no flatterer, believing instead that "reproof, obedient and in order, / Fits kings, as they are men . . ." (I.ii.43–44). Pericles, when explaining his recent trip to Antioch, says that he "sought the purchase of a glorious beauty . . ." (72). But he also clarifies the purpose of the mission: "From whence an issue I might propagate" (73); such royal progeny would be "arms to princes and bring joys to subjects" (74). While such a purpose may be implicit in the Gower and Twine sources, it is not so stated. At such a moment, Pericles is the Jacobean prince, fulfilling his duty to the kingdom to marry and provide royal issue. These are, of course, the instructions of James to Prince Henry in *Basilicon Doron;* such marriage intentions are of increasing importance in the Stuart royal family at the time when Shakespeare writes. Shakespeare clearly attends another text. We saw in chapter 2 how James's royal children provided "arms" to the king and "joy" to the subjects of the realm. As prince, Pericles knows his political duty to his kingdom: provide for orderly succession through his family.

Not only has that hope been dashed in Antioch, but also fear arises that Antiochus may invade Tyre. Wanting to forestall Antiochus's threat and thus be a peacemaker, Pericles articulates the problem: "How I might stop this tempest ere it came . . ." (98). Helicanus, assessing that the danger will come either from "public war" or "private treason" against Pericles' life, counsels the prince to travel. Heeding the advice, Pericles decides to go to Tharsus. Being a wise prince, alert to political needs of his realm, Pericles places Helicanus in charge: "The care I had and have of subjects' good / On thee I lay, whose wisdom's strength can bear it" (118–19). In accepting the task, Helicanus demonstrates, Pericles says, "a subject's shine, I a true prince'" (124). This action has a historical analogue in James, who made similar provisions when he left Scotland to cross the seas to fetch Anne of Denmark. Shakespeare never shows Pericles in Tyre again, though he does spend additional time there. Part of his quest seems to be to regain his kingdom in full stability and peace. His concern for the political welfare of Tyre pervades his thought throughout the play.

Helicanus meanwhile functions as ruler-substitute. In I.iii he explains to the assembled lords: "His [Pericles'] seal'd commission, left in trust with me, / Doth speak sufficiently he's gone to travel" (12–13). He does fill in some of the details about Antioch that have prompted Pericles' departure. Thaliard, come from Antioch to kill Pericles, overhears and decides to report that Pericles has perished at sea. Thus the decision to travel has achieved Pericles' political purpose: Tyre will endure no invasion from Antioch. By II.iv Helicanus can report to Escanes the spectacular deaths of Antiochus and his daughter, consumed by a fire from heaven. A fire of another sort burns in Tyre: political restlessness, brought on by the absence of Pericles. Not knowing whether Pericles lives or not, the lords are anxious for certainty and stability. They propose to seek Pericles; the Second Lord has another plan: that Helicanus become the sovereign. This plea rests on the recognition that "this kingdom is without a head" (35). Helicanus mollifies their concern by urging the Lords to wait another twelve months; if Pericles has not returned, he will "with aged patience bear your yoke" (48). The scene closes with Helicanus's ringing endorsement of the unity of kingdom: "When peers thus knit, a kingdom ever stands" (58)—a commonplace idea but a situation devoutly to be desired by rulers.

The political circumstances in Tyre are precarious at best: no royal issue for succession and an absent ruler. Eventually Helicanus's letters reach Pericles in Pentapolis, where he has married Thaisa. Amidst that joy and the expected birth of a royal child, Pericles must heed the call of Tyre. Gower reports Helicanus's message that "if King Pericles / Come not home in twice six moons, / He [Helicanus], obedient to their dooms, / Will take the crown" (Chorus, Act III, 30–33). Fearful for the life of the baby born at sea, Pericles alters the course toward Tyre and sets forth to Tharsus instead. There he leaves Marina with Cleon and Dionyza and sails toward Tyre again: ". . . I must needs be gone; / My twelve months are expir'd, and Tyrus stands / In a litigious peace" (III.iii.1–3). Though married and a father, Pericles returns to Tyre, separated from this family. He is not able to satisfy the political future of Tyre until the closing moments of the play, when at the prospect of Lysimachus's marriage to Marina, Pericles announces: "Our son and daughter shall in Tyrus reign" (V.iii.82). The royal family will provide the desired political stability, a situation as real in the Jacobean court as in Shakespeare's fiction. The deliquescent quality of the play, with its constant motion, compounds the difficulty of achieving permanence. But Tyre provides a center, because the political realities and demands of it are never far from Pericles' mind.

Threatening Tyre and Pericles is Antioch. The incestuous relationship of King Antiochus and his daughter not only imperils normal, healthy family ties but also imposes harm on the state. Though not in Beaumont and Fletcher's sense, Antiochus is "a king and no king"; that is, he is the opposite of what a king and royal father ought to be, in contrast to King Simonides. Pericles' excursion to Antioch threatens him and his kingdom also; the quest for a wife and a father runs aground at Antioch. Going in search of "a glorious beauty," Pericles finds instead grotesque corruption.

The experience at Antioch, more explicitly than elsewhere in this play, opens the question of interpretation. To borrow Stephen Greenblatt's phrase, the family exists *sub specie semioticae*; it becomes Pericles' task to interpret Antiochus and his daughter, as it is ours to interpret the larger play, just as Shakespeare has interpreted Gower and his other texts. The basic critical, interpretive assumption seems to be, in the words of Pericles, that "Kings are earth's gods" (I.i.104). As Jonathan Goldberg makes quite clear, there were ongoing efforts to understand and interpret James. The king meanwhile often remains deliberately, consciously an "opaque text" (*James I*, p. 135). It suits James's purposes to be both known and unknown, transparent and opaque—a glass through which we might peer but darkly. Antiochus represents the position of James as one who possesses state secrets that may or may not be fathomed. The risk of interpretation pervades the predicament of Pericles, who because he understands correctly, stands in danger of losing his life. Could not Robert Cecil and other courtiers in the Jacobean court confirm this risk? As Pericles observes at one point: "Who has a book of all that monarchs do, / He's more secure to keep it shut than shown . . ." (I.i.95–96). I think that the motif of interpretation of the king and the royal family runs throughout the Romances. Shakespeare emphasizes this art and activity in ways not found in his acknowledged sources. I find this theme consistent with the dramatist's apparent fascination with the Stuart royal family.

The compelling image of the play's opening scene is the array of heads of those who have died in pursuit of Antiochus's daughter: "So for her many a wight did die, / As yon grim looks do testify," says Gower (39–40). Antiochus himself warns Pericles: "with speechless tongues and semblance pale," the former princes, "martyrs slain in Cupid's wars," "advise thee to desist . . ." (I.i.37, 39, 40). This gruesome image contrasts with the alluring beauty of the daughter, who appears "clothed like a bride" (6). When Pericles first sees the daughter, he notes her beauty: "Her face the book of praises, where is read / Nothing but curious pleasures . . ." (16–17). In this instance, Pericles misreads the "text" that he sees; fortunately, when he confronts the text of the riddle, he reads it correctly—to his horror. Creating the aura of the quest of romance, Antiochus describes his daughter in terms that epitomize beauty and risk: "Before thee stands this fair Hesperides, / With golden fruit, but dangerous to be touch'd . . ." (28–29). Wanting to save the daughter for himself, Antiochus has created danger: the golden fruit is not rich with fecund possibilities but rather is corrupt and sterile.

Before he ventures and hazards for the daughter, Pericles says to Antiochus, "As I am son and servant to your will" (24); when Antiochus interrupts with "Prince Pericles," Pericles responds: "That would be son to great Antiochus" (27). The issue of Pericles' becoming the "son" to Antiochus is not in Shakespeare's sources, and it adds another familial dimension to Pericles' quest. As is the case for any Renaissance prince, like the young King James, marriage into another royal family creates an extended family in which the father-king becomes a father to his son-in-law. Dynastic implications are great: will the kingdoms of Tyre and Antioch, for example, be united? Later in the scene, as Antiochus starts to realize that Pericles understands the secret, Antiochus begins to refer to him as "son" (119). Pericles, however, no longer uses the term, recognizing that he cannot become part of this perverse family. No political or personal union will take place between the potential son and father.

The image that Pericles uses in describing his adventures sounds thoroughly Renaissance; certainly it is not in Shakespeare's sources: "Like a bold champion I assume the lists . . ." (62). But when, in a variation of the scheme in *The Merchant of Venice*, Pericles chooses the "casket," he reads the riddle, which, unlike the sources, is told from the daughter's perspective. The riddle hinges on the definition of family: "I sought a husband, in which labour / I found that kindness in a father. / He's father, son, and husband mild; / I mother, wife, and yet his child" (67–70). Pericles becomes, in his words, "pale to read it [the riddle]" (76). He reads and interprets correctly what the riddle implies; thus, he turns to the daughter and says tersely: "Good sooth, I care not for you" (87). Antiochus begins to understand: "he has found the meaning; / But I will gloze with him" (110–11). Though "gloze" means to use specious language, as the Arden editor says, does it not also carry the sense of "to gloss," to indulge in exegesis? Pericles has apparently unraveled the riddle, and Antiochus will seek to interpret him. To unravel the riddle is to expose the desecration of this royal family and to illustrate the vulnerability of the political state. Sounding more like King James in one of his speeches to Parliament than like Apollonius of Tyre, Pericles reminds Antiochus that "Kings are earth's gods" (104). By such a measure one can judge the falling-off that has occurred in Antioch. Pericles flees, having found neither wife nor father in that city.

Tharsus, a place of desolation and famine, which Pericles redeems, becomes, however, a breeding ground for envy and corruption, leading to the presumed death of Marina, whose nurture had been the task of the ruling family. Devoid of the incest of Antioch, Tharsus nevertheless contains a royal parent determined to protect the politics of the city by destroying the surrogate child. When

Pericles first comes to Tharsus, he finds a community ravaged by famine. In a horrifying image, Shakespeare illustrates the threat that this famine poses, especially to families. Cleon, the ruler, observes: "Those mothers who, to nuzzle up their babes / Thought nought too curious, are ready now / To eat those little darlings whom they lov'd" (I.iv.42–44). The Gower and Twine sources do not contain such a graphic rendering of the suffering of Tharsus.

Though now vulnerable, Tharsus had not always been in such a predicament. Cleon describes a former glory in which "plenty held full hand" (22); and the city's "towers bore heads so high they kiss'd the clouds, / And strangers ne'er beheld but wond'red at . . ." (24–25). Though F. David Hoeniger in the Arden edition says that the "towers" referred to derive "surely" from the image of the Tower of Babylon, I suggest that Shakespeare may be glancing at "the cloud-capp'd towers," the magnificent triumphal arches constructed for James's 1604 royal entry into London. One of the arches, seemingly reaching the clouds, honored Peace and Plenty, which had been Tharsus's lot. Indeed, one can see Pericles' function here as the embodiment of peace and plenty. When the citizens spot Pericles' ship, they are relieved to see the white flags of peace. Pericles comes, he says, not "to add sorrow to your tears, / But to relieve them of their heavy load . . ." (90–91). His ship, laden with corn, he generously shares with Tharsus—emblematic of the rich gift giving of a royal prince. He finds a grateful people, who, fearing destruction, have found life instead. The people of Tharsus could say what Lorenzo says of Portia and Nerissa in *The Merchant of Venice:* ". . . you drop manna in the way / Of starved people" (V.i.294–95).

The royal father gives his greatest gift to Tharsus in Act III: his infant daughter Marina, as he hurriedly makes his way back to Tyre. Cleon and Dionyza, once redeemed from famine by Pericles, assume the role of substitute parents for the royal child. Pericles implores them "To give her princely training, that she may / Be manner'd as she is born" (III.iii.16–17). The situation recalls how British royal children spent their childhoods in other families: James and Prince Henry in the household of the earl of Mar, Prince Charles in the Robert Carey family, and Princess Elizabeth in the John Harington family. Cleon and Dionyza reassure Pericles, who specifically instructs Dionyza: "Good madam, make me blessed in your care / In bringing up my child" (31–32). Reflecting actual practice in the Jacobean royal family, this episode echoes the several texts that Shakespeare uses in *Pericles*.

Tharsus in Act IV is a threatening place, like the earlier Antioch, this act recapitulating some of the dangers Pericles experienced in Act I. The royal child Marina, now fourteen years old, becomes the victim of Dionyza's envy; the mother substitute becomes the child destroyer, a sinister perversion of family life parallel to that of King Antiochus and his daughter. The presumed death of Marina in Tharsus resembles Thaisa's "death" at sea. In IV.i Dionyza engages Leonine to kill Marina; Dionyza finds Marina's beauty and virtues galling because they overshadow those of her own daughter. Dionyza echoes Iago's justification for attempting to kill Cassio: "If Cassio do remain, / He hath a daily beauty in his life / That makes me ugly . . ." (*Othello*, V.i.18–20). Moral desolation in Tharsus, embodied in Dionyza, seeks with narrow personal and political intention to destroy a thing of beauty.

Running counter to this attempt to kill Marina is her own search for her father and mother: genealogy is destiny. She aptly captures the plight of her whole royal family: "Ay me! poor maid, / Born in a tempest, when my mother died, / This world to me is as a lasting storm, / Whirring me from my friends" (IV.i.17–20). The play's "whirring" action has separated this family. Marina nevertheless recalls what she has been told about her mother and father, especially by Lychorida, the faithful nurse and companion. Dionzya tells her that "We every day / Expect him [Pericles] here . . ." (33–34). Living in that hope, Marina rejects the false overtures of love from Dionyza. As she talks to Leonine, her appointed murderer, she recalls her birth and her father, information supplied her by Lychorida. Marina vividly describes the scene of her birth: "My father, as nurse says, did never fear, / But cried 'Good seamen!' to the sailors, galling / His kingly hands, haling ropes . . ." (52–54). This recovery of her past reminds us of Pericles' discovery of his rusty armor in Act II in Pentapolis and the recollection there of his father. Marina's recalling her father is not in Shakespeare's sources, but it underscores again the play's preoccupation with royal lineage and heritage. If not united in fact, the royal family gains some unity through memory. Marina escapes the murderous clutches of Leonine by being seized by pirates in what appears a dubious rescue. Leonine determines to swear "she's dead / And thrown into the sea" (98–99). He thereby resembles Thaliard, appointed to kill Pericles. The image of throwing Marina into the sea of course echoes Thaisa's being cast overboard in III.i. Marina later makes the connection herself, wishing that she had been killed or tossed into the sea by the pirates, "for to seek my mother!" (IV.ii.63).

The remainder of the experience at Tharsus consists of reaction to Marina's presumed death: Dionyza, the heartless instigator, and Cleon, horrified at what she has done. Cleon poses the fundamental question for them: "What canst thou say / When noble Pericles shall demand his child?" (IV.iii.12–13). Dionyza answers quickly and unashamedly: "That she is dead" (14). Cleon emphasizes a point not in the sources—namely, that Marina is "a princess / To equal any single crown o'th'earth . . ." (7–8). She is no ordinary child, but a royal child—hence the magnitude of the crime and the potential for political repercussions. But Dionyza's rationalization for what she has done is as clear as it is perverse: "And though you call my course unnatural,— / You not your child well loving—yet I find / It greets me as an enterprise of kindness / Perform'd to your sole daughter" (36–39). In the name of protecting her own daughter's political and personal status, Dionyza has destroyed a rival. At such a moment, Tharsus resembles Antioch.

The final movement in Tharsus consists of Gower's description of Pericles' arrival there "To see his daughter, all his life's delight" (IV.iv.12). Instead, he finds death, further destruction of his royal family. A dumb show depicts his reaction: "Cleon *shows* Pericles *the tomb; whereat* Pericles *makes lamentation, puts on sackcloth, and in a mighty passion departs*" (IV.iv.22 S.D.). The extended epitaph, written by Dionyza, much longer than in the sources, calls attention to Marina's lineage, like the scroll placed in Thaisa's coffin: "*She was of Tyrus the king's daughter* . . ." (36). Pericles, believing Marina dead, decides to let "his courses to be ordered / By Lady Fortune . . ." (47–48). He becomes a wanderer again, not returning to Tyre. Pericles' lamentation represents the grief of the Stuart royal family at the deaths of the royal daughters, Mary and Sophia, even as it recalls Shakespeare's other sources. Like Antioch, Tharsus thus presents threat and destruction, neither place solving the matter of political and familial succession for the kingdom of Tyre.

For Marina the bleak, dangerous experience in Tharsus finds its complement in the nightmare world of Mytilene, to which she is taken by the pirates and sold into prostitution. Against considerable odds, Marina retains her virginity and virtue: prostitution constitutes another major challenge to family life in the play. Marina cries out for assistance: "Diana, aid my purpose!" (IV.ii.147). A question that comes from Bawd epitomizes the mood of Mytilene and may remind us of the tone of many Jacobean comedies: "What's her price, Boult?" (47). Bawd's question finds its counterpart in satiric plays, and it underscores the threat to Marina and to family stability in general. By dint of her will and virtue, Marina survives; she even works deeds of transformation in the brothel, changing, for example, Lysimachus's tawdry purpose into recognition of her qualities. He says: "Thou art a piece of virtue . . ." (IV.vi.111). By her encounter with Lysimachus, Marina enters the political world of Mytilene, pointing out to him that he has desecrated his office as ruler by his immoral behavior. She bluntly speaks to Lysimachus: "Do you know this house to be a place of such resort, and will come into't? I hear say you're of honourable parts and are the governor of this place" (IV.vi.78–80). Chastened, Lysimachus leaves; the relationship between the two will eventually develop into a healthy one. Antioch, Tharsus, and now Mytilene constitute a profound threat to the politics of the family and even to the survival of the family itself. What we witness is the *discordia* experience of the royal family.

To turn to Pentapolis is to turn away from the night world of the other cities and toward potential hope and fulfillment. At Pentapolis, Pericles finds a wife and a father, solving one of the major political and familial quests of the drama. The emphasis on King Simonides as the model king and father is altogether Shakespeare's invention. With his peaceable kingdom, Simonides represents King James. As Gower introduces the change in tone and action for Act II, he closes: "What shall be next, / Pardon old Gower,—this 'longs the text" (Chorus, II, 39–40). Hoeniger suggests that " 'longs the text" means "belongs to" the text. Certainly that would be appropriate, since the Gower figure sings the old songs of romance captured in the texts of Gower and Twine. I think the phrase also could mean "prolongs the text"; such would be consonant with romance convention, when episode follows episode, closure being deferred. The "text" may also be extended, prolonged, to include other texts. The play, not merely about Pericles' romantic quests, also concerns the testing of Pericles as a prince, the political issue. Like Prince Hal in Shakespeare's fiction or Prince Henry of the Stuart royal family, Pericles undergoes training and testing to make him a worthy ruler. Pentapolis reinforces the idea of the politics of the family, as Shakespeare heeds the text of the Jacobean royal family.

Pericles' experience at Pentapolis begins inauspiciously enough: "*Enter* Pericles, *wet*" (II.i. S.D.); this will not be the last time that Pericles will suffer a shipwreck. He washes ashore at Pentapolis, where three fishermen (only one in Shakespeare's sources) greet and assist him. Two important matters grow out of the encounter with the fishermen; the first is their identification of the place and their characterization of Simonides, the "good Simonides" (II.i.98), as one of the fishermen calls him. When Pericles asks why the king is called "good," the fisherman responds: ". . . he deserves so to be call'd for his peaceable reign and good government" (100–101). Pericles comments: "He is a happy king, since he gains from his subjects the name of good by his government" (102–3). This ideal ruler contrasts sharply with the one whom Pericles had encountered at Antioch. The second contribution of the fishermen is their recovery of some "rusty armour."

Pericles acknowledges that the armor is his; more important, it had belonged to his father. The armor and the recollection of Pericles' father are not in Shakespeare's traditional sources. I suggest that this episode becomes another means of re-presenting the royal family, as it underscores the significance of genealogy. Pericles even quotes his father's words to him about the armor: " 'Keep it, my Pericles; it hath been a shield / 'Twixt me and death' " (125–26). The shipwreck "now's no ill, / Since I have here my father gave in his will" (132–33). Pericles then tells the fishermen: "He lov'd me dearly . . ." (137). A loving father and a grateful son—the ideal emblem of a royal family. Recovery of the armor is recovery of the family heritage. Finding his father, Pericles will also see him embodied in Simonides.

Learning also from the fishermen about the birthday celebrations for Simonides' daughter, Thaisa, Pericles sets forth to join in the tourney for her love: "This day I'll rise, or else add ill to ill" (II.i.165). The tournament for Thaisa is thoroughly medieval or Renaissance and not found in the play's sources; it makes literal the image that Pericles used in Antioch. The devices and mottoes that the knights carry in honor of Thaisa come from the tradition of Renaissance emblem books. Pericles enters the lists wearing his rusty armor, unaccompanied and without a shield. The armor joins the issues of pursuit of father and pursuit of wife. Because it is rusty, it may also be an emblem of peace, all the more appropriate as Pericles seeks the hand of a peacemaker's daughter. In the banqueting scene that follows the tournament, Pericles sees his father in Simonides: "Yon king's to me like to my father's picture, / Which tells me in that glory once he was . . ." (II.iii.37–38). Having recovered his father's armor, Pericles is particularly sensitive to the image of a royal father; knowing one's lineage is, of course, crucial in royal families.

Politics and family receive considerable emphasis in Pentapolis. As Simonides and Thaisa take their seats in the pavilion for the tournament, he says of her: ". . . our daughter, / . . . Sits here like Beauty's child, whom Nature gat / For men to see, and seeing wonder at" (II.ii.4, 6–7). Their special position and the gazing of the crowd render literal King James's metaphor in the *Basilicon Doron*—namely, that a king is "as one set on a stage," whose every action is noticed. Simonides tells Thaisa that "princes are / A model which heaven makes like to itself" (10–11). The image of the sovereign as God's lieutenant on earth permeates several of James's speeches to Parliament. Simonides further instructs Thaisa in the banquet scene: "O, attend, my daughter: / Princes, in this, should live like gods above, / Who freely give to every one that come to honour them . . ." (II.iii.59–60). Peace-loving, generous in gift giving, sensitive to the public's gaze, and having a loving concern for the royal daughter's welfare in marriage—all characterize Simonides and the court at Pentapolis. Not in Shakespeare's usual sources, these qualities of the royal family at Pentapolis re-present, I argue, the Stuart royal family.

In the last scene of Act II, Simonides sends away all the knights except Pericles, telling them that for twelve months Thaisa will not marry (II.v.3–4). But of course Thaisa will marry; and her choice will be Pericles, who is put through a testing by Simonides (33ff.). Doubtless recalling his experience at Antioch, Pericles fears that Simonides intends to kill him (43–44). Pericles' courage in fact reassures Simonides, who finally awards Thaisa to him. Simonides' aside again raises the question, however, of Pericles' heritage: ". . . for aught I know, / [Pericles] May be (nor can I think the contrary) / As great in blood as I myself"(II.v.77–79). Simonides' instincts are, of course, correct. Gower says in the Chorus of Act III that from the sexual union of Pericles and Thaisa "A babe is moulded" (11); and in the dumb show, we find this direction: "*Then enter* Thaisa *with child, with* Lychorida, *a nurse.*" Like the court of King James at the prospect of the births of the royal children Sophia and Mary, the court of King Simonides must have been similarly caught up in such expectation of joy. Not only is political succession in Pentapolis secure through Thaisa, but she now readies for the birth of an heir. Future rulers of Pentapolis will succeed through the female line.

But the political world of Tyre intrudes in Pentapolis. Word has come, as Gower reveals, that Pericles should return to Tyre to quell the disturbed spirits there. The beneficial side of this news occurs in the recognition in Pentapolis that Pericles is indeed of royal blood. Such information, Gower says, "Y-ravished the regions round . . ." (Chorus III, 35). Pericles, now referred to as "heir-apparent," is thus worthy to inherit the kingdom of Pentapolis through Thaisa. Simonides therefore has a royal son to succeed him; he has found a son as Pericles has found a father. The marriage of Thaisa and Pericles thus has dynastic significance, as most royal marriages have. The journey back to Tyre with his pregnant wife endures a cruel twist of fate: the child is born at sea, and Thaisa, presumably dying in childbirth, is cast overboard in a coffin. Pericles cries out: "O you gods! / Why do you make us love your goodly gifts, / And snatch them straight away?" (III.i.22–24). Painful awareness of mortality constitutes a major feature of family relationships, as Lawrence Stone has documented. Few in the Globe Theatre, watching *Pericles,* could have been impervious to the reality of Pericles' cry. In the storm and in Thaisa's death we witness what Northrop Frye calls the demonic or night world of romance. What had seemed a comic resolution to Pericles' quest in Pentapolis transforms into tragic possibilities at sea.

When the family finally reunites in V.iii, the recollection of Pentapolis and King Simonides assures identification. Thaisa, for example, identifies Pericles partly by the ring he wears: "The king my father gave you such a ring" (V.iii.39). This ring, not in Shakespeare's sources, echoes the experience of the rusty armor in Act II and the remembrance of Pericles' father. Here the father recalled is Thaisa's. Her rather awkward revelation, "My father's dead" (V.iii.78), opens a political possibility. In fact, as heir apparent, Pericles determines that in Pentapolis "ourselves / Will in that kingdom spend our following days" (80–81). The political and familial world of Pentapolis is as ideal as any in the play. By virtue of his experience, suffering, and attributes, Pericles is worthy to succeed the noble Simonides, which he does by means of marriage to Thaisa. He re-presents Simonides, and together they re-present the Jacobean royal family. Through the politics of the family, Pericles now controls Tyre and Pentapolis. Rusty armor and now a ring—symbols of the reality that genealogy is destiny. Like King James, Pericles will rule another kingdom because of the female line.

Though Mytilene is a place of danger, it has another side: the experience of the reunion of Pericles and Marina off the coast of Mytilene. For the first time in fourteen years the royal family begins to reunite. Though the emphasis is on personal and family concerns, politics has its part in the reunion also. Pericles in his ship, trimmed with "banners sable," contrasting with the white flags with which he first arrived in Tharsus to rescue that city, has not spoken for three months, eating only to prolong his grief (V.i.24–26). Helicanus explains: "This was a goodly person, / Till the disaster that, one mortal night, / Drove him to this" (35–37). In a sense, the play since

Act III has been "one mortal night" for the royal family. Lysimachus of Mytilene is himself unable to rouse Pericles from melancholy, but he does suggest that Marina should be summoned in the hopes of restoring Pericles. Like Cerimon, Marina arrives as a holy physician. In addition to her music, she brings the commiseration of her own suffering: "I am a maid, / . . . hath endur'd a grief / Might equal yours, if both were justly weigh'd" (84, 87–88). The word that triggers a response from Pericles is "parentage"; he sees the similarity between this young girl and his lost wife. Marina tells Pericles that her name was given her by "My father, and a king" (149); and later, "My mother was the daughter of a king . . ." (157). Shakespeare insists on these family identifications far more than do his sources.

Finally and wonderfully, recognition dawns on Pericles, and he says to Marina:

> O, come hither,
> Thou that beget'st him that did thee beget;
> Thou that wast born at sea, buried at Tharsus,
> And found at sea again. (194–97)

Marina has given life to her father. Pericles' image of begetting, not in the sources, corresponds to the idea of procreation common in the Romances and in the Stuart royal family. But even in this moment of ecstatic joy, Pericles makes the political connection by referring to Marina as "the heir of kingdoms" (206). Much in this scene reminds us of the reunion of another royal father and daughter, Lear and Cordelia in IV.vii of *King Lear*, even to the point of the king figure's getting fresh garments. Finding Marina alive not only brings unspeakable joy to a father; it also offers a politically stable future for Tyre: that which was lost has been found—an "heir of kingdoms." The final vision of Diana deters Pericles from his revenge on Tharsus and sends him to Ephesus instead.

"Where am I? Where's my lord? What world is this?" (III.ii.107). These are the questions that Thaisa asks when she awakens, thanks to Cerimon's healing power, in Ephesus, shortly after giving birth to Marina during the storm. Ephesus is the last city of *Pericles*; it is a place of wonder and reunion of the entire royal family. Just as Pericles' being washed ashore at Pentapolis resulted in a new beginning when all seemed lost, so Thaisa's unceremonious coming ashore in a coffin at Ephesus renews life for her. The scroll left in her coffin identifies her by her royal marriage and royal lineage: "*I, King Pericles, have lost / This queen, worth all our mundane cost*" (72–73); "*She was the daughter of a king"* (75). Uncertain about whether she actually gave birth and fearful that she will never see Pericles again, Thaisa enters the "vestal livery" of Diana in Ephesus.

As the rest of the family years later comes to Ephesus, Gower reports of the intended marriage of Lysimachus and Marina: "So he thriv'd, / That he is promis'd to be wiv'd / To fair Marina . . ." (V.ii.9–11). The royal daughter has been promised in marriage to one deemed worthy by the royal father. Pericles now echoes the role of Simonides, who awarded Thaisa to him. At Diana's temple Pericles recapitulates his story from the wedding at Pentapolis to the reunion at Mytilene. Interestingly, Pericles' story enumerates all the cities, with the exception of Antioch, of the play, calling attention to his journeys and, by implication, to the qualities of these different places. His tale is efficacious, producing recognition in Thaisa, an attendant at the temple. She asks Pericles: "Did you not name a tempest, / A birth, and death?" (V.iii.33–34). Establishing their identities, Pericles bids Thaisa to be buried "A second time within these arms" (44). D. W. Harding observes: "In *Pericles* and *The Winter's Tale* the father's recovery of the loved woman and of his capacity to love her occurs simultaneously with the recovery of his effectiveness as a ruler and with the establishment of the succession."[12] For the first time, Thaisa sees her daughter, "flesh of thy flesh" (46), as Pericles calls Marina. The scene closes not only with this glorious reunion but also with the mingling of family and politics. Lysimachus and Marina will be married at Pentapolis and then reign in Tyre, while Pericles and Thaisa will rule in Pentapolis. Domestic family life ceaselessly intertwines with the public political life of the royal family. The family's journeys are over; a new journey begins.

Pericles is a long way from "romance chaos," I think, despite its constant movement. Shakespeare in fact skillfully interweaves romance quest with the practical politics of who shall rule. The emphasis on the politics of family, much stronger in this play than usually supposed, comes, I have argued, from the text of the Jacobean royal family and provides a center for the play. The issue is not identification of James with Pericles, or of Anne with Thaisa, though one can note that Pericles at the end is probably about the age of James and certainly that Marina is the age of Princess Elizabeth. Shakespeare chose to dramatize the old story of Apollonius of Tyre because he saw some relevance for the present moment.

In the play, comments about kingship, about parentage and lineage, and about succession may all derive from Shakespeare's royal text, the royal family of James. Pericles, after all, has set out to acquire a wife in order ultimately to have royal issue, a point not made in the conventional sources. What could be more pertinent for the royal court of James? Pericles does not find the wife at Antioch but at Pentapolis, where the good King Simonides rules. By virtue of this marriage, Pericles becomes "heir apparent" in Pentapolis, a claim that he presses at the end of the play. Meanwhile his royal child, the kingdom's heir, will rule at Tyre. The development of the play thus assures peaceful succession—a hallmark of James's achievement. Pericles will give way to Marina and Lysimachus in Tyre as Simonides has given way to Thaisa and Pericles in Pentapolis. The new generation of royal children supplants in orderly transition the older generation. Certainly such is the plan of King James as he negotiates for the marriages of his children Henry and Elizabeth. Pericles' acquisition of the throne at Pentapolis has its analogy in James's gaining the English crown.

The royal family of James casts its oblique light on and through *Pericles*, compelling us to see the urgency of political issues for Pericles and his family. At one of the play's most poignant moments—the reunion in Ephesus—the great personal and private joy of the family carries with it also the recognition that as a royal family they must get on with the business of ruling. The politics of the family insists that the royal family, as in actual life, must perform the role expected of them. The royal issue, in this case Marina, gives "arms" to Pericles by strengthening his position; she also brings "joy" to the subjects and, of course, to her parents. Gower may sing an old song, but Shakespeare differs from it; in that difference lies the centrality of political issues, inspired, I argue, by that other text flowing into his consciousness: James's royal family.

CYMBELINE

If *Pericles* has at times seemed an unwanted child in the Shakespeare canon, *Cymbeline* has also come in for its share of severe criticism. At least it is included in the first Folio, though grouped with the tragedies. From Samuel Johnson, who referred to the play's "unresisting imbecility," through Bernard Shaw, who also condemned the play, to several more recent commentators, the play has seemed at best intractable, unduly complicated, and incoherent with its romance and historical plots. Simon Forman, who probably saw a performance of *Cymbeline* in 1611, seems at least to have been able to follow the action. Is there some way out of the apparent morass of plot complications of the play? How might early audiences have understood the play? Did they perceive any link between the reigns of the first-century Cymbeline and the seventeenth-century James?

There is, of course, no way to settle these questions definitively, but since 1947, several critics have focused on the historical and nationalistic issues in the play. In many ways, as will become apparent, *Cymbeline* is highly susceptible on first glance of a topical reading. It is interesting to note that Jonathan Goldberg chooses to close his book *James I and the Politics of Literature* with a brief glimpse at *Cymbeline*, a play, he suggests, that captures the images of rule that were "the ruling images of James's reign" (p. 240). I will argue that the royal family of James clearly is one of the texts for this play, a drama that centers on a royal family in ancient Britain of the first century A.D. G. Wilson Knight, in his 1947 book *The Crown of Life*, ignited the spark of historical interpretation; others have fanned the flame. *Cymbeline* is, Knight says simply, "to be regarded mainly as an historical play."[13] Knight adds that the play blends "Shakespeare's two primary historical interests, the Roman and the Britain, which meet here for the first time" (p. 130). Posthumus comes to embody many great virtues that Knight associates with the British character. Knight's nationalism aside, he has performed an invaluable critical service by opening the interpretation of this play to historic issues. J. P. Brockbank calls attention to the importance of Holinshed for having furnished the background for the play,[14] and Robin Moffet focuses on the most important single event during the reign of Cymbeline: the birth of Jesus.[15] My own historical interpretation examines the family of Augustus Caesar as a possible paradigm for the Cymbeline family, some of the British characters thereby taking their cue from accounts of the reign of Augustus that Shakespeare could have known.[16] Shakespeare thus fuses the Roman and British worlds.

Beginning in 1961 with Emrys Jones's review essay, critics have expanded the historical interest to include the topicality of the play.[17] "The topical elements of *Cymbeline*," Jones writes, "have received no scholarly attention, yet they must have contributed to its theatrical success" (p. 89). Jones makes the connection between the play and the "character and foreign policy of James I," the drama paying "tribute to James's strenuous peace-making policy" (p. 89). Jones is the first to note that "Cymbeline (in Shakespeare, though not in

Holinshed) has one daughter and two sons; so did James I'' (p. 96). Put this way, the statement misleads somewhat, since Holinshed does indicate that Cymbeline had two sons; Shakespeare's invention is the daughter. In any event, here is the critical beginning of identifying the characters with members of James's family. Jones even confronts the problem of the wicked Queen: "It would have been undesirable for Cymbeline's wicked Queen to be approximated, in the minds of the audience, with James's virtuous consort, Anne of Denmark" (p. 97). Therefore, he argues, she is purposely made grotesque in the play. Of course, such an answer rather begs the critical question. My own answer about the Queen is that she takes her inspiration from Livia, Augustus's wife; the parallels between the two are striking.

A few years after Jones, Bernard Harris explored the historical basis of *Cymbeline*, again paying some attention to topicality.[18] Harris writes: "It seems certain that the Stuart audience would be capable of reading into that final peace and pardon a testimonial to King James's larger desires" (p. 227). James the peacemaker and Cymbeline the maker of peace seemingly constitute an irresistible connection. Philip Edwards has, however, tried to dampen this enthusiasm by observing "how diametrically opposed to the spirit of the ending of *Cymbeline* were the policies being actively and personally pursued by James in Ireland at the very time when Shakespeare was writing his play."[19] Edwards's cautionary note reminds us that we should not expect to find exact parallels between the fictional and actual worlds. In fact, James consistently portrayed himself as a peacemaker, however at odds this image might have been with reality, a point that I noted in chapter 2 concerning his relationship with Arbella Stuart.

Topical approaches to the Romances and to *Cymbeline* in particular culminate, as I demonstrated in chapter 1, in the criticism by Frances Yates and Glynne Wickham. Dame Frances, we may recall, insists that Shakespeare has sided with Prince Henry and Princess Elizabeth and that *Cymbeline* reveals his predilections. Indeed, Shakespeare presumably revised the play so as to capture that moment in the Stuart royal family when the marriage negotiations for Elizabeth had been completed and Henry had not yet died—thus sometime in late 1612. She eagerly embraces the idea that the three children in the play parallel James's children. She says not a word about the Queen. Wickham follows suit in much of this, though he does disagree about the date of the play. He asserts that *Cymbeline* was performed "at Court in the autumn of 1609"; "*Cymbeline* received its first performance in the autumn of 1609."[20] Alas, there is no evidence to support this insistence; the theaters themselves were closed for most of 1609 because of the plague, and there is no record of a court performance of the play in 1609. In the last sentence of his essay, Wickham reveals why he wants 1609 to be the date for the first performance; if it is, "This clears 1610 for the composition of *The Winter's Tale* and restores legitimacy to its claim to being the Investiture play" (p. 113). Of course, even if one could make a convincing case for the 1609 date for *Cymbeline*, that argument in and of itself scarcely demonstrates anything about the composition of *The Winter's Tale*. Wickham insists on these dates because he has a scheme for the Romances and their topicality, specifically their correspondence to several events in the life of the royal family.

The traditional sources for *Cymbeline* include accounts from Holinshed for the historical plot and from Boccaccio's *Decameron* and *Frederyke of Jennen* for the wager plot. In addition I have suggested in my essay on the Roman nature of the play that writers such as Plutarch, Tacitus, and Suetonius may have helped shape the nature of several characters, especially the Queen and Cloten. Much more so than in *Pericles*, Shakespeare has invented his material; none of the presumed sources here provides the kind of outline and details that *Confessio Amantis* does for *Pericles*. How slight the historical matter is can be revealed by citing part of what Holinshed wrote about Cymbeline's reign:

> Kymbeline or Cimbeline the sonne of Theomantius was of the Britains made king after the decease of his father . . . This man (as some write) was brought up at Rome, and there made a knight by Augustus Caesar. . . . Little other mention is made of his dooings, except that during his reigne, the Saviour of the world . . . was borne of a virgine, about the 23 yeare of the reigne of this Kymbeline . . . some writers doo varie, but the best approved affirme, that he reigned 35 years and then died, and was buried at London, leaving behind him two sonnes, Guiderius and Arviragus.[21]

The whole issue of the tribute due Rome receives uncertain treatment from Holinshed: whether the conflict "was occasioned by Kymbeline, or some other prince of the Britains, I have not to avouch" (8:44). One reads the Holinshed account in vain search for Imogen, Posthumus, the wicked Queen, Belarius, and, of course, the wager action. What's past is surely but prologue for Shakespeare's *Cymbeline*.

Joining these pre-texts for the play are several con-texts. The love and sexual struggle in *Cymbeline*, involving imagined unfaithfulness and testing, may remind us of Chapman's *The Widow's Tears* or even Middleton's *Michaelmas Term*, where Quomodo in effect makes a wager with himself as to how the wife and son will react to his presumed death. What I see as a kind of sexual sterility in *Cymbeline*[22] finds its counterpart in a play such as Jonson's *Epicoene*, in which family values are inverted and perverted, leading away from the healthy, procreative functions of love and marriage. Examining the political world of Jacobean comedy, one finds two plays especially relevant for *Cymbeline*: Rowley's *A Shoemaker a Gentleman* and Beaumont and Fletcher's *Philaster*. With its ancient British setting, its Roman invasion, its royal children and royal birth, and the eventual peace between Rome and Britain, Rowley's play certainly moves in a direction similar to that of *Cymbeline*. Struggles over the kingdom, the nature of kingship, and love dominate *Philaster*, a play that has long been linked to *Cymbeline*. Bullough, in his consideration of sources, decides that *Philaster* is an analogue for Shakespeare's play (8:6); I think this is a reasonable position to take. Given the uncertainty about the dates of these plays, one resists making dogmatic claims.

We have no way of knowing finally whether these texts by Rowley and by Beaumont and Fletcher entered Shakespeare's imagination or not. What may have prompted all of these dramatists at approximately the same time to explore royal families in a historical-romance mode is the presence of the Jacobean royal family. *Cymbeline* is, I think, an intertextual mixture of several texts, known and unknown, fictional and real, that come together in the artist's mind, sparking his production of a text that differs from the others.

As Wickham, Yates, and others have noted, one of the possible connections of James to *Cymbeline* is the Brutus/Troynovant myth of history, used by the Tudors and then by James to assert an ancestral relationship to Brutus, the mythical founder of Britain. Cymbeline, like Lear, is presumably a descendant of Brutus. In the magnificent royal entry for James in 1604, Dekker and Jonson link James both to Brutus and to Augustus Caesar. The theme that runs through these associations is peace and union. Anthony Munday pursues this idea in his first Lord Mayor's Show, *The Triumphs of Re-United Britannia* (1605), in which there is much praise of James. Munday traces the lineage of Brutus's sons, especially Albanact, who presumably ruled over Scotland and who has given rise to James "our second *Brute*" "by whose happye comming to the Crown, *England, Wales,* &

Scotland, by the first Brute seuered and diuided, is in our second *Brute* re-united, and made one happy *Britania* again: Peace and quietnesse bringing that to passe, which warre nor any other meanes could attaine vnto."[23] A figure representing Brutus in the pageant precisely states this idea: James has "knit againe in blessed vnity" that which had been separated (sig. B3ᵛ).

In a civic pageant that probably took place close to the time of the composition of *Cymbeline,* Munday, in an entertainment for the investiture of Henry as Prince of Wales (1610), again explores the Brutus connection. One of the speakers represents Cornwall and its link to Brutus: "I, the good Angell or *Genius* of *Cornea,* Queene to Brutes noble Companion *Corineus,* the first of fayre Britaynes Regions, and your [Henry's] owne worthie Dukedome."[24] Henry's gracious response Munday likens "to the large extended winges of *Ioues Birde* the Eagle" (sig. C3). The other speaker, impersonated by Richard Burbage, represents Wales. The ancient past of Brutus and his progeny may well serve as a prologue to Shakespeare's *Cymbeline.* Obviously several texts available to Shakespeare join the Stuart royal family to the Brutus tradition. Shakespeare has already explored part of that tradition in *King Lear;* he turns to it again in *Cymbeline.* Tempting is the speculation that *Cymbeline* may have been written partly in response to the celebrations for Prince Henry in 1610. At the least, I believe that in his play Shakespeare re-presents James's family.

What about the royal family in *Cymbeline?* The king-father is, of course, Cymbeline; all the principal characters link to him by blood relationship or through marriage. He is husband to "the Queen" (never named in the play), but she is his second wife and not the mother of his children. She, in fact, has a son of her own, the inimitable Cloten. Just as Cymbeline has remarried in order to replace his dead wife, so he "adopts" Cloten and Posthumus as sons to substitute for his lost sons, Guiderius and Arviragus, stolen some twenty years before the play opens. Ironically, this new definition of the royal family falls apart: the Queen is impossibly wicked, Cloten a fool and unworthy to be a royal son, and Posthumus banished for marrying Imogen. Further, Imogen disappears from the court, and suddenly Cymbeline stands vulnerable not only to the invasion of the Romans but also to the internal dissolution of his family. Despite his efforts to solidify the royal family, he has no heir. The threat of separation, as great in this play as in *Pericles* though without shipwrecks, has political as well as familial consequences. In *Cym-*

beline the political future of the kingdom is at stake, which cannot be resolved until the original family is recovered. Delving the past—family heritage and lineage—helps to define and determine the future: genealogy is destiny.

The essential political problems are how to guarantee future stability of the kingdom through orderly familial succession and how to deal with the immediate threat of the Roman invasion. At moments, the latter seems easier to solve than the former. The dramatic problem is how to reunite Imogen with her father while getting him to acknowledge and accept Posthumus as her husband. The discovery of his long-lost sons constitutes the kind of bonus that romance is capable of delivering. Thus Cymbeline, who through much of the play seems the inverse of good King Simonides in *Pericles*, comes by the end to resemble Simonides by establishing a good and peaceable government. Though the royal family takes several configurations, I will consider first Cymbeline, his Queen, and Cloten; then Imogen and Posthumus; and finally Cymbeline's sons, Guiderius and Arviragus, and their guardian, Belarius. In the play's last scene, a dazzling and complicated one, Cymbeline finds his family: they reunite for the first time in at least twenty years. We may say of the close what Mary Queen of Scots embroidered at Sheffield: "In my end is my Beginning."

At the play's beginning, two anonymous Gentlemen, assuming a Gower-like function, summarize the basic strife within the royal family. The First Gentleman reports about Cymbeline's family:

> His daughter, and the heir of's kingdom (whom
> He purpos'd to his wife's sole son—a widow
> That late he married) hath referr'd herself
> Unto a poor but worthy gentleman. (I.i.4–7)[25]

Shakespeare crams many facts about the domestic and political life of the family into those four lines: Cymbeline is distraught that his presumed heir of the kingdom and daughter has married Posthumus rather than Cloten, the new Queen's son. Apparently Cymbeline and his wife have agreed on a dynastic arrangement by having Imogen marry Cloten. Such a marriage would presumably solidify family bonds and assure the stability of the kingdom. Though none of this material appears in his historical sources, Shakespeare need not have looked further than James's family for a pattern of negotiations and marriage arrangements, all moving in high gear about the time of *Cymbeline*.

After drawing the contrast between Cloten and Posthumus, the Second Gentleman asks: "Is she [Imogen] sole child to th' king?" (56). The First Gentleman replies: "His only child. / He had two sons . . . / . . . from their nursery / Were stol'n . . ." (56–57, 59–60). Imogen is in effect the only royal child, her brothers having been stolen away some twenty years earlier. This is the reason for her assuming such importance in the politics of the realm: on her rests the future of the kingdom, a future to be assured through the female line. By choosing Posthumus, however, Imogen betrays her father's wishes. Two separations occur in this royal family: one imminent (Imogen's departure) and one in the past (the disappearance of the royal sons).

Angered by Imogen's marriage to Posthumus, Cymbeline first banishes him: "Thou basest thing, avoid hence, from my sight!" (I.ii.56). At least two meanings reside in Cymbeline's accusation: "Thou'rt poison to my blood" (59): Posthumus is poisonous to the family, and he is harmful to royal blood. Cymbeline reinforces this political implication in his charge against Imogen: "Thou took'st a beggar, wouldst have made my throne / A seat for baseness" (72–73). The distraught Imogen wishes that she were not a royal child: "Would I were / A neat-herd's daughter, and my Leonatus / Our neighbour-shepherd's son!" (79–81). Imogen would deny her heritage as she later will deny her sex by pretending to be a male. How Cymbeline can regard Posthumus as "base," having himself nurtured Posthumus at court is puzzling; but that is Cymbeline's narrow interpretation of what it means to be noble. In a way Shakespeare stands on its head the situation of Bertram and Helena in *All's Well*. Part of Cymbeline's poison, his "blood," comes as the result of an apparent agreement with the Queen about marrying Imogen to Cloten. Being both father and king, Cymbeline insists on his royal prerogative to determine who will marry his royal child. The Stuart royal family offers a living text on this issue, as James pursues marriage negotiations for his royal children.

The relationship of the Queen and Imogen is poisonous, neither trusting the other. With soothing words of assurance the stepmother greets Imogen: ". . . you shall not find me, daughter, / After the slander of most stepmothers, / Evil-ey'd unto you" (I.ii.1–3). To which Imogen later responds: "O / Dissembling courtesy!" (15). The Queen cannot serve as a mother substitute for Imogen, primarily because her own designs run counter to Imogen's welfare. "Lack of affect" seems too small a phrase to characterize the Queen; she is strongly evil, as we see in her delight in using poison to effect her will (I.vi). The Queen seems a mixture of the wily serpent in the Garden of Eden, of Augustus's wife Livia, and of Dionyza, who would not shrink from murder in order to advance her own child. The Queen obviously constitutes a major threat to the stability and even to the survival of Cymbeline's family. Her game is political power.

The politics of the royal family finds particular expression in the images of rule provided by Cymbeline and his Queen. I suggest that these two characters represent two sides of James's rule: opaque and transparent texts, subject to interpretation. Like Antiochus in *Pericles*, the Queen posseses dark secrets that affect the rule of the kingdom. By fair or foul means the Queen grasps for political power; love of power motivates her. For many of the characters, especially for her husband Cymbeline, she remains an unfathomable text. That is why he can incredulously ask the rhetorical question in the play's last scene when learning of his wife's treachery: "Who is't can read a woman?" (V.v.48). Unlike James who boasted of his interpretive skills in his 1605 address to Parliament shortly after the Gunpowder Plot, Cymbeline has been incapable of reading the text of his wife's actions. Cymbeline himself represents the open, forthright image of rule—nothing mysterious or devious here. James, who in his 1605 Parliament address wished that there were a crystal window so that all could see into his heart and who said the same thing again in 1607, had decided, by the time of his 1610 address to Parliament, that he indeed offered "a great and a rare Present, which is a faire and a Christall Mirror, . . . as through the transparantnesse thereof, you may see the heart of your King."[26] Cymbeline as king is something like that: clear in his intentions and actions with the Romans and with his daughter, if at times misguided. By a peculiarity of the play we actually see very little of Cymbeline: he appears in only seven scenes of the play and speaks just over 260 lines out of some 3260 lines; up to the final scene he has spoken a mere 100 lines. The final scene, in fact, calls attention to the necessity of interpretation, because many texts have to be analyzed, as we will see. This fictional royal family, like the actual Stuart royal family, is subject to and in need of interpretation. By Shakespeare's pursuit of this theme in the Romances he represents the Jacobean royal family.

The clear picture that emerges of Cymbeline and his Queen is of an unsuspecting husband, done in by his wife. One would not want to use Sanderson's misguided phrase that described James and Anne as a "matchless pair." When Cloten exits in II.i, the Second Lord analyzes the play's royal family: Cloten is an "ass" and his mother "a crafty devil"; Imogen is caught "Betwixt a father by thy step-dame govern'd, / A mother hourly coining plots . . ." (57–58) and a repugnant wooer. The Second Lord closes with a hope for the royal child: ". . . that thou mayst stand, / T'enjoy thy banish'd lord and this great land!" (63–64). Running through this sentiment is a concern for the political future of the kingdom, which Imogen represents, and it implies both the private and the public life of the royal family. The Lord's statement also sums up the basic dramatic problem to be resolved in the remainder of the play.

Cloten, both would-be lover to Imogen and would-be son to Cymbeline, is a somewhat mindless pawn in his mother's political scheme as she attempts to shape the politics of this royal family. Cloten's wooing of Imogen appears at points amusing, and at times perverse. He says that he "loves" her, but that seems far-fetched; only her contempt of him exceeds his ineptitude. Reflecting failure to understand his daughter, Cymbeline advises Cloten: Imogen still laments the loss of Posthumus; "some more time / Must wear the print of his remembrance on't, / And then she's yours" (II.iii.41–43). And Cymbeline refers to Cloten as our "dear son" (59). Cloten's bootless effort to win Imogen does carry one interesting point. He chides her for disobedience: "You sin against / Obedience, which you owe your father . . ." (110–11). He also claims that her contract with Posthumus is invalid because he is unworthy. Cloten rightly points out the limitations on royal children as they think of marriage partners: "Yet you are curb'd from that enlargement [freedom], by / The consequence o'th' crown . . ." (119–20). We recall Prince Henry's letter to James, in which he says that he would "love" whomever his father chose for him to marry.

Cymbeline's substitute family meets the political force of the Romans head-on in III.i, when Caius Lucius arrives from Rome and provides an answer to Cymbeline's opening question: "Now say, what would Augustus Caesar with us?" (1). What Caesar wants is payment of the yearly tribute of three thousand pounds, lately "left untender'd" (10). Resistance to the Romans' demand, curiously championed by the Queen and Cloten, draws its resolve in part from the recollection of the ancestral past, another instance of the play's probe and recovery of the past. The Queen's appeal begins, "Remember, sir, my liege, / The kings your ancestors . . ." (17–18). These ancestors reinforce Cymbeline's resistance, even at the risk of war. Another past, however, also intrudes: Cymbeline's experience at the

145

court of Augustus: ". . . my youth I spent / Much under him; of him I gather'd honour . . ." (70–71). Ironically, that honor now teaches him to refuse Caesar. The faith of his British fathers leads Cymbeline to defy his Roman fathers. Caius Lucius sees the politics of the royal family at work. Surely the Queen views this opposition as a means of making herself and Cloten indispensable to Cymbeline.

War is imminent. But these great matters of state dissolve into domestic concerns when Cymbeline asks: "Where is our daughter?" (III.v.30). When the report comes that her doors are all locked, Cymbeline cries out: "Grant heavens, that which I fear / Prove false!" (52–53). The Queen, not at all distraught, says:

> gone she is,
> To death, or to dishonour, and my end
> Can make good use of either. She being down,
> I have the placing of the British crown. (63–66)

This naked statement of purpose again recalls Dionyza. The Queen's regard for her husband shines through her comment when learning of Cymbeline's despair: "All the better: may / This night forestall him of the coming day!" (69–70). This perverse wish for Cymbeline's death turns out to be the Queen's final statement in the play. Cloten, meanwhile, sets out to find Imogen, to be revenged on her by raping her and killing Posthumus—like mother, like son.

This unnatural and insidious part of the royal family finally can come to no good; it carries with it the seeds of destruction and tragedy. Shakespeare, having invented Cloten and the Queen, will have to dispose of them if the family is to attain some stability and survive: a part will have to be destroyed to assure the whole. Cloten meets death in Wales at the hands of Guiderius, a moment of some poetic justice, since Guiderius is one of the long-lost sons of Cymbeline. Cloten has gone to Wales in pursuit of Imogen and with a kind of naïve, if misplaced, confidence in his mother's power. If Imogen should complain of his actions to her father, Cloten says that his mother, "having power of his testiness, shall turn all into my commendations" (IV.i.20–22). He tries futilely to deal with Guiderius by saying, "I am son to th' queen" (IV.ii.93). But Guiderius responds: "I am sorry for't: not seeming / So worthy as thy birth" (93–94). Despite Cymbeline's complaint that Posthumus is base and unworthy of Imogen, obviously Cloten is the one truly base and ignoble. Cloten, separated from his mother, meets his death by being beheaded at the hands of one who is stronger and more noble than he. The Queen, bereft of her son, will die in the play's last scene. They have apparently sustained one another, but their relationship is eventually consumed by that which nourished it.

Cymbeline, meanwhile, feels lost. He comments on his situation in IV.iii:

> A fever with the absence of her son;
> A madness, of which her life's in danger: heavens,
> How deeply you at once do touch me! Imogen,
> The great part of my comfort gone: my queen
> Upon a desperate bed, . . . her son gone. . . . (2-7)

His legitimate and understandable conclusion is that the royal family has been destroyed. Quite apart from his familial feeling, Cymbeline has no prospective heir for the kingdom, now that Cloten and Imogen are both gone. The threatening presence of the Romans exacerbates the problem. Cymbeline cries out: "Now for the counsel of my son and queen, / I am amaz'd with matter" (27-28). But when the battle comes, neither the Queen nor Cloten is able to assist him. Instead, Belarius, Guiderius, and Arviragus, reinforced by Posthumus, rescue Cymbeline. The true royal family is emerging, though Cymbeline will not know this until the revelation in the play's last scene. Shakespeare economically capsulizes in the "dumb show" about Cymbeline's rescue in V.ii the shifting nature of the family's definition. Cloten and the Queen become the past which must be discarded because it is false: in their end is Cymbeline's beginning.

Turning to Imogen and Posthumus, one examines an ahistorical plot, parts of which Shakespeare seems to have borrowed from Boccaccio. In a sense, this couple faces the problem inherent in many comedies and not a few tragedies: obstinate parental will that thwarts their romantic love. One recalls *A Midsummer Night's Dream* and *Romeo and Juliet*, to cite obvious examples. Shakespeare's immediate dramatic problem for the lovers is somehow to reconcile them. Interestingly, they do not reunite until their relationship to the royal family clarifies. Why should this somewhat traditional love plot be appropriate to the political goings on in ancient Britain and Rome?

I think that, given what he knew of the Jacobean royal family, Shakespeare saw in it the potential conflict of political purpose and domestic desire, especially on the question of marriage. The future of the kingdom is the issue, not simply the satisfaction of personal fancy. Certainly James's family was to give tangible evidence of this conflict in the marriage negotiations for Princess Elizabeth, Queen

Anne being particularly difficult in this matter, as shown in chapter 2. Further, the Imogen/Posthumus story ties in closely with family issues. Imogen and Posthumus move in different directions, she busily cutting herself off from her royal family and he searching for his family. They also offer a variation of the Widow of Ephesus story, partly dramatized in Chapman's *The Widow's Tears*. The main difference, of course, is that Imogen remains faithful, despite what Posthumus, thanks to Iachimo's wily devices, comes to believe. Likewise, Imogen assumes that Posthumus has been false. This couple raises several other issues as well. Division and self-division characterize their plight; by this I mean that each separates from a family, divides; and each struggles with internal divisions also. Part of the play's task is to resolve these divisions which, if allowed to persist, would have serious political implications. Of necessity, both Posthumus and Imogen actively engage in trying to interpret the text of the other one. Imogen finds Posthumus a heretical text; and Posthumus in effect asks Cymbeline's question: ''Who is't can read a woman?''

Posthumus' search for his family ultimately has political implications for Britain, because this seeking brings clarity and change in him and helps Cymbeline accept him as the husband of his royal daughter. In the opening scene the First Gentleman says of Posthumus: ''I cannot delve him to the root'' (I.i.28). We do learn, however, that Posthumus's father, Sicilius, had rendered distinguished service for Cassibelan against the Romans, had died of grief at the loss of two sons in battle, and had lost his wife when she gave birth to Posthumus. Bereft of family, Posthumus comes into the royal family of Cymbeline, who nurtures him and brings him up at court. Cymbeline thereby gives him something of what he himself had gained at the court of Augustus. The Vision of Jupiter and of Posthumus's family in V.iv completes the process of finding his family. Meredith Skura suggests the connection between this quest and his marriage to Imogen: ''. . . there is no way for him to find himself as husband until he finds himself as son, as part of the family he was torn from long ago.''[27] Though he gains a genealogy, Posthumus must also come to terms with Cymbeline, his father substitute.

The first two acts concentrate on the separation of Imogen and Posthumus from each other and on the subsequent wager, a presumed test of Imogen's fidelity. Like many conventional lovers, they exchange tokens in I.ii: she gives him a ring, and he gives her a bracelet, accompanied by the usual vows of eternal love. He goes off to Rome, banished by Cymbeline, who eventually must acknowledge Posthumus as a surrogate son. Imogen sees her father as the interrupter of their love; she and Posthumus could not even grab a parting kiss, she complains, because "comes in my father, / And like the tyrannous breathing of the north, / Shakes all our buds from growing" (I.iv.35–37). This superb image captures the problem of their thwarted sexuality and the disruptive nature of Cymbeline;[28] indeed, he resembles the north wind that caused such havoc for Pericles' family in III.i of that play. Not knowing that Posthumus has entered into a wager with Iachimo about her faithfulness, Imogen nevertheless assesses her predicament: "A father cruel, and a step-dame false, / A foolish suitor to a wedded lady . . ." (I.vii.1–2). Here is sufficient reason for Imogen's desire to leave this royal family. When Iachimo makes his "assault," Imogen rebuffs him: "The king my father shall be made acquainted / Of thy assault" (149–50). If Cymbeline should tolerate the likes of Iachimo, "he hath a court / He little cares for, and a daughter who / He not respects at all" (153–55). Whatever Imogen's disaffection from her father, she recognizes his political authority and patriarchal function.

This mingling of political and personal occurs also in II.iv where Posthumus accepts Iachimo's ocular proof of Imogen's infidelity. Early in that scene Philario and Posthumus discuss the impending Roman threat to Britain (10–26); Posthumus is confident of the British resistance to the Romans. From this certainty he moves to uncertainty about Imogen, as attested to by Iachimo. Part of his outburst centers on wondering about the faithfulness of his own mother: "yet my mother seem'd / The Dian of that time: so doth my wife . . ." (158–59). All is called into doubt; the center does not hold. Reflecting something of self-division, Posthumus explores "The woman's part in me" (172). That part of him accounts for all vices that man experiences. Having enumerated these vices, Posthumus claims: "I'll write against them . . ." (183), thereby producing a text to be interpreted. Like King James writing against the evils of tobacco, this future royal son would make part of himself manifest in a text.

Acts III and IV belong to Imogen as she sets off to Wales in quest of Posthumus. In III.iv Pisanio shows her the letter that Posthumus has written accusing Imogen of being a strumpet. Her response echoes Posthumus's own: "O, / Men's vows are women's traitors!" (54–55). Having read the text of the letter, Imogen interprets the text of Posthumus: "What is here? / The scriptures of the loyal Leonatus, /

All turn'd to heresy" (81–83). She even blames Posthumus for "My disobedience 'gainst the king my father . . ." (90). Pisanio urges her to return to the court; but she says: "No court, no father, nor no more ado / With that harsh, noble, simple nothing, / That Cloten . . ." (133–35). Cutting herself off from her heritage, Imogen in fact opens herself to experience in Wales which will lead to other discoveries.

Unwittingly, she meets her long-lost brothers in Wales, eventually establishing the family's genealogy. We appreciate the irony of her comment: ". . . would it had been so, that they / Had been my father's sons . . ." (III.vii.48–49). Later, "I'ld change my sex to be companion with them, / Since Leonatus false" (59–60). Effectively she has done that since she is now disguised as a male. Like Posthumus who contemplates the woman's part in him, Imogen engages in self-division by assuming the role of a man. Taking the potion that Pisanio has provided, Imogen seems to die only to awaken in a bizarre situation when she finds Cloten's headless corpse and believes it to be that of Posthumus. It will be the business of the play's last scene to bring her back to her father in harmony, to regain Posthumus, and to discover her brothers.

Posthumus reenters the play in Act V a changed person, chiding himself for his action towards Imogen and ready to fight in her father's behalf. He cries out: "Let me make men know / More valour in me than my habits show. / Gods, put the strength o' th' Leonati in me!" (V.i.29–31). Invoking his family, he surges into battle, vanquishing Iachimo, and helping rescue Cymbeline. Posthumus changes his garb, taking on the guise of a "Briton peasant" (24) and says: "so I'll fight / Against the part I come with" (24–25). James Nosworthy glosses "part" to mean "side, party"; but I suggest that this term also carries a hint of self-division: he fights against his former self, perhaps also against the woman's part in him. He changes yet again, putting on his Italian clothes: ". . . I have resumed again / The part I came in" (V.iii.75–76). Since this comment follows his help in rescuing Cymbeline, he may mean that he will eventually resume the part—or the position at court—that he formerly held. At least the play works out that way.

In assisting Belarius, Guiderius, and Arviragus to redeem Cymbeline, Posthumus has become, so Skura argues, "a proper son," "brave, but not overbearing; accepting his position as nameless third son" (p. 209). This paves the way for the vision of his family in V.iv. Imprisoned and in a state of remorse, his own version of the night-world experience, Posthumus is ready for the vision, one that recovers his family for him. His father, mother, and two brothers all enter as apparitions while he sleeps. They provide a wonderful summary of familial responses to Posthumus. The father, Sicilius, knows that if he had lived, he would have "shielded him / from this earth-vexing smart" (V.iv.41–42), providing fatherly care for his son. In despair the family invokes Jupiter, who makes a spectacular entrance and assures the family: "Be content, / Your low-laid son our godhead will uplift" (102–3). His mission completed, Jupiter ascends to his "palace crystalline" (113); and the family vanishes too.

What an extraordinary vision that provides the roots of Posthumus's familial lineage, assuring his genealogy, healing his self-division, and making him worthy of the royal child Imogen. He awakes, not like Imogen earlier to a nightmarish experience, but to a recollection of his family and a discovery of a "book," the tablet that Jupiter has left containing an unfathomable riddle, a text to be interpreted. Unable to understand its promise for him, Posthumus reads that if certain conditions are met, "then shall Posthumus end his miseries, Britain be fortunate, and flourish in peace and plenty" (143–45). In the fulness of time these conditions will be satisfied and this hopeful ending realized. The inescapable link between personal fortune and political destiny occurs in royal families.

In Wales, to which Imogen and Posthumus go, there is another family, established for twenty years: Belarius and his two surrogate sons, Guiderius and Arviragus.[29] The past and the present that Shakespeare creates allow for an examination of the personal lives of Guiderius and Arviragus long before their identity is confirmed and their political future opens before them. Out of the thin materials that Holinshed provides, simply that Cymbeline had two sons, Shakespeare weaves a whole fabric of romance. Strong emotional bonds exist in Belarius's household: the two young men believe that Belarius is their father and are unaware that the king is their true father. As in the case of Imogen, the dramatist focuses on the lives of these royal children, who are crucial to political succession in the kingdom.

Isolated and insulated, Guiderius and Arviragus, in contrast to their sister, know little of the political world. All that they know comes from Belarius, who on occasion contrasts their idyllic life with that of the court, as when he claims:

> O, this life
> Is nobler than attending for a check:
> Richer than doing nothing for a robe,
> Prouder than rustling in unpaid-for silk. (III.iii.21–24)

151

A Jacobean audience may hear an implicit condemnation of Stuart court life. But Arviragus recognizes the limitations of their present life: "What should we speak of / When we are old as you? When we shall hear / The rain and wind beat dark December?" (35–37). "We have seen nothing," he asserts. Belarius responds by expanding on the subject of the court's corruption. Belarius also suggests that he is a text: "O boys, this story / The world may read in me: my body's mark'd / With Roman swords . . ." (55–57). As these royal sons listen to Belarius's story, they become part of his text. Guiderius, for example, lets his "spirits fly out," Belarius says, "Into my story" (90–91), putting "himself in posture / That acts my words" (94–95). At such a moment Belarius may seem a dramatist and Guiderius an actor, suiting the action to the word. Arviragus's response is less immediate, less a matter of action than of contemplation or interpretation: he "shows much more / His own conceiving" (97–98). Captured here is an image of Shakespeare's representation of texts, including the Jacobean royal family, which the dramatist has responded to with "his own conceiving."

The family in Wales cannot be immune to the world of politics, as is demonstrated first by Belarius's delving into their past. He rehearses his disaffection from Cymbeline and his exile: ". . . this twenty years / This rock, and these demesnes, have been my world . . ." (III.iii.69–70). He is a Prospero without the latter's power. At the least, in the security of their cave, "we will," Belarius asserts, "fear no poison, which attends / In place of greater state" (77–78). Cymbeline's court already gives ample evidence of poison at work. Belarius also reveals to us: "These boys know little they are sons to th' king, / Nor Cymbeline dreams that they are alive" (80–81). Belarius gives a pre-text and his pretext: he has taken these royal children, "Thinking to bar thee [Cymbeline] of succession as / Thou refts me of my lands" (102–3). The innocent royal sons have thus become pawns in the game of politics. In order for the royal family of Cymbeline to be reestablished and the political future of the kingdom made secure, this little family in Wales must dissolve, displacing its twenty-year past with a future that brightens with hope, both political and personal.

The force that begins the disruption and eventual redefinition of Belarius's family is Imogen, who wanders into their cave, disguised as a young man and searching for Posthumus. This family's well-established routine appears in the opening of III.vii where Belarius outlines their chores: "Cadwal [Arviragus] and I / Will play the cook and servant . . ." (2–3). Such domesticity reflects the orderly life that has been created here as it also comments on the simple ways in which families function. When they discover Imogen, they accept her freely and openly, as Arviragus vows, "I'll love him as my brother" (44). The delicious irony is that they are in fact related, all being children of the royal Cymbeline. Arviragus asks Imogen later: "Are we not brothers?" (IV.ii.3). The threatening presence of Cloten in IV.ii represents a menacing assault on their lives and a foretaste of the battle to come: the world starts reaching in to touch the lives of the Belarius household. Guiderius, of course, kills Cloten by beheading him; Belarius is quite fearful because he knows that Cloten is the son of the Queen. In the destruction of Cloten, which we cannot truly lament, there is nevertheless the re-presentation of Belarius's abduction of the royal children.

Stage directions capture poignantly the second blow to the Belarius family: "*Re-enter* Arviragus *with* Imogen, *dead, bearing her in his arms*" (IV.ii.193 S.D.). Imogen's presumed death marks the symbolic death of Belarius's family; it will now be caught up in battle and will eventually be reconnected to Cymbeline. The touching and genuine response of Guiderius and Arviragus to the "death" of Imogen leads them to bury her "By good Euriphile, our mother" (234), who was actually their nurse. Through it all, Belarius insists that Cloten also receive a decent burial; after all, "He was a queen's son, boys" (244) and should be buried "as a prince" (251). Belarius, the original transgressor, is always ready to affirm a sense of order and decency. He, of course, has a political perspective lacking in the young princes, who nevertheless exhibit nobility by that "invisible instinct" that framed them "To royalty unlearn'd, honour untaught" (177–78), according to Belarius.

By IV.iv the Belarius family has decided to enter the fray against the Romans, though Belarius at first says, "the king / Hath not deserv'd my service nor your loves . . ." (24–25). Belarius nevertheless gives in to their determination: "Lead, lead. The time seems long, their blood thinks scorn / Till it fly out and show them princes born" (53–54). In the battle they are instrumental in rescuing Cymbeline from the Romans (V.ii). Posthumus speaks at some length about the valor of the old man and "two striplings"; he sums it up in a quasi riddle: "Two boys, an old man twice a boy, a lane, / Preserv'd the Britons, was the Romans' bane" (V.iii.57–58). By helping save Cymbeline, Belarius ironically risks the possibility of losing the boys and perhaps his own life. But such unselfish acts also open the play to the possibility of the final scene, to which I now turn.

The rupture of family relationships heals in V.v, a scene remarkable for its alleged twenty-four denouements, or what Philip Edwards calls its "poly-anagnorisis," and even more for what happens in the way of reconciliation and reunion. A skeleton outline of the scene reveals that the Queen dies; Imogen and Posthumus reunite; Cymbeline accepts them joyfully; Iachimo is forgiven; Belarius reveals that Guiderius and Arviragus are Cymbeline's sons; and Britain, having won the war, agrees to pay the Roman tribute. Concern for the politics of the royal family pervades the scene. Not only do problems of plot resolve here; but also the dramatist clarifies issues of succession, genealogy, and interpretation—all related to the Stuart royal family. Cornelius—with an account of the Queen—Iachimo, Posthumus, and Belarius all have a story, a text to tell. Belarius has the oldest story, which immediately settles questions of succession and genealogy. These interpretations join the Soothsayer's interpretation of Posthumus's mysterious text and the Soothsayer's reinterpretation of an earlier vision. With so many acts of interpretation, Shakespeare reflects his position as one who re-presents the Jacobean royal family, a book open and known to him.

Like King James, Cymbeline cannot separate his familial and political roles. As king, for example, he knights Belarius, Guiderius, and Arviragus for their valor in his behalf, "you whom the gods have made / Preservers of my throne" (V.v.1–2). Ironically, Belarius had twenty years ago disrupted the throne, trying to thwart the succession of the royal issue. When Cymbeline starts to pursue the heritage of the old man and his sons, Cornelius interrupts with news of the Queen's death.

In the dramatic strategy of this scene, the Queen's death precipitates other revelations. Cymbeline must understand the truth about his wife before he is able to be restored to the rightful and loving members of his family. The Queen has been a wicked force in the family who needs to be exorcised before the family can be healed. Astounded, Cymbeline learns that "she never lov'd you: only / Affected greatness got by you: not you: / Married your royalty, was wife to your place: / Abhorr'd your person" (37–40). In response to Cornelius's report, Cymbeline asks the question: "Who is't can read a woman?" (48). The Queen has been another of those unfathomable texts; life in the Romances often seems a riddle.

When Iachimo makes his confession, Posthumus steps forward to reveal his identity and to accept blame for the death of Imogen, who stands nearby disguised. Posthumus cries out: "O Imogen! / My queen, my life, my wife, O Imogen, / Imogen, Imogen!" (225–27). She starts to interrupt, and he strikes her, believing her to be an impertinent page. Here we have a representation of Pericles' striking Marina. It is Pisanio who blurts out that the page is Imogen. Cymbeline is incredulous: "Does the world go round?" (232). With embraces, Posthumus and Imogen reunite, thereby assuring political succession. Posthumus utters the line so dear to Tennyson: "Hang there like fruit, my soul, / Till the tree die" (263–64). The ripeness is all. Imogen also kneels to her father for his blessing; he says: "My tears that fall / Prove holy water on thee . . ." (268–69). These baptismal tears make a new creature in the father-daughter relationship, cleansing the past and opening the future—spiritual procreation.

One more step will make the royal family complete: the establishment of a royal genealogy. Belarius begins this final movement by revealing who he is. Cymbeline orders: "Take him hence, / The whole world shall not save him" (321–22). But Belarius says: "First pay me for the nursing of thy sons . . ." (323). These children, the sons, save Belarius and save Cymbeline. Belarius tells Guiderius and Arviragus that they are not his children; he turns to Cymbeline: "They are the issue of your loins, my liege, / And blood of your begetting" (331–32). Belarius begets Cymbeline, who begat these sons. When the full wonder of the truth hits Cymbeline, he asks: "O, what am I? / A mother to the birth of three? Ne'er mother / Rejoic'd deliverance more" (369–71). He echoes the sentiment of the Abbess at the end of *Comedy of Errors:* "After so long grief such Nativity!" Cymbeline is both father and mother, as he witnesses the birth anew of his sons. His travail is over; the family is whole, new-born. The procreative, nursing instincts of the mother fuse with the father's patriarchal concern for sheltering the family and for being patriarch of the kingdom.

Just as Pericles in the midst of such familial ecstasy remembered to think of the political destiny of the kingdom, so Cymbeline says to Imogen: "Thou has lost by this a kingdom" (V.v.374). That is, her position as sole heir to Cymbeline has been usurped by the older male children. She does not care: "No, my lord; / I have got two worlds by't" (374–75). She has lost a kingdom but gained two worlds, her brothers. Such simple joy may recall the unvarnished affection that existed between the royal brothers and sister in James's family. Cymbeline captures the emblematic moment: "Posthumus anchors upon Imogen; / And she . . . throws her eye / On him: her brothers, me: her master hitting / Each object with a joy'' (394-97). These veritable stage directions arrest a moment of ineffable joy. Cymbeline welcomes Belarius into the family: "Thou art my brother; so we'll hold thee ever" (400); and Imogen says to Belarius: "You are my father too . . ." (401). Belarius has lost his surrogate sons and gained a royal family.

Peace and harmony in the private life of the royal family beget the prospect for peace in the kingdom. Symbolizing this new condition, Philharmonus comes in to interpret Jupiter's text, left for Posthumus. Lucius says: "Read, and declare the meaning" (435). The cedar of the riddle is Cymbeline; the two lopped branches, his lost sons. The tree now revives, "whose issue / Promises Britain peace and plenty" (458-59). Pericles brought peace and plenty to the despairing and starving streets of Tharsus; Peace and Plenty greeted James in 1604 at one of the triumphal arches. The royal children, the "issue," offer hope for the future, assuring peace and plenty. As in the fiction, so in the court of King James. The Soothsayer also reinterprets the vision that he had in IV.ii.346-51. Under those different circumstances he had foreseen Roman victory; but that same dream now yields different results: the soaring eagle means that imperial Caesar "should again unite / His favour with the radiant Cymbeline . . ." (475-76). Like visions, texts are subject to ongoing interpretation. Like James and his family, Cymbeline and his family need interpretation.

As peacemaker, Cymbeline submits to Rome from his position of strength and magnanimity: "Never was a war did cease, / . . . with such a peace" (485-86). Cymbeline as king now embodies the "peaceable reign and good government" of King Simonides in *Pericles;* or as Anthony Weldon wrote about King James, he "left all his Kingdoms in a peaceable condition." Strife, disorder, and separation dominate the royal family at moments in the play until these conditions reverse and give way to peace and hope. Small wonder that Cymbeline cries out: "Laud we the gods, / And let our crooked smokes climb to their nostrils / From our blest altars" (477-79). There is nothing like any of this in Shakespeare's known texts; but in his emphasis on the royal issue, on succession, on deliverance and peace, I think that Shakespeare reads the text of the Stuart royal family and re-presents it.

The rain and wind that "beat dark December," in Arviragus's phrase, give way to a restored cedar and the tree of fruitfulness that is ripe with possibility. The winter's tale is over. Expectancy rests with the new generation of royal children. The restored domestic life of the royal family assures political efficacy. Such events and ideas must have struck a responsive chord in Jacobean audiences as they did in the dramatist responding to the Stuart royal family. The holy waters that Cymbeline refers to become a great stream of cleansing for the family and for the body politic. The words of an Old Testament prophet seem appropriate: "But let judgment run down as waters, and righteousness as a mighty stream" (Amos 5:24). The judgment that rushes through *Cymbeline* celebrates finally the power of love which has triumphed over the love of power: a peacemaker king, secure in the future of his kingdom through the royal issue, offers magnanimous reconciliation to a vanquished foe. That final ruling image coincides with the images of rule of James and his family.

THE WINTER'S TALE

If *Pericles* and *Cymbeline* have suffered varying degrees of neglect, no such fate has attended *The Winter's Tale*, especially recently. Whole books discuss this single play; performances of it are regular if not frequent. Some of the greatest actresses have tackled the role of Hermione. The first recorded court performance was on 5 November 1611, the anniversary of the Gunpowder Plot; the play was presented at court again during the wedding festivities for Princess Elizabeth and Frederick Palatine in February 1613. Certainly the play's emphasis on the reunion and deliverance of the family—Hermione even escapes apparent death—would be compatible with the national celebration of the Gunpowder event. A play that includes the death of a royal son and the anticipated wedding of the royal daughter would coincide with events in the Stuart royal family by February 1613: the death of Prince Henry in November 1612 and Elizabeth's wedding provide a paradigm of tragicomedy on the national level. Like Hermione in the statue scene who seems to be art but is life, so the play itself exhibits an intermingling of artifice and actuality, as the play re-presents the Jacobean royal family.

There is a built-in topical flavor to any Jacobean play that refers, as does *The Winter's Tale*, to "Whitsun pastorals," "puritans," and "bear-baitings," just to cite references from Act IV. The dance of the twelve Satyrs in that same act has been linked to a similar moment in Jonson's *Oberon*, a masque performed at court on 1 January 1611, with Henry as Oberon. A Servant observes in the play: "One three of

them, by their own report, sir, hath danced before the king . . .''
(IV.iv.337–38).[30] It seems probable that this refers to *Oberon*, in which
members of the King's Men may have performed. Something slightly
self-reflexive emerges from the comment of the First Gentleman,
responding to the reunion of father and daughter: ''The dignity of
this act was worth the audience of kings and princes; for by such was
it acted'' (V.ii.79–80). Given the Jacobean court audience in November 1611, this statement is all the more appropriate. Whether inten-
tional or not, Shakespeare's observation rings true for the court
audience that witnessed the larger play on at least two occasions.
Members of such an audience would have watched the Stuart royal
family watching a play that is preoccupied with royal families—a play
fit for kings.

On the matter of the possible Jacobean relevance of the play,
opinions, of course, vary. Glynne Wickham, as discussed in chapter
1, is the prime exponent of the play's connection to James's family,
even to the point of identifying some of the characters with members
of the royal family, hinting that the sixteen-year gap in the play
corresponds to the time between Mary's execution and James's
gaining the English throne, and arguing that the play was written for
the festivities of Henry's investiture as Prince of Wales in the summer
of 1610. On the latter, no external evidence survives. Attacking
Wickham's position, Hallett Smith denies such topicality in the play,
arguing instead that Shakespeare ''drew very little of contemporary
concerns, public affairs, gossip, sensations into his plays.''[31] In
contrast, Charles Barber, without tying the play to the royal family,
two decades ago found the play to be a reflection of Jacobean society,
especially the conflict between court and country. He writes: ''I
suggest then that the play is about the process of social change in
seventeenth-century England.''[32] Barber's essay lacks specific historical information to indicate that these problems and changes that he
enumerates are in fact germane to the first decade of the seventeenth
century. One can surely find the conflict between court and country
in *As You Like It*.

To say that *The Winter's Tale* is ''about'' social change in England
sells the play short, reduces its vast richness. Something of the same
problem inheres in a recent quasi-topical interpretation. ''*The Winter's
Tale*,'' Peter Erickson writes, ''enacts the disruption and revival of
patriarchy. The male-oriented social order undergoes a series of
challenges and crises.''[33] Erickson provides no theoretical or historical basis for his understanding of patriarchy, a system that is a given

in Shakespeare's plays and in the Jacobean political world. I think, on the other hand, that patriarchy is not under attack in this play, however much the men may be found wanting. Erickson suggests that in the final scene Leontes resumes "political control" (p. 826), the women thereby losing power.

A political problem clearly exists in the play—more a matter of royal succession than some seemingly petty squabble of what Erickson calls "sexual politics." One could just as easily argue that since the lost heir, Perdita, has been found, the potential political power for women opens at the end of the play rather than diminishes. Erickson moves in a curious biographical direction when he suggests that in the play Shakespeare can be seen as " 'forgiving himself' . . . in relation to women" (p. 827). That presumably is the dramatist's personal reason for the play. But specifically why should Shakespeare need to "forgive himself," and why is *The Winter's Tale*, and not some other play, the moment and means by which he achieves such forgiveness? Is Erickson offering some updated reason for Shakespeare's being on the Dowdenian heights at the end of his career?

If we assume that *The Winter's Tale* was written in 1611, the play contains several interesting parallels to James's family. Wickham's explanation of the sixteen-year gap in the play, needlessly far-fetched, has not generally been accepted. If we focus instead on Perdita as being sixteen years old at the play's end—a fact that Shakespeare found in his principal source, Greene's *Pandosto*—we can note that Princess Elizabeth was in her sixteenth year. The attention given to the royal son Mamillius early in the play may recall similar attention paid to Prince Charles after his arrival in England in 1604; he was the only young royal child in the Jacobean court. Following Maynard Mack's suggestion that Mamillius would likely be about seven years old,[34] I think that Leontes must be about thirty years old, because he refers to the twenty-three years since he was Mamillius's age: "Looking on the lines / Of my boy's face, me-thoughts I did recoil / Twenty-three years, and saw myself un-breech'd . . ." (I.ii.153–55). Leontes would thus have been thirty when Perdita was born; so was James when Elizabeth was born.

The number "twenty-three," not in Shakespeare's source, is referred to two other times: Leontes says that the messengers sent to Delphos have been gone twenty-three days (II.iii.197—"three weeks" in *Pandosto*), and the Shepherd refers to the "age between ten and three-and-twenty" (III.iii.59–60). James was twenty-three when he married Anne, and at the time of the court performance of the play, they were in their twenty-third year of marriage. At the end of the play Leontes would be roughly the age of King James—and of Shakespeare. We note that in the source Pandosto is fifty years old at the conclusion. We can, if we choose, dismiss these parallels as happy coincidence, and I certainly do not want to exaggerate their importance; but taken altogether, they do raise the possibility that Shakespeare has the Stuart royal family in mind as he reworks his source and fashions his play.

Perhaps one event that drew Shakespeare to Greene's Elizabethan romance was its death of the young prince and the forthcoming wedding of the princess. By 1611, James's family had endured the deaths of two infant princesses, Mary and Sophia, and was in the midst of Elizabeth's marriage negotiations. Because the only extant text of *The Winter's Tale* is the 1623 one, we have no way of knowing whether it represents the performances of 1611 or 1613 or some other. Given that the only eyewitness account of the play, Simon Forman's 1611 description, makes no mention of Hermione's restoration, one naturally wonders if this startling event, a radical departure from *Pandosto*, occurred in the early performance. Certainly, several textual scholars have at least entertained the possibility that the 1623 text of the play represents a revision.[35] If we can for the sake of argument accept such a possibility, then 1613 seems the likely occasion for revision, as Greg suggests. The restoration of Hermione and the attendant joy would therefore be much more in keeping with the court festivities in February 1613 than her death would have been. If, as I have suggested earlier, the theater is a place of speculation, then I offer the conjecture that events in the personal and political life of the Stuart royal family may have helped shape the action of *The Winter's Tale*. My argument for the interconnection of the play and James's family does not rest on this speculation, however. I do believe that the Jacobean royal family was one of the texts that entered the construction of the play, which is the intertextual result of Shakespeare's creative process.

If Shakespeare created the whole fabric of *Cymbeline* out of a thread found in Holinshed's account, he was able in *Pandosto* to find an abundance of material. Two questions arise: why did Shakespeare resort to Greene's musty romance, and what did he do with it? The latter question has been ably dealt with by Bullough.[36] Shakespeare closely follows *Pandosto*, but he also diverges from it in significant ways. He reverses the countries, for example, placing Leontes in Sicily, not in Bohemia. The most striking change, of course, is that

Shakespeare lets Hermione live whereas Bellaria in *Pandosto* dies at the news of the death of her son, Garinter. Melancholy, Pandosto takes his own life at the end, after his incestuous attraction to his daughter, Fawnia. Shakespeare adds Paulina, Antigonus, and Autolycus. Bellaria is the one who requests that the mission be sent to Delphos to get the oracle from Apollo.

One of the facts that Shakespeare leaves out is Egistus's arranging a marriage for his son Dorastus to Euphania, daughter of the king of Denmark. Since James had himself married a daughter of the king of Denmark, why didn't Shakespeare include this incident? I think he wanted to avoid such a potentially explicit reference to the royal family, which might have confused his fiction with reality. Since Dorastus steadfastly, to his father's chagrin, refuses to accept this marital scheme, that would have been most awkward for the dramatist. Shakespeare, nevertheless, found in *Pandosto* a romance compatible with exploring the interconnections of politics and royal family. Most of the changes that he makes mitigate the harshness of Greene's fiction and thereby render it more palatable for the Jacobean audience in the Globe and at court.

Unlike *Pandosto*, in which the Shepherd has a shrewish wife, in the play he has a son. Given his primary source and the dramatic contexts of such plays as *1 The Honest Whore* and *The Woman's Prize*, Shakespeare might reasonably be expected to have retained the Shepherd's shrewish wife. The change, I argue below, suits the play's structure of fathers and sons. But deviating from a source is nothing new for Shakespeare, as we have already seen in our consideration of *Pericles*. The issue of jealousy, of such terrible importance in *The Winter's Tale*, finds full-scale treatment in *Cupids Whirligig*. But instead of the frivolous Timothy Troublesome, Shakespeare provides the more serious Leontes, whose jealousy has severe political consequences. The irrationality, suspicion, and disruption that plague Sir Timothy and his wife find, however, their counterpart in Shakespeare's play. The dubious, problematic reunion of Sir Timothy and his wife Shakespeare renders with certainty and glory in Leontes and Hermione. Out of the petty world that characterizes *Cupids Whirligig* Shakespeare creates a mythos of the family and the political state, compatible with but different from the experience in his own *Othello*. The importance of the royal child and the return of the lost daughter in *The Winter's Tale* remind us more of Day's *Law-Tricks* and Rowley's *The Shoemaker a Gentleman* than of the contemporary satiric drama.

As Shakespeare chooses a royal focus, he moves away from the depoliticized world of much Jacobean comedy. He accents a royal family that survives its crises, finds its lost heir, and in a burst of wonder in the final scene obtains a future that opens before them with unexpected hope. Things die, but things are new-born. Matters of political succession, royal genealogy, and interpretation wind their way through the drama, much as they do in the other Romances.

Within the play itself, texts determine the royal family's destiny. I have in mind specifically the trial scene of Hermione, III.ii, which represents the climax of the first half of the play. The future of the ruling family of Sicily is at stake. The politics of the family and its domestic life intertwine, as this moment epitomizes the several openings and closings of the play. The trial of Hermione with its formal, legal structure belies the chaos that grips Sicily at that moment, the result of Leontes' jealousy. Hermione's defense of herself is a rousing answer to the charges against her: it is calculated, logical, honest, studied, and full of controlled passion. On this I certainly disagree with Erickson, who sees Hermione as adopting "a stance of patience and stoic passivity" (p. 825). Her argument comes as the immediate response to the formal indictment that is read. But another text answers this one and highlights a major issue for the royal family.

At the end of her defense, Hermione cries out: "Apollo be my judge!" (III.ii.116), an appeal to an authority greater than the puny, mortal Leontes, who is ready to have her executed. Cleomenes and Dion, the Delphic messengers, are summoned. After they swear that they have not broken the seals on the scroll or read its secrets, Leontes orders: "Break up the seals and read" (131). That breaking is emblematic of the splitting of the family bond. The Oracle, of course, exonerates everyone except Leontes, who is designated "a jealous tyrant" (133). Reaction to the reading of this text ranges from the Lords who cry, "Now blessed be the great Apollo!" (137) and Hermione's simple "Praised!" to Leontes' question: "Hast thou read truth?" (137–38).

The text of the oracle is closed; now the interpretation begins.[37] The Officer assures Leontes that the scroll was read "As it is here set down" (139). To Leontes' ambiguous question the Officer responds only that he has accurately and truly read the text. But Leontes attacks the "truth" of the text: "There is no truth at all i' th' Oracle: / The sessions shall proceed: this is mere falsehood" (140–41). Leontes misreads, misinterprets the message. The Apollonian oracle, both clear and cryptic, retrospective and prophetic, judges the past—finding Hermione, Camillo, and Polixenes all blameless and Leontes guilty—and opens a riddlelike future: ". . . the king shall live without an heir, if that which is lost be not found" (134–36). The past of the royal family closes; the future opens with uncertainty. In the twinkling of an eye, word arrives that the royal heir, Mamillius, has died, and with that, the royal mother presumably dies. The judgment of the gods, swift and sure, breaks the obstinate Leontes across their will.

Suddenly Leontes, utterly alone, having already cast off his infant daughter, is apparently no longer a royal father or a royal husband. This moment represents great personal loss not only in the royal family but also in the kingdom: there is no heir. The question of succession becomes a major motif in the play, and it underscores the inextricable link between royal family and politics. Shakespeare does not let us lose sight of the political problem that Leontes' actions have produced. If there is to be a comic solution to this winter's tale, then the royal family must be reunited in some way, and the kingdom must be assured of an heir.

Two important questions sum up much of the play's concern about its royal families: the disguised Polixenes asks his son Florizel, "Have you a father?" (IV.iv.393); and Leontes asks about the Perdita whom he does not recognize: "Is this the daughter of a king?" (V.i.207). Florizel answers Leontes' question: "She is, / When once she is my wife" (207–8); that is, once he marries her, his father will also be hers. She will then be a royal heir. Of course, Shakespeare explores the irony of this situation, for Perdita is the blood daughter of a king, namely Leontes; that will be revealed in the next scene. She is the lost heir who is found. Florizel impertinently answers his father's question, saying, I have a father, "but what of him?" (IV.iv.393). Shortly after this, Polixenes reveals his identity and disinherits the son, leaving himself and the kingdom without an heir.

Though the crucial, determinate importance of women in this play can scarcely be exaggerated—an importance greater than elsewhere in the Romances—I will focus on fathers and sons, a subject not often explored.[38] The Jacobean court audience watching the play in 1611 could not have been insensitive to or unaware of the conflict between James and his son Henry, documented in chapter 2. The court audience seeing the play in February 1613 would have been sobered by the death of Mamillius, Henry's death painfully fresh in their minds. The family of history and the family of art invade each other.

In addition to Leontes and Polixenes, other fathers inhabit the play. Antigonus, who has the dubious distinction of meeting one of the cruelest deaths in Jacobean drama, has three daughters (II.i. 144–45), a point curiously never mentioned by his wife, Paulina. The wily rogue Autolycus, who stood out vividly in Forman's 1611 account of a performance, refers to his father as the one who has named him (IV.iii.24). Florizel creates for Perdita a fictional father when they arrive at Leontes' court: she has come, he says, from Libya, where she is the daughter of Smalus (V.i.156–59). The Shepherd who becomes father to the infant Perdita in Bohemia also has a son, known in the play as Clown. As if to emphasize father/son relationships, Shakespeare gives the Shepherd a son instead of a shrewish wife, as in *Pandosto*. For sixteen years the Shepherd cares for and nurtures Perdita. What was to have been her death by Leontes' neglect has become life, thanks to the Shepherd; her surrogate father also acts as mother, his wife apparently having died (IV.iv.55).

The Shepherd and Clown become a parody of Leontes and Mamillius or Polixenes and Florizel. They in fact become part of the extended royal family as the two kings accept them and reward them. Their final conversation is rather touching as they come fresh from the experience of the reunion of Leontes and Perdita. The Shepherd, some eighty-three years old (IV.iv.454), tells his son: "I am past more children, but thy sons and daughters will be all gentlemen born" (V.ii.127–28). The Clown reports their acceptance by the royal family: ". . . the king's son took me by the hand, and called me brother; and then the two kings called my father brother; and then the prince, my brother, and the princess, my sister, called my father father; and so we wept . . ." (140–44). What a marvelous redefining of the royal family, extending to and acknowledging the contribution of the Shepherd and Clown. James's relationship with the earl of Mar's family, Henry's care for Phineas Pett, and Elizabeth's familial ties with the Haringtons illustrate how the Stuart royal family often extended its boundaries beyond blood ties. The Clown says that the tears he shed were "the first gentleman-like tears that ever we shed" (145). And his father responds ambiguously: "We may live, son, to shed many more" (146). As another father, the same age as the Shepherd, reminds us, we come crying hither into this world.

Turning now to the royal sons and fathers, I focus first on Mamillius, who dies but is fulfilled in Florizel. By the 1613 performance, something of the same thing has happened in James's family when, after Henry's death, Charles becomes the only royal son and heir apparent, trying to complete Henry's potential. Mamillius and Florizel in their similarity represent the youth of Leontes and Polixenes. The play's opening scene, a conversation between Camillo and Archidamus, dwells on the relationship between the two kings and on Mamillius. Archidamus from Bohemia describes the Sicilian prince: "You have an unspeakable comfort of your young prince Mamillius" (I.i.34–35). Camillo agrees and expands the subject: "it is a gallant child; one that, indeed, physics the subject, makes old hearts fresh: they that went on crutches ere he was born desire yet their life to see him a man" (37–40).

Nothing like this extensive attention to and praise of the Mamillius figure exists in *Pandosto*. In this praise of Mamillius one can hear exactly the same kinds of comments being made about Prince Henry by 1611, as political hopes increasingly attended his promise. It is interesting to contemplate the royal family's hearing the comments about Mamillius and recalling similar observations being made about Henry. If they recollected such comments in 1613, it would have been a poignant memory. Like Mamillius, Henry's great promise was not to be realized. Archidamus closes the scene: "If the king had no son, they would desire to live on crutches till he had one" (44–45). The play eventually dramatizes that "if." Even as the play opens by celebrating the royal sons, it raises the specter of what things would be like without such an heir. The Oracle in III.ii brings into sharp focus the plight of the king and kingdom without an heir. Old hearts will be made fresh at the play's end, but by Perdita, not Mamillius. The female line will be established.

Mamillius is the only young royal child in the Romances. We witness Marina's being born in *Pericles*; but she is soon separated from her father, and we do not see her again until she is a teenager. Similarly in this play, Perdita, born and soon taken to Bohemia, disappears for sixteen years before we see her. Leontes' outburst of jealousy governs his conversation with Mamillius in I.ii. He asks a question that is the obverse of the one that Polixenes will later ask of his son: "Art thou my boy?" (120), a question full of doubt as Leontes begins irrationally to suspect the faithfulness of Hermione. All the evidence suggests, even to Leontes, that Mamillius is a copy of his father. Looking at his son, Leontes recalls his own childhood some twenty-three years earlier: "How like, methought, I then was to this kernel, / This squash, this gentleman" (159–60). He sends the son away as he readies to enlist Camillo's aid in destroying Polixenes.

In II.i Mamillius appears in the company of his mother and her ladies, who care for him. This confirms that he is still quite young, not yet in the regular company of men, as Prince Henry was by the age of six. I do not recall any other moment in Shakespeare's plays, outside of a few minor ones in the history plays and in *Macbeth*, where we gain such a portrait of a young child, full as Mamillius is of wit and mischief, vexing his mother. Hermione opens the scene: "Take the boy to you: he so troubles me, / 'Tis past enduring" (II.i.1–2). Ironically, those same words could have been spoken by Leontes, but in quite a different context. Mamillius taunts the ladies, accusing them of treating him as if he "were a baby still" (6). Hermione finally gets him to settle down and tell her a story, a winter's tale "of sprites and goblins" (26).

Leontes, disturbed by the escape of Polixenes and Camillo and full of accusations against Hermione, interrupts this domestic scene. He begins with a command: "Give me the boy: I am glad you did not nurse him" (56). This conflict between mother and father over the son may remind us of the struggles that James and Anne had over their children, especially Henry. That Hermione did not nurse Mamillius of course reflects common practice. Leontes has a final command about the son: "Bear the boy hence, he shall not come about her . . ." (59). Mamillius exits, not to be seen in the play again—a fateful exit. We learn later of his illness (II.iii.10–11), and by III.ii of his death. With his death the political question of succession opens. Mamillius remains for Leontes an ever-present memory; he winces with pain when he recalls his son, and he sees in Florizel in Act V his own son. A year after the court performance of this play in 1611, James was to share in Leontes' sense of loss, life thus imitating art.

Florizel, the other royal son in the play, re-presents Mamillius, even to the point of being the same age; so Paulina notes in V.i: "Had our prince / (Jewel of children) seen this hour, he had pair'd / Well with this lord: there was not full a month / Between their births" (115–18). Not only are they virtually identical in age, but the regard that their fathers hold for them is similar. Thus, one reason for Polixenes' desire to return to his kingdom is to see his son, whom he describes to Leontes:

He's all my exercise, my mirth, my matter:
Now my sworn friend, and then mine enemy;
My parasite, my soldier, statesman, all.

> He makes a July's day short as December;
> And with his varying childness cures in me
> Thoughts that would thick my blood. (I.ii.166–71)

Mamillius demonstrates his playful nature, his "varying childness," in II.i with his mother. Unfortunately, Leontes' warped mind cannot find in this child the curing, healing power that Polixenes refers to. As we see throughout the Romances, royal children provide hope and deliverance both in the private, domestic life of the royal family and in the kingdom. James's children, we remember, were referred to as the "joys" of the kingdom.

We do not even learn the name of Polixenes' son until Act IV, when we find Florizel in Bohemia in love with Perdita, presumably a mere shepherdess. The closing of Mamillius's life has opened the exploration of Florizel's life in the dramatic structure. Sixteen years have brought youthful manhood to Florizel, now presumably twenty-three years old. Florizel's younger life remains, in the words of Time, a "wide gap" (IV.i.7). At the opening of IV.iv, Perdita refers to Florizel as "The gracious mark o' th' land . . ." (8), reflecting the esteem that he enjoys in Bohemia. It is she who is fearful of what his father's reaction might be to Florizel's love of a shepherdess: "even now I tremble / To think your father, by some accident / Should pass this way . . ." (18–20). But Florizel, a bit headstrong and confident, dismisses the fear, assuring Perdita that nothing would mean anything to him without her. Confrontation between father and son does occur, for Polixenes has come to the festival by design, not by accident. One could argue that their encounter constitutes the "trial" of Florizel, reaching its climax when Polixenes asks Florizel if he has a father. But Florizel, impertinent and insistent, thinks that his father need not know of his business.

If the question were only one of love, then perhaps Florizel is right; but as a royal child and heir, he should know that the issue is, as always, much greater. Political necessity and parental will circumscribe prerogatives of royal children. Despite Perdita's warning, "Of your own state take care" (449), Florizel tells her: "Lift up thy looks: / From my succession wipe me, father; I / Am heir to my affection" (480–82)—brave but foolhardy words. Surely he wants to impress Perdita with the depth of his love for her, but he seems a bit foolish—perhaps even selfish. The political conflict between father and son and the issue of succession do not appear in *Pandosto*; Shakespeare again emphasizes the politics of the family in ways not in his source.

The royal child, such as Prince Henry, knows his duty to the kingdom, sometimes having to submerge one's own personal desires to the greater claim of the politics of the family.

Florizel continues to insist: "Not for Bohemia, nor the pomp that may / Be thereat glean'd . . . / . . . will I break my oath / To this my fair belov'd" (489–90, 92–93). He tells Camillo that concerning his father, "I mean not / To see him any more . . ." (495–96). Not only has the father disinherited the son, but now the son will disown his father, promising never to see him again. Florizel becomes the lost heir, eager to marry the lost heir of Sicily. Fortunately for his sake, and for the kingdom's, Camillo becomes his counselor and guide, much as he had been first for Leontes and then Polixenes. Polixenes had in fact respected Camillo as his "father" (I.ii.461). Camillo becomes the father substitute for Florizel, even as he functions as dramatist, shaping the destiny of Florizel and Perdita, often writing their script and arranging their costumes.

Reflecting his own desire, Camillo urges the couple to make for Sicily. His fertile mind envisions their reception at Leontes' court:

> Methinks I see
> Leontes opening his free arms and weeping
> His welcomes forth; asks thee there 'Son, forgiveness!'
> As 'twere i' th' father's person; kisses the hands
> Of your fresh princess. . . . (IV.iv.548–52)

Act V, scene i, realizes Camillo's dramatic imagination. His description in IV.iv underscores how Florizel will be a son for Leontes. Having put on Autolycus's garments, Florizel says: "Should I now meet my father, / He would not call me son" (657–58), a statement filled with several ironies. But Camillo has at least put this royal pair on the right course; and his own desires will be satisfied: "I shall review Sicilia, for whose sight / I have a woman's longing" (666–67). One can argue that Act V functions precisely as a "re-viewing" of Sicily: the royal children represent the ones whom Leontes has lost; the royal friends, Leontes and Polixenes, renew their love; Hermione returns to life. The re-view of Sicily offers a perspective not seen before; Time has helped bring many changes. The winter's tale is over; Leontes' tears and penance have been his re-creation, a renewing that the kingdom also shares.

One of the topics discussed by Camillo and Archidamus in the play's opening scene is the loving relationship of Leontes and Polixenes; their love is the predicate of Act I. Camillo reports: "They were trained together in their childhoods, and there rooted betwixt them then such an affection which cannot choose but branch now" (I.i.22–24). Delving their roots is simple, unlike the case of Posthumus in *Cymbeline*. Though their "more mature dignities and royal necessities" (25) have separated them, they have remained linked by "interchange of gifts, letters, loving embassies, [so] that they have seemed to be together, though absent; shook hands, as over a vast . . ." (27–30). Their love has endured not a breach but an expansion, like gold to airy thinness beat. This mood carries over to I.ii, where Polixenes refers to Leontes as "brother" and "best brother" (4, 148).

Polixenes, who has been visiting in Sicily for nine months, intends to return to Bohemia. Anxious about political affairs there, he says: "I am question'd by my fears, of what may chance / Or breed upon our absence . . ." (I.ii.11–12). We recall the uncertainty in Tyre while Pericles was gone, which only Helicanus could mitigate. Hermione urges Leontes: "Tell him, you are sure / All in Bohemia's well" (30–31). The irony becomes that all is not well in Sicily. The ugly development of Leontes' jealousy counters Polixenes' description of the innocence of their youth:

> We were as twinn'd lambs that did frisk i' th' sun,
> And bleat the one at th' other: what we chang'd
> Was innocence for innocence: we knew not
> The doctrine of ill-doing, nor dream'd
> That any did. (67–71)

But they have since known temptation.

The innocence associated with Mamillius, Perdita, and Florizel as children reflects their fathers' youthful innocence. Particularly in scenes i and ii of Act I the description of Mamillius and Florizel recapitulates Leontes and Polixenes. Polixenes discovers again what a fleeting thing innocence is when Camillo informs him that Leontes intends to kill him. Puzzled by what he has read in Leontes' face, Polixenes describes it: "The king hath on him such a countenance / As he had lost some province, and a region / Lov'd as he loves himself" (368–70). That is precisely what has happened; what has been lost is not some political entity but rather, as Leontes thinks, the faithfulness of his wife and friend. Camillo correctly describes Leontes' condition as a "sickness" (384). Polixenes sees the danger: "as his [Leontes'] person's mighty" (453), Leontes' reaction is likely to be violent. To escape the jealous wrath of his friend, Polixenes commits himself to Camillo's plan—what his own son will do some sixteen years later.

Polixenes passes into the gap of time and space. A chapter of his life closes in Sicily but opens in Bohemia. He is not entirely forgotten: the Oracle exonerates him in III.ii, and Leontes pledges: "I'll reconcile me to Polixenes . . ." (III.ii.155). When in Act IV Camillo voices his desire to return to Sicily, Polixenes says: "Of that fatal country, Sicilia, prithee speak no more; whose very naming punishes me with remembrance of that penitent . . . and reconciled king, my brother; whose loss of his most precious queen and children are even now to be afresh lamented" (IV.ii.20–25). Thinking of Leontes' children, Polixenes asks: ". . . when sawest thou the Prince Florizel, my son?" (26), a question that echoes the inquiry that Henry IV makes about Prince Hal. Polixenes notes further in a statement that King James would have understood: "Kings are no less unhappy, their issue not being gracious, than they are in losing them when they have approved their virtues" (27–29). The statement resonates with both personal and political concern.

With Camillo's help Polixenes decides to go to the festival to spy on Florizel. Though Perdita gives them rosemary and rue (IV.iv.74)—emblems of remembrance and grace—certainly little grace governs Polixenes' encounter with his son. He does try to reason with Florizel, pointing out that a father "Is at the nuptial of his son a guest / That best becomes the table" (396–97). And he insists on the father's prerogative in matters of marriage: "The father (all whose joy is nothing else / But fair posterity) should hold some counsel / In such a business" (409–11). Again, the issues are even more profoundly significant when that son is a royal heir. Polixenes expresses his concern for the future, for succession, and for the politics of the royal family; these issues do not appear in *Pandosto*.

When Polixenes removes his disguise, he strikes at everyone, especially Florizel for his disobedience and insensitivity to the needs of the kingdom. Polixenes says:

> Mark your divorce, young sir,
> Whom son I dare not call; thou art too base
> To be acknowledg'd: thou a sceptre's heir,
> That thus affects a sheep-hook! . . .
> . . . .
> . . . we'll bar thee from succession;
> Not hold thee of our blood, no, not our kin. . . . (418–21, 430–31)

Like Leontes before him, Polixenes casts off his child and now has no heir. Bohemia resembles Sicily. Polixenes' wrath against his son, Perdita, and the Shepherd sadly echoes that of Leontes.

The play reviews royal family relationships and finds them in disarray: the bond cracks between father and son—'tis strange. Sixteen years after the play began, two fathers, once best of friends, separate from one another and from their families. The kingdoms, once so full of promise of the royal issue, now teeter on the brink of potential disaster because they have no heir. The winter's tale of the first three acts deepens in Bohemia; only the love of Florizel and Perdita, the new generation of royal children, offers much reason for hope. These lovers demonstrate that the play world has not entirely closed; it remains open to possibilities. The kingdom may yet find the heirs who seem lost.

Nothing quite prepares us for Leontes' "Too hot, too hot! / To mingle friendship far, is mingling bloods. / I have *tremor cordis* on me" (I.ii.108–10). He unleashes his jealousy, the consequences of which destroy his family. The ceremony of innocence is drowned, and all is called into doubt. As a jealous husband, Leontes resembles somewhat Timothy Troublesome in *Cupids Whirligig* or Don Zuccone in *The Fawn*, except that here the obsession has potentially tragic consequences, as in *Othello*. In a string of questions that cascade from Leontes, beginning "Is whispering nothing? / Is leaning cheek to cheek? is meeting noses? / Kissing with inside lip?" (284–86), he confirms his suspicions, being his own "putter-on." He believes that all have betrayed him; conspiracy abounds. If the accusations he makes are not true, then Bohemia is "nothing, / My wife is nothing, nor nothing have these nothings, / If this be nothing" (294–96). He would not venture such charges, he assures Camillo, and sully "The purity and whiteness of my sheets" nor "Give scandal to the blood o' th' prince, my son" (327, 330), without being certain. Camillo tries to pull him from the precipice of his despair and wrath by urging him to take Hermione to him "Even for your son's sake" (337), thereby quelling the likely stir in the "courts and kingdoms / Known and allied to yours" (338–39). Political danger inheres in the domestic strife within the royal family.

Accusations lead to action directed against the family: Leontes sends Mamillius away from his mother, accuses Hermione of being an adulteress, and casts away his newborn daughter in the last scene of Act II. Leontes, who has "drunk, and seen the spider" (II.i.45), proceeds on a new assumption: "All's true that is mistrusted" (48). Sounding like Othello, Leontes says: "if I mistake / In those foundations which I build upon, / The centre is not big enough to bear / A school-boy's top" (100–103). If all that he assumes is not true, then

171

chaos has come again. He sends Hermione to prison, where she gives birth to their daughter. No joy or celebration attend the birth of this royal child. Doubly imprisoned by being in the womb of her jailed mother, this child gains only a limited freedom; for Leontes' mind creates another prison, Sicily itself.

Paulina's assumption that the presentation of the babe to Leontes will soften his heart and mitigate his harshness against Hermione proves false. Early in II.iii we learn that Mamillius is ill; further, Leontes himself knows no rest or peaceful sleep. Thus Paulina arrives with the infant, promising to bring sleep for Leontes. She in fact engages in a "needful conference / About some gossips for your highness" (40–41). The gossips would be needed for the baptism of the child; but the only baptism that Leontes has in mind is one by fire: "Commit them to the fire!" (94). Leontes is the only traitor present, according to Paulina: "for he, / The sacred honour of himself, his queen's, / His hopeful son's, his babe's, betrays to slander . . ." (83–85). Leontes harms the politics of the family by sullying its honor. If no one will burn the child, "The bastard brains with these my proper hands / Shall I dash out" (139–40), Leontes says. Putting such harshness to shame, Antigonus takes on the task of caring for the babe—"anything possible"—"To save the innocent" (166). If not by fire, then by desertion: Leontes orders Antigonus to take the child "To some remote and desert place . . . Where chance may nurse or end it" (175, 182). Even pointing out to Leontes how the child resembles him, as Paulina does (97–107), fails to lessen the perversity of this royal father's intentions. Sending away the innocent child destroys any remaining shred of innocence in Leontes. The state will also pay the price for this action.

The whole family is on trial in III.ii, a trial ordered by Leontes; it shall proceed "Even to the guilt or the purgation" (III.ii.7)—the last word carrying with it the sense of "acquittal" and of "catharsis"; both accompany this experience. In many ways it is a magnificent scene for Hermione as she convincingly defends herself against Leontes' false charges, being resolute in her innocence. Leontes in the opening lines notes Hermione's heritage, a point to be pursued throughout the trial: ". . . the party tried / The daughter of a king, our wife . . ." (2–3). Part of Hermione's defense rests on her family ties, her genealogy; she is, after all, the queen on trial. Hermione describes herself: "A fellow of the royal bed, which owe / A moiety of the throne, a great king's daughter, / The mother to a hopeful prince . . ." (38–40). These simple facts themselves raise doubts about the purpose of the procedures. If Hermione possesses a "moiety" of the throne, then Leontes is also on trial. To try her puts to question the structure of the royal family. Hermione invokes the family as she enumerates her losses: "The crown and comfort of my life, your favour"; "My second joy, / And first-fruits of my body, from his presence / I am barr'd"; "My third comfort / . . . is from my breast / (The innocent milk in it most innocent mouth) / Hal'd out to murder . . ." (94, 96–98, 98–101). She has even been hauled to court before she has had time to recover from childbirth.

Before the Delphic messengers enter, Hermione again identifies herself as the daughter of a king:

> The Emperor of Russia was my father:
> O that he were alive, and here beholding
> His daughter's trial! that he did but see
> The flatness of my misery, yet with eyes
> Of pity, not revenge! (119–23)

In his essay Erickson says that with these comments Hermione "submits her case to an earlier patriarchal authority" (p. 825). But I understand her to be appealing rather to the sympathy of her father, underscoring her familial ties. Ultimately her appeal to authority will be to Apollo, not to her dead father. From her father she would derive support, not a judgment of the proceeding. Making the emperor of Russia Hermione's father is but another way in which Shakespeare alters his source *Pandosto*, for there it is Egistus's wife, not Pandosto's, who makes this claim. The family bonds here stretch into Hermione's past, even as this scene mingles past, present, and future. Just as Queen Anne could base part of her authority on being the daughter of the King of Denmark, so Hermione can make a similar claim.

Despite the appeals to family, past and present, it takes the message of the Oracle to change the inevitable direction of the trial's verdict, as discussed earlier. The Oracle functions in part like the report of a jury, judging the trial. Only Leontes resists its conclusion, though he, too, changes after the death of Mamillius and the apparent death of Hermione. The last part of the scene forms Leontes' trial, as Paulina relentlessly rehearses his sins. He sums up the error of his mind: "I have too much believ'd mine own suspicion" (151). He plans to change by reconciling himself to those whom he has wronged. But for Camillo's disobedience, even more harm would have been done; Leontes praises Camillo: "how he glisters /

Thorough my rust!'' (170–71). The rust, the dross, of Leontes' soul will now be burned away by years of contrition and penance as he enters the crucible of the loss of his entire family, knowing that he will have no heir "if that which is lost be not found" (135–36). He sets forth on a plan of redemption: "Once a day I'll visit / The chapel where they [Mamillius and Hermione] lie, and tears shed there / Shall be my recreation" (238–40). These holy tears will not be the holy waters of joy that flowed from Cymbeline upon reunion with Imogen, not tears of advent or birth, but of death and judgment. And yet they will be efficacious, re-creative, producing a cleansing in Leontes and eventually in the kingdom. There will be an empty tomb as this brazen world of Sicily transforms into a golden world in the play's last scene.

The politics of the royal family pervades Act V; as Leontes' family reunites, it provides redemption for the kingdom. The principal political problem of no heir in Sicily, or in Bohemia for that matter, resolves. Nowhere in *The Winter's Tale* is it clearer that Shakespeare attends some text other than *Pandosto*, because the divergence from that romance is profound in this last act. The text of the Stuart royal family may have provided the immediate example of the intermingling of politics and family. Woven throughout the fabric of this play runs the bright thread of the quest for an heir, its prominence apparent in the last act. The voices of V.i echo with concern for the kingdom in ways that find no parallel in *Pandosto*.

As Act V opens, Cleomenes urges Leontes, who has performed "A saint-like sorrow," to "forgive himself" (V.i.2, 6). Recalling Hermione, Leontes experiences anew the loss of her and recognizes "That heirless it hath made my kingdom . . ." (10). The other Delphic messenger, Dion, argues that Leontes should remarry; any who do not desire this "pity not the state, nor the remembrance / Of his most sovereign name . . ." (25–26). Dion asks the listeners to consider "What dangers, by his highness' fail of issue, / May drop upon his kingdom, and devour / Incertain lookers on" (27–29). What, Dion says, could be "more holy / Than to rejoice the former queen is well?" (29–30); that, of course, is impossible. Failing that, Leontes should remarry and produce an heir and subsequent stability for the kingdom. The private life of the royal family has political consequences, as the Jacobean audience knew well. Paulina, however, persuades Leontes to let her determine whom he should marry and when: "That / Shall be when your first queen's again in breath: / Never till then" (82–84)—a riddlelike statement that proves prophetic. Paulina is sure that "The crown will find an heir" (47). As King James had instructed Prince Henry, a ruler marries for the sake of the kingdom in order to provide a successor.

Having raised the succession problem, Shakespeare provides an answer, though Leontes does not know it yet: namely, the arrival of Florizel and Perdita, who have fled Bohemia and the wrathful father to come to Sicily where Leontes welcomes them. Florizel and Perdita closely re-present the lost royal children. Leontes looks at them and cries out: "O, alas! / I lost a couple, that 'twixt heaven and earth / Might thus have stood, begetting wonder, as / You, gracious couple, do" (130–33). Instead, Leontes has been left "issueless" (173). "What might I have been," Leontes says, "Might I a son and daughter now have look'd on . . ." (175–76). Unknown to him, he looks on his daughter and son-to-be, who, of course, also recalls Mamillius. Leontes welcomes Florizel as the son of his dear friend Polixenes, his "brother," a "graceful gentleman," and "holy father," as Leontes calls him. He repents anew the "sin" that he committed against Polixenes. Florizel recapitulates Mamillius and Polixenes, and Perdita evokes recollection of Hermione: "I thought of her," Leontes observes, "Even as these looks I made" (226–27). The reception of Florizel and Perdita by Leontes fulfills the text of Camillo's vision in IV.iv. To their dismay, Polixenes has also arrived in Sicily. What seems like threat transforms to reconciliation in the following scene. Sicily, closed, incarcerated for sixteen years, starts to open to dreams that become reality. The royal families stand on the verge of reunion; the kingdom awaits the answer of the lost heir.

For reasons that have puzzled interpreters of *The Winter's Tale*, the reunion of father and daughter takes place offstage; we get only a report of it, unlike the comparable situation in *Pericles* and *Cymbeline*. But what a report! That which has been lost is found: Leontes and Sicily have an heir. Today in our hearing the text is fulfilled. Perdita's return solves the riddle of the Oracle and offers a political assurance to the state. Just as the scroll of the Oracle's message had been opened in III.ii and read, so here an opening leads to the fulfilling of that same Oracle. The First Gentleman reports: "I was by at the opening of the fardel, heard the old shepherd deliver the manner how he found it" (V.ii.2–3). Opening the shepherd's bundle leads to the richness of family reunion; he brings proof of Perdita's heritage. Thus the father substitute provides Perdita with her true father. One report captures the wonder of the occasion: "there was speech in their dumbness, language in their very gesture . . ." (13–14). Not surprisingly, everywhere "Nothing but bonfires: the Oracle is fulfilled; the king's daughter is found" (22–23). Capsulizing Leontes' reaction is the Third Gentleman's report of Leontes, who cries to Perdita, " 'O, thy mother, thy mother!' then asks Bohemia forgiveness; then embraces his son-in-law . . ." (52–54). We may agree with the Gentleman's statement: "I never heard of such another encounter . . ." (57–58).

Certainly Shakespeare did not hear it in Greene's romance where Pandosto imprisons Dorastus and lusts after Fawnia, his daughter. The celebrations for the deliverance of the Stuart royal family after the Gunpowder Plot, the bonfires lit for the births of the royal daughters, the festivities associated with Henry's investiture—all underscore delight and joy in the family of history that find their counterpart here in the royal family of art. To have seen what we have seen, to have heard what we have heard, compels us to concur with the First Gentleman's assessment: "Every wink of an eye, some new grace will be born" (110–11). The twinkling of an eye will produce yet another grace in the final scene, as the spectators and royal family go to see Hermione's statue. Such scenes make old hearts fresh.

If V.ii fulfills the Oracle, then V.iii completes the trial scene, in some ways the obverse of that trial. One radical difference: here the trial is of faith, not of law. That which the trial had severed comes back together, except for Mamillius. The gap in the royal family closes in this last scene, as new life opens before them in ways that they could only dream of: Leontes reunites with Hermione, believed dead for the past sixteen years, and Hermione and Perdita greet one another for the first time since they shared a prison cell. Paulina delights in the visit of the royal families to her house to see Hermione's statue: "It is," she says, "a surplus of your grace, which never / My life may last to answer" (V.iii.7–8). In fact, Paulina will herself provide a surplus of grace in the renewal of Hermione. Gathered before the statue are the kings of Sicily and Bohemia, and the "Heirs of your kingdoms . . ." (6). They have come to be spectators, but in the twinkling of an eye, they become participants in the drama that unfolds. In order to see the statue of Hermione, Paulina must open a curtain behind which it stands. The opening of the Oracle's text, the opening of the Shepherd's fardel, and now the opening of the curtain all point in the direction of revelation of the past, believed closed, that becomes prologue to a brighter future for the royal family. Each incident provokes its own sense of wonder and redefinition of the family.

The statue is not, as it seems, a representation of Hermione but is a re-presentation of her. It mocks the onlookers with its art, an art that translates into life before their startled eyes. This cold pastoral teases them out of thought and opens an eternity before them. Paulina usurps the function of Julio Romano and becomes Oracle-like in this scene. She holds the mystery of Hermione in her hands; she unfolds the curtain, and behold she shows them a mystery: we shall not all sleep, but some will be raised to life. Perdita, kneeling before the statue, says: "Lady, / Dear queen, that ended when I but began, / Give me that hand of yours to kiss" (43–45). In Hermione's apparent ending was Perdita's beginning; so it is often true in the Romances: Marina can say the same of Thaisa. Paulina "afflicts" them with the statue; but as Leontes rightly says: "For this affliction has a taste as sweet / As any cordial comfort" (76–77). This "unlawful business" (96), as Paulina calls it, ends when, having awakened their faith, she causes the statue to move. Spectators in the court audiences, as today, share in the delicious wonder of those in the play when Hermione moves and speaks.

Though Hermione and Leontes do not immediately engage in conversation, they do embrace; surely there is "speech in their dumbness, language in their very gesture." Perdita now kneels not to the statue but to her mother, as Paulina says to Hermione: "Our Perdita is found" (121). This surplus of grace not even Paulina could have anticipated during those sixteen years. Hermione speaks for the first time since her trial: "You gods, look down, / And from your sacred vials pour your graces / Upon my daughter's head!" (121–23). Such a moment emphasizes the importance of the royal child. Hermione insists that she has "preserv'd / Myself to see the issue" (127–28). A mother speaks, and so does a queen. Holy waters of baptism now pour down on Perdita, this one who represents the future of the kingdom. In his closing speech Leontes asks Hermione's forgiveness and pardon (the past) and introduces her to Florizel (the future): "This your son-in-law, / And son unto the king, whom, heavens directing, / Is troth-plight to your daughter" (149–51). The royal family is intact, and so is the kingdom; the final stage emblem confirms that. Paulina, who has led them to this Promised Land and who has gained in Camillo a husband, is to lead them back to the court, where in leisure and security they will explore "this wide gap of time, since first / We were dissever'd" (154–55). Shakespeare burnishes the brazen world of Sicily until it resembles gold; a holy fire of separation, affliction, and penance has not consumed but has nourished.

177

Shakespeare opened the text of *Pandosto*, read it, closed it, and then offered his interpretation from that closed book. Shakespeare opened the book of kings, the text of the Stuart royal family, read it, closed it, and opened his fiction to its interpenetrating presence. In the years immediately before *The Winter's Tale*, the royal family had experienced domestic family strife, the threat of destruction but deliverance in the Gunpowder Plot, the births and deaths of two royal children, the coming to court of Princess Elizabeth, the investiture of Prince Henry, and marriage negotiations for the royal children. If not these precise events, then surely the general pattern of the intertwined nature of royal family and politics, only vaguely hinted at in *Pandosto*, finds its way into the intertextual nature of *The Winter's Tale*. The statue of Hermione may be a paradigm for this intermingling of life and art. She seems a fiction but is real—thus in the play. The family of history invades the family of art, providing thereby a re-presentation of the Jacobean royal family. To close his various texts is not to discard them, for Shakespeare finds in these closings an aperture. In words that seem especially appropriate for *The Winter's Tale*, Northumberland in *Richard II* says: "Even through the hollow eyes of death, / I spy life peering" (II.i.270–71). The court audience of 1613 must have seen that idea in the play as the royal family renews, expands itself through marriage, even though a royal son has died. In England, as in Sicily, a royal heir exists, offering hope and stability for the kingdom.

THE TEMPEST

Though there are several travel pamphlets that we think Shakespeare knew and that may have influenced him in writing *The Tempest*, in fact little in these accounts corresponds to the overall structure and development of the play, despite an occasional parallel.[39] The royal families in the play owe part of their inspiration, I argue, to the text of the Jacobean royal family in which the dramatist could see for himself the interrelationship between the life of that family and the political issues of the kingdom. Along with *The Winter's Tale*, *The Tempest* received court performances in November 1611 and again in February 1613 at Princess Elizabeth's wedding festivities. No evidence exists for a performance earlier than the first one at court. Thus within a few days in 1611 and again in 1613, the royal family was able to watch performances of both plays. These plays re-present the politics of the Stuart royal family.

What did the royal family watching *The Tempest* see in it? Why was it performed at court again in 1613? If we had absolute answers to these questions, we would of course understand much about courtly aesthetic taste. What did the court audiences watching the royal family watching the play perceive about them and the play? Was the reaction in 1613 different from that of 1611? Certainly significant events had occurred in the royal family between these two performances. Responses to these teasing questions trail off into speculation because we cannot know the answers in any verifiable way. I think it unlikely, however, that James's family could have been impervious to the problems of the royal families in the play. James and his family had a perspective different from that of the rest of the audience—not only their physical location during performance but also their understanding of what a royal family is and does. At such a court performance I suspect a coalescence of the family of history and the family of art—a coming together of texts that Shakespeare was aware of. At court the living text of the Stuart royal family confronts the fictional text, just as each had faced the other in Shakespeare's mind. In the fictional rendition Shakespeare explores the politics of the family.

Many critics have chosen to view *The Tempest* as Shakespeare's valedictory to the stage; the Epilogue comes in for special scrutiny on this issue. Prospero is therefore Shakespeare's personal spokesman, if not Shakespeare himself. I think we must resist such an interpretation, however comforting it may be, however much we would like to put our finger on a given play and be assured that at that moment we have found the dramatist in his art. In fact, since *Henry VIII* was presumably written after *The Tempest*, we immediately encounter difficulties with the earlier play's being Shakespeare's farewell to the theater.

Subordinating the magic and mystery of the play, several critics have focused on its politics. Christopher Morris, for example, has called attention to the political nature of *The Tempest*, with its themes of imagined ''state of nature'' and of a Utopia. Morris suggests: ''It may not be entirely fanciful to suppose that, among all the layers and levels of his last play *The Tempest*, there lies concealed Shakespeare's political testament.''[40] Morris's emphasis on politics in the play is surely on the right track, though whether we can find Shakespeare's personal ideas on politics therein is doubtful. Glynne Wickham has linked politics and James's family by identifying characters in the play with members of the royal family. Thus, Miranda, for example, is

Princess Elizabeth and Ferdinand, one of Elizabeth's suitors.[41] Wickham argues that the prospects for peace brighten throughout Europe if "men will only follow James's example in abjuring revenge and placing their faith in the 'brave new world' of the younger generation: wage peace, not war" (Wickham, p. 13). Certainly, as I demonstrated in chapter 2, James was not beyond practicing a little revenge himself, especially if one considers the sad case of his relationship with and treatment of Arbella Stuart, or if one considers his policy toward Ireland. The moral, uplifting political vision that Wickham suggests, however desirable, cannot reflect actual practice, nor are the political ideas of the play quite that simple.

For Gary Schmidgall the play contains "a statement about *homo civilis*—about the 'fair and reasonable blending together' of men into a society, about the renovation of a political structure, and about the self-education of its fallen ruler in the skills and magnanimity of an ideal governor."[42] Prospero and Caliban are "complex political archetypes," and the central themes "are eminently political" (p. 155). Of the themes that Schmidgall discusses, I particularly want to examine two: the theme of peaceful succession and the theme of royal lineage and heritage. Both tie in with the politics of the family. Two related ideas permeate the royal family in *The Tempest:* redemption and adoption. Redeeming the political state by repairing relationships in the royal family and expanding the political and dynastic base by adopting others into the family constitute a major part of the play's emphasis on the politics of the family.

As has been evident in the other Romances, so here in *The Tempest:* acts of interpretation tie in to the text of the royal family. Jonathan Goldberg writes with regard to *Measure for Measure:* "Representation includes acts of restatement and of interpretation as well as the dramatic act of renaming."[43] Such is true also in *The Tempest* where representation occurs as substitution and replacement, primarily the removal of the false substitute Antonio so that Prospero may be eventually represented by Miranda—the by now familiar situation of succession through the female line. Like King James, Prospero will be replaced by his progeny: such succession forms an integral part of the politics of the royal family, whether real or fictional. More than elsewhere in the Romances, Shakespeare explores here the issue of the false claimant to power, a possible representation of King James's arduous efforts to block claimants to the English throne. In the ultimate union of Naples and Milan, not by treachery but by a royal marriage, Shakespeare echoes the situation in *Pericles, The Winter's Tale,* and, to a lesser extent, *Cymbeline,* where Pentapolis and Tyre, Sicily and Bohemia, and Rome and Britain experience a new union. In the Romances the persistent pattern of concern for two kingdoms in each play represents the ongoing attempt to define the precise links between England and Scotland, not that Shakespeare's mythical kingdoms are Scotland and England, but rather that the political issue prevails in the actual and fictional situations. One recalls James's desire for and pursuit of a formal Act of Union, an action that Parliament perversely chose not to take. I will argue then that James and his family are re-presented in *The Tempest* through the issues of peaceful succession, royal genealogy, interpretation, and the union of the kingdoms. Politics and especially politics of the royal family predominate in a play that at first glance may seem remote from the rough-and-tumble world of political reality. But D. W. Harding observes that "the last act of *The Tempest* keeps in sight the realities of power and politics in a Renaissance court."[44] In pursuit of these topics I will focus on the political worlds of King Alonso and his family (his daughter Claribel and his son Ferdinand); Prospero, his brother, and Miranda; and on Caliban, who serves primarily as a parody of the royal families.

Unlike the other Romances, *The Tempest* begins with "*a tempestuous noise of thunder and lightning heard*" (S.D.),[45] prelude to a seastorm. Amidst the desperate and unsuccessful efforts of the sailors, we also see King Alonso of Naples, his son Ferdinand, his brother Sebastian, the counselor Gonzalo, and Antonio, brother to Prospero. What these members of royal families are doing together, where they have been, and why they have come to this island, the opening scene does not answer. In fact, the scene in many ways is puzzling. Despite life-threatening circumstances, the scene has what no other storm in Shakespeare has: a sense of humor.[46] The Boatswain, for example, accuses the King's party of getting in the way: "You mar our labour: keep your cabins: you do assist the storm" (I.i.13–14). He wryly urges Gonzalo as counselor to the king to try his skills at calming the storm. Gonzalo notes the Boatswain's gallows-type humor. Antonio and Sebastian in contrast chide the Boatswain severely: Sebastian says, "A pox o' your throat, you bawling, blasphemous, incharitable dog!" (40–41); and Antonio says, "Hang, cur! hang, you whoreson, insolent noisemaker" (43–44). Their harshness corresponds to what we see of them later, as it also duplicates the storm itself.

The storm's turbulence represents, as Schmidgall has suggested, discord in the political state. Of course, we cannot know that yet, but it does become a symbol for the political disturbance of twelve years earlier in Italy where Prospero was deposed. It may also epitomize, I think, conflict in the royal families, thereby affecting politics. A note of resignation, perhaps peace, comes in Gonzalo's portrait of the King and his son: "The King and Prince at prayers, let's assist them, / For our case is as theirs" (53–54). Prospero, another royal father, will echo Alonso and Ferdinand in the play's Epilogue: "*And my ending is despair, / Unless I be reliev'd by prayer . . .*" (15–16). In this case Prospero asks for our assistance. The opening scene closes with the desperate cries of the sailors and Gonzalo's statement of resignation: "The wills above be done! but I would fain die a dry death" (66–67). Never has the beginning of a play seemed so like an ending. We have apparently just witnessed the destruction of a royal family and others.

What is Shakespeare doing? For one thing, he plays on the double meaning of *tempus:* both "storm" and "time." What appears to be the end of time is in fact the beginning of a measure of time, one afternoon on Prospero's island in the Mediterranean. We may recall Mary Queen of Scots's statement: "In my end is my Beginning." Shakespeare imposes another sense of time by carefully observing the unity of time, as he had in *The Comedy of Errors*, also set in the Mediterranean world, but certainly not observed in the other Romances, where as much as sixteen years may transpire. Allowing for differences, one may generalize and say that *The Tempest* begins in Act IV of *The Winter's Tale*. Because time is so short in the play, we get a truncated view of the royal families, a glimpse by comparison with the other late plays.

Shakespeare also emphasizes the time preceding the play, that is, the twelve years before the play opens. Though we see only one afternoon, it resonates with all the experiences that have preceded it: the past is prologue, as Antonio notes (II.i.248). By interweaving the twelve preceding years into the experience of an afternoon, Shakespeare enables us to understand more about the families than we could have if only allowed to view them from the perspective of a few hours. Paradoxically, in narrowing the focus to a brief moment in time, Shakespeare actually opens the lens to a much larger view. We cannot capture the royal family in a single moment without also perceiving the events that led to that instant. The court audience watching James and his family at the performances of the play must have felt similarly about them: November 1611 and February 1613 resound with the experiences that constitute that moment. Hence, given what the Stuart family had endured by 1613, the audience is likely to view the family somewhat differently from November 1611. Gazing on the Stuart royal family in 1613, rejoicing beyond a common joy at the wedding of Elizabeth, the audience also saw a family that had recently suffered the death of its Prince Henry. In seeing Prospero on his island one storm-interrupted afternoon, we also see him in Milan twelve years earlier, losing his political kingdom.

When we learn in I.ii that Prospero has caused the storm to suit his purposes, we gain another meaning of time: this is the right time, the propitious moment. Events unfold by design, not by accident. The time has come not only for Prospero to gather his enemies on the island but also to reveal to Miranda her true royal heritage. By so doing, Prospero grants her new life as daughter to the Duke of Milan. Twelve years intervene before Prospero deems the moment ripe for giving Miranda a new identity. Redeeming himself and his political foes and "adopting" Miranda as a royal daughter and eventually Ferdinand as son, Prospero gains control of his Italian kingdom and solidifies his dynastic lineage. The politics of the royal family clearly operates. Time in the play is therefore both *chronos* (a measure) and *kairos* (a quality).

On the subject of the ripeness of time, Lancelot Andrewes, one of King James's favorite preachers, spoke eloquently in a sermon preached before the royal family in Whitehall on Christmas Day 1609. Andrewes's sermon takes as its text a portion of a Pauline epistle: "when the fulness of the time was come, God sent forth his Son, made of woman, made under the law, to redeem them that were under the law, that we might receive the adoption of sons" (Galatians 4:4-5, King James Version). I do not contend that Shakespeare necessarily heard or knew the sermon, but several of Andrewes's ideas intersect *The Tempest,* I think. The fulness of time that Andrewes examines is, of course, the Nativity; the topic inherently links the process of time and family life—a link that I also see in *The Tempest.* Speaking of the two kingdoms in his first address to Parliament (1604), James said: "In the end and fulnesse of time vnited, the right and title of both in my Person, alike lineally descended of both the Crownes, whereby it [kingdom] is now become like a little World within it selfe."[47] Through his royal genealogy, James claims both kingdoms at the appropriate time, the kairotic moment.

Andrewes pursues the meaning of the "fulness of time," suggesting that it can mean either *plenitudo temporis* (fulness of time) or *tempus plenitudinis* (a time of fulness).[48] Time is a "measure; it hath a capacity; that hath a fulness," Andrewes writes (p. 47). He uses the metaphor of time as a "cask" that is filled, but "that wherewith it is filled doth more concern us" (p. 50). Andrewes defines this time of fulness:

> For till then all was but in promise, in shadows and
> figures and prophecies only, which fill not, God knows.
> But when the performance of those promises, the body of
> those shadows, the substance of those figures, the
> fulfilling or filling full of all those prophecies came,
> then came "the fulness of time," truly so called. (P. 49)

Dreams realized equal a time of fulness; so *The Tempest* also demonstrates. The preceding twelve years and the voyage of Alonso's party constitute the *plenitudo temporis;* subsequent events on the island provide the *tempus plenitudinis.* Surely the play is also about redemption, which Andrewes defines as "a second buying, or buying back of a thing before aliened or sold" (p. 57). The alienation and separation of twelve years will yield to reconciliation and redemption as Prospero forgives his brother and King Alonso.

Andrewes reminded his listeners on Christmas that there are twelve days to the season, a time of fulness, in which they are to celebrate the birth, a "fulness of thanks or thankfulness" to follow the "fulness of joy" of the Nativity (1:61). I would like to call *The Tempest* a "Twelfth Night" play, using that designation as a metaphor for the play. The twelve years of *The Tempest* correspond to the Twelve Days of Christmas, culminating in Epiphany. My suggestion complements John Bender's imaginative essay in which he draws religious and liturgical connections between the play and the date of its first recorded performance, Hallowmas 1611.[49] "Read as a play for Hallowmas," Bender writes, *"The Tempest* becomes a conjuration against winter, a miniature reenactment of the annual endeavor to countermand the cold, dark fearful out-of-doors through indoor revels" (p. 244).

Prospero makes manifest his identity and power to the travelers who have come to the island; such a revelation changes some of the characters and certainly redefines their relationships. These travelers, Alonso's party, had gone to a wedding at Tunis but end up at a "birth" on an enchanted island: birth of their redemption and reconciliation to Prospero and birth of the relationship of Ferdinand and Miranda. In a metaphorical sense, the shipwrecked party has been traveling twelve years to reach this moment and this island, where in the fulness of time revelation will come. The epiphany experience generates love and forgiveness, solidifying the royal families and setting free those captive to their own guilt. Like the Magi in Matthew's gospel account, the travelers and Prospero and Miranda will return home another way (Matthew 2:12), implying transformation. They will not be the same people who first came ashore on the island. What seemed like certain death to King Alonso, his family, and companions at the end of the play's opening scene turns out to be life; the sense of miracle is inescapable. Something wondrous happens: apparent closure actually becomes an aperture. The royal family survives, renewed in time, a time of redemption.

On Prospero's island three political spheres operate: Alonso, Caliban, and Prospero, each calling attention in a different way to the politics of the family. Before we see Alonso and his group safe, we hear Prospero assure Miranda that no harm has come to those on the ship (I.ii.14) and Ariel's testimony of what he has done: "In troops I have dispers'd them 'bout the isle. / The King's son have I landed by himself . . ." (I.ii.220-21). We will shortly see Ferdinand wandering about alone, separated from the others. Accompanying ships, the rest of the fleet, have headed "sadly home for Naples; / Supposing that they saw the King's ship wrack'd, / And his great person perish" (235-37). If so, they will return to Naples aware of the political problem of succession, the royal family having apparently been destroyed. But, in fact, they are all very much alive, as we see in II.i.

Their appearance in II.i opens with the cheerful words of Gonzalo: "Beseech you, sir, be merry; you have cause, / So have we all, of joy; for our escape / Is much beyond our loss" (II.i.1-3). For Gonzalo at least it is a time of joy. He refers to "the miracle, / I mean our preservation . . ." (6-7). That is exactly what it must seem like to this shipwrecked party, so overwhelming had been the prospect of death during the storm. Glynne Wickham has suggested that in Caliban's plot, one may see a reference to the Gunpowder treason. If the Stuart royal family watching this play wanted to make such connections, it might see in the miraculous deliverance of King Alonso such an analogy. Lancelot Andrewes, as I noted in chapter 1, preached the first Gunpowder sermon on 5 November 1606, calling attention precisely to the miracle of deliverance of the royal family. He observes that desolation was defeated: "All those, the King, Queen, Prince, Nobles, Bishops, Judges, both houses; alive all; not a hair of any of their heads perished; not so much as 'the smell of fire' on any their garments."[50] He repeats the image in his sermon of 5

185

November 1612. Perhaps Andrewes is the inspiration for Ariel's observation that of the shipwrecked group "Not a hair perish'd; / On their sustaining garments not a blemish . . ." (I.ii.217–18). Gonzalo pursues the miracle of their garments, which, despite being drenched in the sea, hold "their freshness and glosses, being rather new-dyed than stained with salt water" (II.i.60–62). Gonzalo's perspective recalls Edgar's comment to his blind father, who has ostensibly plunged from the cliff of Dover but has survived: "Thy life's a miracle" (*Lear*, IV.vi.55).

We hear several different voices in II.i: the cheerful, optimistic voice of Gonzalo; the despairing voice of Alonso, who has lost his royal son; and the cynical, conspiratorial voices of Antonio and Sebastian. The scene falls into two parts: the experience of relief at their safety yet the sense of Ferdinand's loss and the conspiracy of Antonio and Sebastian. Gonzalo's perspective on the world and life culminates in his vision of the ideal commonwealth (143–52, 155–64). A lack of strife and a spirit of innocence characterize Gonzalo's vision, leading him to assert: "I would with such perfection govern, sir, / T' excel the Golden Age" (163–64). This utopian dream of the political state prompts Alonso to say: "Prithee, no more: thou dost talk nothing to me" (166). Since utopia means "nowhere," Alonso may be punning on that concept. Because some people claimed that the early years of James's rule were a kind of Golden Age, a Pax Britannia, Gonzalo may be giving voice to that idea. But Alonso's response and the facts of the play demonstrate the impossibility of such a commonwealth. Watching this, King James must have been aware of the gap between such a vision and the facts of his own island kingdom: instead of a land of milk and honey, he found an empty treasury. The time of fulness surely had not come in the Jacobean court. Antonio and Sebastian's witty exchange with Gonzalo further deflates Gonzalo's grandiose, optimistic view of the world. Even on Prospero's island, for all its magic, the world is decidedly brazen, not golden.

The issue of political succession in the royal family permeates Alonso's thinking. With his daughter Claribel married in faraway Tunis and his son Ferdinand presumably dead, Alonso resembles a Cymbeline or a Leontes. Or a King James, who, when he saw the performance in 1613, had lost a son through death and was losing a daughter in marriage to a husband in another country, never to see her again. Though Prince Charles remained as heir to the throne, his sickly childhood raised doubts about the possibility of his serving as sovereign. Life imitates art, and art represents life. Alonso becomes a father-king in search of his son. His silence, contrasted with the garrulous voices of Gonzalo, Antonio, and Sebastian, testifies to the loss that he feels. To Gonzalo's initial cheerful urging that they all be merry, Alonso says simply, "Prithee, peace" (II.i.9). He tries to stifle the verbal sparring among the other three: "I prithee, spare" (24). The issue of Claribel opens when Gonzalo, waxing enthusiastic about their garments, observes that they are as fresh as when they put them on in Africa, "at the marriage of the King's fair daughter Claribel to the King of Tunis" (67–68). Sebastian responds ironically: " 'Twas a sweet marriage, and we prosper well in our return" (69–70). For the first time in the play we learn what Alonso's group has been doing before the storm and arrival on the island.

Responding to the talk about the trip to Tunis, Alonso eventually cries:

> You cram these words into mine ears against
> The stomach of my sense. Would I had never
> Married my daughter there! for, coming thence,
> My son is lost, and, in my rate, she too,
> Who is so far from Italy removed
> I ne'er again shall see her. (102–7)

His brother Sebastian puts the blame squarely on Alonso: "Sir, you may thank yourself for this great loss" (119), choosing to "loose" Claribel to "an African" rather than to some prince of Europe. "You were kneel'd to," Sebastian continues, "and importun'd otherwise, / By all of us . . ." (124–25). Exactly why Alonso has made this political decision regarding the marriage he does not clarify. At the moment the politics of this royal family seems all awry, highlighting the seriousness of the consequences of decisions about marriages for the royal children, a point doubtless in the minds of the court audience in both 1611 and 1613. Did Princess Elizabeth or James later reflect on *The Tempest* as her life got ensnared in the political and military problems of Europe; did they remember Alonso and Claribel? Certainly those who had opposed Elizabeth's marriage to Frederick, such as Queen Anne, may have seen a special relevance in the Alonso-Claribel plight.

Sebastian finally says to his brother, "The fault's your own"; and Alonso quietly responds: "So is the dear'st o' th' loss" (131). Despite assurances from Francisco that Ferdinand "may live" (109–18), Alonso believes to the contrary: "No, no, he's gone" (118).

When Alonso awakens from his sleep, what almost became a nightmare, he urges: ''. . . let's make further search / For my poor son'' (318-19). Alonso begins another journey, looking for his son and heir. Without Ferdinand, Naples might well have no heir. Having survived the storm, having barely escaped death at the hands of Antonio and Sebastian (an action that re-presents the storm), Alonso desperately travels into the island, where in the fulness of time his son will be revealed to him, and epiphany will occur. Only then will the question of familial succession be resolved.

The *''Open-ey'd conspiracy,''* as Ariel calls it (296), of Antonio and Sebastian is blatantly political, a grab for power by destroying part of the royal family. Antonio and Sebastian thereby resemble Dionyza in *Pericles* and the Queen in *Cymbeline*, all willing to disrupt royal families for personal political gain. The tempter is Antonio, Prospero's brother and usurper of Milan; his arguments touch on political, historical, and moral issues. The fits and starts of Antonio's temptation echo the techniques of an Iago: ''What might, / Worthy Sebastian?— O, what might?— No more:— / And yet methinks I see it in thy face, / What thou shouldst be'' (199-202). Finally he reveals what he sees in his mind's eye: ''My strong imagination sees a crown / Dropping upon thy head'' (203-4). Sebastian begins vaguely to perceive what Antonio is suggesting: he sees in Antonio's manner ''a birth, indeed, / Which throes thee much to yield'' (225-26). Antonio gives birth to his idea of regicide and usurpation, a perverse ''birth'' to say the least. The scheme proceeds on Antonio's assumption about Ferdinand: '' 'Tis as impossible that he's undrown'd / As he that sleeps here swims'' (232-33). Antonio emphasizes the hopeful prospects ''that even / Ambition cannot pierce a wink beyond, / But doubt discovery there'' (236-38). Not the every wink that brought some new grace at the end of *The Winter's Tale*, this is indeed the opposite. ''Birth'' and ''discovery''—the twelve days of Christmas parodied in Antonio and Sebastian.

Probing the political matter begins with Antonio's question: ''Who's the next heir of Naples?'' (240). Claribel, who ''dwells / Ten leagues beyond man's life,'' is effectively out of the political picture as potential heir in Naples, a point that Alonso had himself made. As Sebastian says: '' 'twixt which regions [Naples and Tunis] / There is some space'' (251-52)—enough space to make plausible Sebastian's act in time. Historical promptings remind Sebastian that Antonio did supplant Prospero: ''True,'' answers Antonio, ''And look how well my garments sit upon me . . .'' (266-67). The past is prologue; ''what to come, / In yours and my discharge," Antonio says (248–49). Antonio and Sebastian ready themselves to enact a representation of the deposing of Prospero twelve years earlier. As brother of the king, Sebastian would assert his family prerogative in taking the crown; the politics of this royal family will take a new turn. Sebastian had earlier said: "Hereditary sloth instructs me" (218), one meaning of which is that the fault of being the younger brother to Alonso has limited his freedom and political potential. So long as Alonso's royal children live, Sebastian has no realistic hope for the kingdom.

Sebastian raises an additional political matter; he says to Antonio: "one stroke / Shall free thee from the tribute which thou payest; / And I the King shall love thee" (287–89). Antonio will be set free of his debt to Naples for assisting in the original overthrow of Prospero from Milan. The wedding of a royal daughter and the loss of a royal son mean for Antonio and Sebastian that the fulness of time has come. Only the intervening revelation by Ariel singing in Gonzalo's ear thwarts their intention; Ariel makes manifest to Gonzalo the danger to the royal person. Pericles, Cymbeline, and Leontes all know how vulnerable their kingdoms are without an heir, a point that King James must have been increasingly aware of early in 1613. Alonso is spared—another miracle in the play.

Wandering in the wilderness of Prospero's island, Alonso and his group grow weary; discouraged, Alonso says: "Even here I will put off my hope, . . . / . . . he [Ferdinand] is drown'd / Whom thus we stray to find . . ." (III.iii.7–9). And he says with resignation: "Well, let him go" (10). But Antonio and Sebastian confer with one another, reminding each other of their intention and hoping to gain the opportunity to strike that evening. Antonio warns Sebastian: "Do not, for one repulse, forego the purpose / That you resolv'd t' effect" (12–13). Two apparitions or epiphanies occur that change the spirit of this group: first, the banquet, which makes them incredulous. Even Alonso, however, decides to eat "since I feel / The best is past" (50–51). But the banquet vanishes when Ariel appears "*like a Harpy*" and addresses Alonso, Sebastian, and Antonio as "three men of sin, . . . you 'mongst men / Being most unfit to live" (53, 57–58).

Not only an epiphany, this is also a judgment. Ariel reminds them of the overthrow of Prospero, "for which foul deed / The powers, delaying, not forgetting, have / Incens'd the seas and shores, . . . / Against your peace" (72–75). Again one can argue that Alonso's group has been traveling toward this island for twelve years. Ariel turns to Alonso: "Thee of thy son, Alonso, / They have bereft; and do

189

pronounce by me / Ling'ring perdition" (75-77). The future is "nothing but heart-sorrow / And a clear life ensuing" (81-82). Alonso seems destined for a period of penance such as that experienced by Leontes. Alonso tells the perplexed Gonzalo what he has heard and reveals his feeling of desperation: "Therefor my son i' th' ooze is bedded; and / I'll seek him deeper than e'er plummet sounded, / And with him there lie mudded" (100-102). The twelve years of enjoying the fruit of Prospero's overthrow now accumulate at this moment to provoke guilt and recollection. Another manifestation will be needed in order to purge this guilt and set the group free—for this they have been spared the ravages of the storm. The process of redemption has begun. Before the day closes, a royal father will also find that which was lost. The political destiny of Naples will be clarified.

Caliban, who never poses a serious threat to Prospero, functions in part as a parody of the political insurrection of Antonio and Sebastian; by extension he may be a parody of the casting out of Prospero twelve years earlier in Milan. Critics have puzzled over what to make of Caliban; Frank Kermode, in the Arden edition, sees him as the "ground of the play" (p. xxv), the "focus of the play's ideas" (p. lxxvi). More recently, Jacqueline E. M. Latham has tried to make a case for King James's *Daemonologie* as a possible source for Caliban.[51] I think that Caliban's principal function, certainly in terms of the play's politics, is to parody the quest for power. At moments he recalls something of the spirit of Jacobean satiric comedy. Several critics, focusing on Prospero's magic, have linked the play to Jonson's *The Alchemist*,[52] but I find other plays by Jonson also appropriate. The acquisitive and sexual energy of Caliban finds its counterpart in the birds of prey in *Volpone*. Indeed, Caliban, a subhuman creature, fits into the animalistic world of *Volpone*, its characters consumed with greed. Sir Politic Would-be, crawling under a tortoise shell, may even look a bit like Caliban. Caliban's threat to orderly family life recapitulates the several dangers to family and marriage in *Epicoene*, in which one of the principal couples is the Otters. Like some of the characters in Middleton's *Chaste Maid*, Caliban would produce children in order to control the island, to gain an inheritance. To the extent that Caliban is a materialist, he resembles dozens of characters from satiric comedy.

Years earlier on the island, Caliban had seemed a member of Prospero's extended family, instructing Prospero about the island and being taught by him. Caliban confesses to Prospero: ". . . I lov'd thee . . ." (I.ii.338). But such familial harmony gave way to discord and disaffection when Caliban attempted to rape Miranda. Such an action represents dissolution in the family structure and harm to the social stability that Prospero has imposed on the island. Prospero explains to Caliban: "I have us'd thee, / . . . with human care; and lodg'd thee / In mine own cell, till thou didst seek to violate / The honour of my child" (347–50). This could be Cymbeline talking to Posthumus as he banishes him. Those brought into and nurtured by the court family sometimes dash expectations. Both Prospero and Cymbeline feel betrayed, let down in their own hopes. Caliban claims that if he had raped Miranda, he would have "peopled . . . / This isle with Calibans" (352–53). Here is the more serious threat of Caliban—not political overthrow with the help of Stephano and Trinculo but violation of the family bond. Caliban also resents Prospero's control of the island, which originally belonged to his mother Sycorax. Caliban says: "This island's mine, by Sycorax my mother, / Which thou [Prospero] tak'st from me" (333–34). He accuses Prospero of usurpation. If Caliban were somehow successful, he would be a threat to royal succession and lineage.

Apparent opportunity comes for him in the persons of Stephano and Trinculo, two who have survived the storm. In a scene (II.ii) that immediately follows Antonio and Sebastian's near success in killing Alonso, the unlikely trio of Caliban, Stephano, and Trinculo joins forces to take political control of the island, thereby parodying Antonio and Sebastian. Ironically, Caliban thinks that Stephano and Trinculo must surely be gods; he thus responds to the drunken Stephano: "That's a brave god, and bears celestial liquor: / I will kneel to him" (II.ii.118–19). Caliban promises: "I'll show thee every fertile inch o' th' island; and I will kiss thy foot: I prithee, be my god" (148–49). Caliban thus repeats his experience of twelve years earlier with the newly arrived Prospero. Having complained about being Prospero's subject, Caliban ironically accepts bondage to the unworthy Trinculo and Stephano.

The twin issues of politics and family permeate the trio's plans. Even though drunk, Stephano makes a shrewd political assessment: "Trinculo, the King and all our company else being drown'd, we will inherit here" (II.ii.174–75). Such an analysis also governs the thoughts of Antonio and Sebastian. But Caliban opens to his partners another world on the island: Prospero and his daughter, an obstacle to overcome before inheriting the island. Trinculo inadvertently captures the inherent limitations of his group's intention: "They say there's but five upon this isle: we are three of them; if th' other two be brain'd like us, the state totters'' (III.ii.4–6). The technique for overthrowing Prospero, Caliban explains, is to catch him asleep and there "thou mayst knock a nail into his head" (60)—shades of Antonio and Sebastian's plan to kill Alonso. Caliban also insists that they steal Prospero's books without which he has no power: ''. . . without them / He's but a sot, as I am . . .'' (90–91).

In addition to the political power that may be wrested from Prospero, potential sexual power awaits in capturing his daughter. Caliban explains to the others about Miranda, "a nonpareil . . .'' (98). He adds: ''. . . she will become thy bed, I warrant, / And bring thee forth brave brood'' (102–3). Stephano has his own vision of a brave new world on the island: "Monster, I will kill this man: his daughter and I will be king and queen, . . . and Trinculo and thyself shall be viceroys'' (104–6). Though ludicrous, this plot has its counterpart in many examples of those who would gain political power, in this case not by orderly succession but by violence. To solidify political gain, the usurper establishes a family and produces progeny to succeed him. In miniature, and making allowances, here is the oft-repeated pattern of political states. As the royal fathers understand throughout the Romances and as King James understood, political control gains in strength and is less vulnerable when heirs exist. Caliban's conspiracy, of course, comes to naught; his partners easily stray from their goal when Ariel dazzles them with glistering apparel. Caliban senses the lost opportunity: "we shall lose our time . . .'' (IV.i.247). Though aware of the fulness of time, Caliban fails in bringing it to fruition.

The third political sphere on the island is Prospero, who in fact controls the other two. Prospero brings into sharp focus the re-presentation of the Stuart royal family. Issues of political succession, royal lineage, redemption and adoption, substitution, and interpretation pervade even the first scene (I.ii) in which Prospero and Miranda appear; here he demonstrates control of the island. This long scene introduces this royal father and daughter, his helpful spirit Ariel, the beast Caliban, and Alonso's son Ferdinand, very much alive. The scene explores both the fulness of time and, at the end, the time of fulness. The dominant tense is the past, though that changes in the final section, where Ferdinand represents both the present and the future. Exploring the past, Prospero endows his royal daughter with an identity as she comes to realize that her father has been a prince, is still rightful Duke of Milan. To understand heritage and lineage is essential for any royal child, as we have seen throughout the Romances. Discussions with Prospero provide Miranda a kind of "birth," an awareness of who she is; the process of this unfolding information resembles an epiphany for her. After fifteen years, she knows who she is and who her father is: self-discovery and familial discovery. Revelations in this scene highlight the twelve years of *The Tempest* that converge in one afternoon because the fulness of time has come. Prospero redeems Miranda's past and adopts her as a royal daughter, all leading to the prospect of a time of fulness.

Putting aside his magical garment, Prospero begins: "The hour's now come; / The very minute bids thee ope thine ear . . ." (I.ii. 36–37); the time is ripe. Prospero as a ruler has been for Miranda until this moment an opaque text, carefully guarding his state secrets. His former life in Milan having been surrounded by books, Prospero highlights the matter of interpretation. Opening the book of rulers and of the past, Prospero unfolds the secrets of his text, of himself. He begins by asking Miranda what she can recollect from the "dark backward and abysm of time" (50). Prospero will shine a great light into that darkness, illuminating the past. The only thing that Miranda remembers is having been attended by four or five women (47), a sign of her royal upbringing. Prospero tells her: "Twelve year since, Miranda, twelve year since, / Thy father was the Duke of Milan, and / A prince of power" (53–55). Miranda is the "only heir / And princess, no worse issued" (58–59). This startling revelation means that Miranda will never be the same again. Recovering his past and exposing it, Prospero begins his own catharsis. It is as important for him to reveal his princely identity as it is for Miranda to learn it. Presumably for the first time in twelve years, Prospero speaks about his own lineage. He becomes, for Miranda at least, duke of Milan for the first time; he begins the process of freeing himself from the political prison of the island. Revealing royal heritage of parent and child surely represents a relationship well understood in the Jacobean royal family. Prospero grants Miranda her royal genealogy as he confirms his own in her—again possible succession through the female line. Having gained his crowns through his mother and Princess Margaret, James gives a royal heritage to his children. The remaining few hours of *The Tempest* will firmly establish the politics of the family.

The story of Antonio's ouster of Prospero from Milan vibrates with the interconnections of politics and family. That Antonio is Prospero's brother compounds the heinous quality of the crime. As Prospero begins this section of revelation, he says to Miranda: "I pray thee, mark me, that a brother should / Be so perfidious!—he whom next thyself / Of all the world I lov'd . . ." (67–69). Much of the blame, of course, rests with Prospero himself as he to his "state grew stranger, being transported / And rapt in secret studies" (76–77). Ironically, the trust that Prospero had placed in Antonio, "Like a good parent" (94), had created falsehood instead. Antonio desired not only revenue but also Prospero's power; ultimately, "he did believe / He was indeed the duke . . ." (102–3). Usurpation comes as a result of Prospero's political negligence and of Antonio's grasping for power. The sacred bond of the royal family has cracked.

One wonders if James saw himself in any of this. I do not mean the identification often mentioned between Prospero as magician-theologian-scholar and James's interest in such matters, though James may have made such connections. I refer instead to the political issue of the prince's neglect of his kingdom. As I documented in chapter 2, James paid attention to problems of state only under intense pressure by the likes of Cecil and others. He much preferred to hunt and indulge himself, and he was occasionally guilty of neglecting his family. Like James in England, Prospero was the wisest fool in Milan. At least on the island, Prospero acknowledges his political fault; he has had twelve years to think about it. The fulness of time has come, and Prospero acts to regain his kingdom.

The problem in Milan, as Prospero tells Miranda, has come because he cast the function of government upon his brother. Antonio becomes the substitute ruler, a representation of Prospero. Unfortunately, Prospero lacks the power-in-absence that the Duke has in *Measure for Measure,* as Goldberg points out, or that Pericles had in Tyre, or that King James had. This quality, Goldberg notes (p. 225), was one of the modes of absolutist power characteristic of James. Prospero refers to the matter of substitution (l. 103) and to how Antonio became a false claimant, clouding the issue of succession. In a puzzling image Prospero says: "To have no screen between this part he play'd / And him he play'd it for, he needs will be / Absolute Milan" (107–9). Antonio violates the principle of re-presentation by becoming the thing itself. With the connivance of the King of Naples, Antonio completes the process of substitution. One thing that Prospero will accomplish before the day is over is to regain his dukedom and to remove Antonio, thereby installing Miranda eventually as the true substitute, the genuine representation of himself. As with King James and the other royal fathers in the Romances, royal children will succeed their parents in an orderly, legitimate succession.

Ferdinand becomes an essential part of Prospero's plan; he opens a political and dynastic future. In fact, the royal families of

Naples and Milan now begin to intertwine in love rather than in the political intrigue of twelve years earlier. He and Miranda jointly will resolve the problem of succession and will help to redeem the kingdoms. Though Ferdinand is the last character to be dealt with in I.ii, he becomes the first. When we initially see him, he describes his plight, "Sitting on a bank, / Weeping again the King my father's wrack . . ." (I.ii.392-93). Ferdinand has been charmed by Ariel's music and brought to this spot by Ariel. Prospero explains to the dazzled Miranda that Ferdinand is not a spirit but a "gallant" who has been in the shipwreck and is "something stain'd / With grief . . ." (417-18). Not even knowing Miranda's name, Ferdinand nevertheless unconsciously reveals it when he sees her: "O you wonder!" (429).

Believing his father dead, Ferdinand asserts his position as king of Naples: "myself am Naples, / Who with mine eyes, never since at ebb, beheld / The King my father wrack'd" (437-39). He promises Miranda: ". . . I'll make you / The Queen of Naples" (451-52). This royal son understands succession quite well; without a father, then he may himself determine who his queen will be—such an intention was for Florizel in *The Winter's Tale* simple impertinence. Antonio and Sebastian, Stephano and Trinculo, and Ferdinand all understand the political implications of King Alonso's death. Ferdinand differs because there is no violence in his purpose. Prospero, however, pretends that Ferdinand has some political design for the island: Ferdinand is "Upon this island as a spy, to win it / From me, the lord on't" (458-59). Such is, in fact, the intention of Caliban's group, not of Ferdinand. Prospero, for Ferdinand, constitutes both an opaque and a transparent text.

If Ferdinand survives Prospero's tests, as he will, then a time of fulness will begin: the personal and political future for Milan and Naples will expand in ways that no one had anticipated. A short afternoon on Prospero's island can lead to a long, ever-extending future as these royal children constitute the next generation of rulers, a clear example of the politics of the family at work. Enduring the toil placed on him by Prospero, Ferdinand assures Miranda: "I am, in my condition, / A prince, Miranda; I do think, a King . . ." (III.i.59-60). Miranda promises to be his wife and queen. At such a moment, they resemble Florizel and Perdita. Their love will, of course, eventually translate into politics, affecting the future of the two kingdoms. In dealing with Ferdinand, Prospero exhibits a kind of political mastery that had been absent twelve years earlier in Milan.

By Act IV, Ferdinand, having passed all of Prospero's tests, gains the assurance of Miranda from Prospero, who says: "here, afore Heaven, / I ratify this my rich gift" (IV.i.7–8). In a sense regaining his daughter by conferring royal identity on her, Prospero resembles the Duke in Day's *Law-Tricks*; in awarding his daughter to Ferdinand, Prospero resembles the King in *Philaster*. Prospero also says that he gives "a third of mine own life" (3) to Ferdinand. Kermode in the Arden edition surveys various interpretations of this puzzling phrase. I find especially interesting the idea that Prospero, who has taken care of Miranda for fifteen years, gives that third, that period of time, to Ferdinand. This would make Prospero forty-five years old (Kermode, p. 93n.3). King James was forty-five at the time of the first court performance, and Elizabeth, fifteen. Soon they, too, would be involved in marriage negotiations for her. By the time of the 1613 performance, all such plans had come to fruition, as James gives his daughter to a foreign prince. No one in the court audience in 1613 could have failed to perceive the relevance. In 1611, Shakespeare and the audiences were aware that James had both a son and a daughter of marriageable age. Without insisting on identification, one at least sees how the play re-presents the Stuart royal family. Ferdinand hopes for "quiet days, fair issue and long life . . ." (IV.i.24)—"fair issue" will, of course, confer stability on the kingdom, a point that King James obviously understood but one that looked different in 1613 from the earlier expectations in 1611.

Celebrating the nuptial agreement, Prospero presents a masque, a "vanity" of his art. Nothing in the Jacobean courtly aesthetic offers a more immediate, more explicit image of the king's power than does a court masque which, among other things, regularly asserts, confirms, and celebrates the absolutist power of James. Texts of Jacobean masques stand behind the text of Prospero's masque. Though James was not the author of the masques performed in his presence, he was the begetter, the sponsor, of them. In the play Prospero creates the masque, a dramatic expression that demonstrates his power of illusion. Certainly this masque reflects a dramatic context peculiar to the Jacobean court. Special pleasure must have attended those at court who watched Prospero's masque and saw in it and through it other masques that honored the court and the royal family. King James and his family watch Prospero and his family watching the masque; in that stage image is a re-presentation of the Stuart royal family. Because the King's Men appeared as performers in court masques and because on at least two occasions they performed *The*

Tempest at court, one readily understands the play's masque as evoking dramatic experiences that the Jacobean court had shared. Prospero's masque interprets, re-presents a Jacobean masque.

Caught up in the spectacle, Ferdinand cries out at one point: "Let me live here ever; / So rare a wonder'd father and a wise [wife] / Makes this place Paradise" (IV.i.122-24). But of course, Ferdinand does not know about the conspiracies of Caliban and of Antonio and Sebastian, which make this island something less than Paradise, help make it indeed human. Perhaps some spectators at Jacobean court masques also thought for a moment their kingdom Paradise; reality, however, always lurked outside the Banqueting House—a kingdom of familial and political strife as well as a place of glorious and spectacular events. Prospero's idyllic and idealistic masque lasts but a moment, a mere illusion, the product of his imagination. Like many actual masques, it serves two purposes: a celebration of the *"contract of true love"* (84) and a bestowing of gifts on the lovers. Celebrating married love focuses on the family. Bestowing the gift of plenty assures a peaceful kingdom.

Much has been said about Prospero's masque (see Kermode's introduction, pp. lxxi-lxxvi), including the idea that it was added for the 1613 performance at the wedding festivities—an attractive theory but difficult to substantiate. With only one text of the play, that in the Folio, we cannot know whether it is a faithful version of the earlier performances. One can argue that the masque works just as well in 1611, if without the 1613 immediacy, because of anticipated weddings for both Elizabeth and Henry. Some critics have explored connections between Prospero's masque and several of Jonson's masques, especially *Hymenaei* (see, for example, Schmidgall, pp. 223-25).

I briefly direct attention to the first masque performed at the new Stuart court, that by Samuel Daniel, *The Vision of the Twelve Goddesses*, performed on 8 January 1604. I do not try to establish indebtedness, but rather I see Daniel's masque, performed at the instigation of Queen Anne, as an analogue to Prospero's (Shakespeare's) masque. Represented by spirits, the three goddesses who appear in the play— Iris, Juno, and Ceres—also have parts in Daniel's masque. Daniel in a letter to the Countess of Bedford, who performed in the masque, describes the costumes for two of the actors: "First Juno, in a sky-colour mantle embroidered with gold and figured with peacocks' feathers, wearing a crown of gold on her head . . ."; "Ceres, in straw colour and silver embroidery with ears of corn and a dressing of the same. . . ."[53] In the masque itself, Iris, "decked like the rainbow" (p.

197

32), descends from a mount. One can easily imagine that the staging of *The Tempest,* at least at court, may have evoked recollections of the costumes of these goddesses.

Daniel's goddesses bring gifts, twelve in number, left on Sibylla's altar, including: kingdoms large, mild love, true zeal, wealth, felicity, justice, concord, plenty, and pleasure (p. 36). The blessings of Juno and Ceres in *The Tempest* are also twelve in number: *"Honour, riches, marriage-blessing, / Long continuance, and increasing, / Hourly joys be still upon you!"* so says Juno (106–8). And Ceres adds:

> *Earth's increase, foison plenty,*
> *Barns and garners never empty; . . .*
> *Spring come to you at the farthest*
> *In the very end of harvest!* (110–15)

Ceres sings of harvest and spring—no winter's tale here. The twelve blessings of Juno and Ceres resemble gifts of the Christmas season, culminating in Twelfth Night.

Why should Juno and Ceres be singled out to bless the marriage of Ferdinand and Miranda? Probably because Juno with her scepter represents power in the kingdom, political mastery; and Ceres embodies the plenty of harvest, a time of fulness. Such is explicit in Daniel's letter to the countess, in which he refers to Juno as "the Goddess of empire and *regnorum praesidi,"* who brings the blessing of power (p. 26), and to Ceres, who brings "plenty." Peace and plenty have been associated with English sovereigns for a long time, especially in James's 1604 royal entry into London. They were embodied in Pericles as he arrived to save the starving people of Tharsus. These ideas capture hope for the younger generation of royal children, enjoying the political peace that may come through "fair issue," as Ferdinand says, and economic plenty. Juno says to Ceres: *"Go with me / To bless this twain, that they may prosperous be, / And honour'd in their issue"* (103–5). This purpose echoes Oberon's instructions at the end of *A Midsummer Night's Dream:* "To the best bride-bed will we, / Which by us shall blessed be; / And the issue there create / Ever shall be fortunate" (V.i.392–95). Venus and Cupid are conspicuously absent from the masque because they imply "wanton" love (94–101). The emphasis here falls on familial love and an implicit political future with royal progeny. Prospero's island, neither Ephesus (the home of Diana) nor Paphos (the home of Venus), centers on family.

In the play, Iris introduces the goddesses and has the concluding speech before the Reapers appear and then suddenly vanish. So in

Daniel's masque. Iris prepares the way for the goddesses in words that echo in the play: ". . . well may'st thou there observe their shadows . . ." (p. 32). The Sibylla wonders if she has merely dreamed the presence of Iris: "It can be but a dream: . . . But what prospective is this? . . . O admirable Powers! What sights are these?" (p. 33). Ferdinand refers to the "most majestic vision" (118) of the masque and wonders if the characters he sees may be but spirits (120). Prospero cuts off the masque when he recalls the threat of Caliban; he also confirms that the actors were all "spirits, and / Are melted into air, into thin air" (149–50). Iris, in Daniel's masque, remarks that the divine powers who have appeared: ". . . having clothed themselves with these appearances do now return back again to the spheres of their own being from whence they came" (p. 36). Prospero reminds us that our little lives are rounded with a sleep. Night, in Daniel's masque, says: "And so, bright visions, go, and entertain / All round about whilst I'll sleep again" (p. 32). As in actual masques, so in Prospero's: the performers are mere representations of mythic or symbolic figures.

Prospero's nuptial vision, imaged in the masque, has its earlier counterpart in Gonzalo's utopian vision of the ideal commonwealth. But Prospero remains fully cognizant of the discrepancy between the imagined world and the brazen world that we inhabit. Both Daniel's masque and Prospero's celebrate the kingdom by the offering of gifts, underscoring again, I think, the inextricable link between royal family and politics. The marriage vision of Prospero's masque is as political as it is fanciful. The masque ratifies the forthcoming wedding of Ferdinand and Miranda, a marriage fraught with possibilities for the kingdoms of Naples and Milan. Dynastic succession will be confirmed in their union; peace will reign in these kingdoms from which Prospero has been disaffected.

The last act brings the families together as Prospero orchestrates his greatest scene, filled with epiphanies and new beginnings: the fulness of time has arrived—"time / Goes upright with his carriage," Prospero says (V.i.2–3). This last act also brings together issues that we have seen operating throughout the play: political succession, royal lineage, interpretation, and union of the kingdoms. The first revelation is self-revelation as Prospero responds to the compassion for Alonso's group demonstrated in Ariel, leading to his great assertion: "the rarer action is / In virtue than in vengeance" (27–28). Prospero acknowledges that the power of love is greater than the love of power. When he abjures his rough magic and promises to drown his book, Prospero turns his back on his immediate past.

Before he makes known his presence to the King's party, Prospero outlines their sins of political ursurpation and familial dishonor and offers his forgiveness, his rarest action. The group stands transfixed, statuelike, until Prospero releases them from the charm and appears to them as himself. Shakespeare in a sense inverts the statue scene of *The Winter's Tale*. Finally after Ariel's song, the figures begin to move and speak. Prospero assures them "that a living Prince / Does now speak to thee . . ." (108–9). Reminiscent of Leontes, Alonso says: "Whether thou be'st he or no, / Or some enchanted trifle to abuse me, / . . . I not know: thy pulse / Beats, as of flesh and blood . . ." (111–14). Prospero is no more a statue or apparition than was Hermione.

Immediately Alonso changes: "Thy dukedom I resign, and do entreat / Thou pardon me my wrongs" (118–19). Alonso responds both as a ruler and as a guilty person. Prospero turns to his brother: "For you, most wicked sir, whom to call brother / Would even infect my mouth, I do forgive / Thy rankest fault . . ." (130–32). He also requires his dukedom from Antonio. Securing Milan, Prospero replaces the false substitute Antonio with his daughter, who will be the true representation of her father. Interestingly, the text provides no hint of how Antonio responds to this forgiveness; whether there is language in his gesture, eloquence in his dumbness, we do not know. Epiphany seems not to touch Antonio very deeply; this is not Paradise.

Given Prospero's knowledge and power, Alonso wants to know where he has lost Ferdinand: "Irreparable is the loss; and patience / Says it is past her cure" (140–41). Prospero insists that he has suffered a "like loss": ". . . I / Have lost my daughter" (147–48). Alonso with a lost son and Prospero with a lost daughter resemble Polixenes and Leontes. Alonso will have no heir if that which is lost be not found. Incredulous that Prospero has endured a comparable loss, Alonso says: "O heavens, that they were living both in Naples, / The King and Queen there!" (149–50), presumably referring to Ferdinand and Miranda—a statement that has prophetic force. Suddenly Prospero reveals "Ferdinand *and* Miranda *playing at chess*" (171 S.D.). Alonso fears that this is but an illusion: "If this prove / A vision of the island, one dear son / Shall I twice lose" (175–77). Alonso wonders if Miranda is a goddess "that hath sever'd us, / And brought us thus together?" (187–88). Ferdinand assures his father that Miranda is mortal, the daughter of Prospero, "of whom I have / Receiv'd a second life; and second father / This lady makes him to me" (194–96).

Ferdinand, who has been "adopted" by Prospero, makes clear the interconnections of the two royal families, a link that has political implications as well.

Gonzalo offers a benediction for this royal couple: "Look down, you gods, / And on this couple drop a blessed crown!" (201–2). In one sense, that has already been done in the masque in Act IV, but of course the goddesses as mere actors melted into air. Gonzalo praises Ferdinand and Miranda further: "For it is you that have chalk'd forth the way / Which brought us hither" (203–4). The royal children have led them; they stand on the verge of the Promised Land of political peace between Milan and Naples, cemented by the love of these children. Small wonder that Gonzalo launches into his interpretation of the text of the play, his own reading or misreading of what has happened, beginning: "Was Milan thrust from Milan, that his issue / Should become Kings of Naples?" (205–6). This is the new political reality, the new political order, with Prospero restored to his rightful kingdom. Only in a narrow sense can one talk about Prospero's eventual loss of Milan through its being controlled by Naples. The emphasis should be where Gonzalo places it: Prospero's heirs through Miranda will be rulers of Naples, a much greater political entity. Dynastic marriage clarifies succession in the kingdoms. The political situation at the end of *The Tempest* resembles that at the end of *Pericles* and *The Winter's Tale:* Tyre will be linked to Pentapolis, and Sicily and Bohemia will be joined through the marriage of Florizel and Perdita. These kingdoms endure not a diminution but an expansion. James expanded Scottish influence by becoming King of England: the kingdoms unite, and royal issue will assure that union.

Two minor epiphanies remain: the sudden appearance of the Boatswain and others, presumed dead, and the arrival of Caliban, Stephano, and Trinculo. Hearing the Boatswain's story and learning that the ship is as good as new, Alonso rightly observes: "These are not natural events" (227). Puzzled, he insists: "some oracle / Must rectify our knowledge" (244–45), thereby echoing *The Winter's Tale.* But no one in fact needs Apollo, for Prospero possesses sufficient knowledge to explain what has happened. Only the appearance of Caliban, whose treachery perhaps he can understand, gets a rise out of Antonio, who thinks this "fish" might be "marketable" (266). Prospero chides Stephano: "You'ld be King o' the isle, sirrah?" (287); to which Stephano meekly replies: "I should have been a sore one, then" (288). Caliban goes off to Prospero's cell, realizing what a "thrice-double ass" he has been to put his faith in the likes of a Stephano and Trinculo.

One final revelation: Prospero will spend the night recounting "the story of my life," especially the details of his life since he came to the isle. Is this not another re-viewing of the twelve years of *The Tempest*? As he began by revealing the past to Miranda, he will end his stay on the island by rehearsing that same past for the others. Having drowned his books of magic, Prospero opens to his hearers the text of his life, a book that has been opaque for twelve years but that now will be illuminated. In one sense the play comes full circle, beginning and ending with Prospero's interpretation of his story; such interpretation parallels Shakespeare's response to one of the texts for this play: the Jacobean royal family. Having suffered this day on Prospero's island, the visitors from Milan and Naples will while away the night listening to Prospero. Tomorrow the future opens: all will set sail for Naples, returning like the Magi to their homeland but by a different route. The fulness of time will become the time of fulness. What waits in the future is "the nuptial / Of these our dearbelov'd . . ." (308–9). The play has been but a prologue to the hope and expectation that attend the royal children, who assure dynastic succession and peace with a promise of fair issue. These children epitomize the hopes of the Jacobean court.

The play's Epilogue is conventional, not, I think, Shakespeare's farewell to the stage or his apology to King James for having used magic in the play.[54] Prospero does not entirely step out of his role in a self-conscious way to confront us as a mere actor. Indeed, Prospero mentions both the political and the personal accomplishment of his action: ". . . *Since I have my dukedom got, / And pardon'd the deceiver* . . ." (Epilogue, 6–7). Prospero notes that he lacks "*Art to enchant*" (14), which I take as his acknowledgment that his power of illusion has been but an illusion of power—at least in the real political world of Milan and Naples. Surely the last word of the Epilogue emerges from the play as well as reflects on it: "*Let your indulgence set me free*" (20). Characters in the action have been set free from the bondage of the past and from guilt. Naples and Milan have been freed from political uncertainty. Being set free means, of course, to be redeemed. If not entirely correct, Gonzalo comes close to the truth when he asserts that all of them have found themselves "When no man was his own" (V.i.213). Insofar as that has happened, we can echo Gonzalo's command: "O, rejoice / Beyond a common joy! and set it down / With gold on lasting pillars" (V.i.206–8). The royal family is whole; the kingdoms are secure—a hope for Milan and Naples and for England.

Like the discoverers and settlers of the New World, the travelers to this island have had many strange and wondrous experiences. Like the Magi, Ceres and Juno have brought gifts to the new royal couple. Like the Wise Men, Alonso and his group have brought themselves, have experienced the epiphany of Prospero's appearance, and have gone home changed people. Like the Stuart royal family, the royal families in the play have experienced the inextricable link of politics and family life. Like the royal family in 1611 and 1613, Prospero and Alonso stand ready to give away their royal children in marriage, with all the hopeful prospects that this entails. Like life itself, twelve years of existence converge in one small afternoon on a remote, unidentified island. Like the prophet Isaiah, Prospero means, through his actions and his Epilogue, to turn to the future, a time of fulness:

> Cease to dwell on days gone by
> and to brood over past history.
> Here and now I will do a new thing;
>   this moment it will break from the bud.
> Can you not perceive it? (Isaiah 43:18–20, New English Bible)

HENRY VIII

What play was being performed when the Globe Theatre burned in June 1613?"—so goes a common question on objective tests about Shakespeare. The answer is, of course, *Henry VIII*, or at least that is a reasonable conclusion from the external evidence. With that the knowledge of *Henry VIII* ceases for many people; apparently the 1613 fire has consumed their interest in this play. The play may have set the Globe on fire but not the world! Why a decade and a half after his last English history play does Shakespeare return to the subject of English history? Certainly history dramas were out of vogue by 1613. Did Shakespeare have some special reason for reviewing his country's past and Tudor history in particular? Are those earlier plays merely the prologue to this one? I will argue that James's royal family affects the occasion and the writing of *Henry VIII*. This play is, as I suggested at the beginning of this chapter, the culmination of Shakespeare's re-presentation of the Stuart royal family and the most explicit of all the Romances on the interconnection of the family of history and the families of art. The light may no longer be so oblique.

Like the other Romances, with the exception of *Pericles*, the first text of *Henry VIII* is in the Folio. Sir Henry Wotton's letter to Sir Edmund Bacon on 2 July 1613 leads to the conclusion that the play that he refers to as being performed when the theater burned was *Henry VIII*. Wotton writes: "The Kings Players had a new Play called *All is True*, representing some principal pieces of the Reign of *Henry 8*. which was set forth with many extraordinary Circumstances of Pomp and Majesty."[55] Wotton notes that during the masque at Wolsey's house, cannon were fired, and shots landed on the thatched roof of the theater, setting it afire, "consuming within less than an hour the whole House to the very grounds" (p. xxviii). Other evidence corroborates Wotton's letter and points strongly in the direction of Shakespeare's *Henry VIII*. If new, as Wotton says, then presumably the play was written in 1613 for the King's Men. Whether it had been performed along with other plays for the wedding festivities of Princess Elizabeth in February 1613, we cannot be sure, but that certainly seems plausible. Or perhaps Shakespeare wrote it after the wedding to capitalize on the intense interest in the royal family. In any event, 1613 seems the likely date for the play; such will be my assumption.

Like Gower in *Pericles* or Time in *The Winter's Tale*, Shakespeare steps into the wide gap of time, both historical and artistic, when he writes *Henry VIII*. Having ended his historical span with the victory of Henry Tudor over Richard III, Shakespeare during Elizabeth's lifetime never explored the Tudor monarchs. Not since the early 1590s had he approached the Tudor dynasty in his drama. Not since the late 1590s had he written an English historical drama. Thus, well into the Jacobean era, he decides to write about Henry VIII and the birth of the future Queen Elizabeth, King James's kinswoman. G. Wilson Knight suggests: "Finally the poet, copying his analogue Prospero, returns deliberately to a national and contemporary theme, and writes *Henry VIII*. He may have originally purposed such a conclusion, holding it in reserve for his crowning work."[56]

I doubt that Shakespeare had such a grand design and that *Henry VIII* is his "crowning work"; but Knight correctly sees the play as intimately related to the Romances that precede it. It shares more with those plays than it does with the earlier histories. For me, *Henry VIII* is the intertextual result of at least four texts working on Shakespeare's imagination: the historical chronicles, Samuel Rowley's play *When You See Me, You Know Me*, the other Romances, and the Stuart royal family. It may be that in Cranmer's final prophetic vision, rather than in Prospero's, we have Shakespeare's valedictory.

The main historical text is Holinshed's *Chronicles*, which Shakespeare follows closely when it suits him. He apparently also uses Foxe's *Actes and Monuments* for the plot against Cranmer in Act V. Shakespeare, as is his wont in history plays, freely rearranges the chronology of the twenty-year span covered in the play to fit his dramatic purposes. Bullough sees four reasons for Shakespeare's use of Holinshed: "to show the evil ambitions of papist churchmen . . . ; to portray the King's own self-willed nature and its bad and good effects; to present some major people and incidents involved in these two themes; to suggest the alternation of tragic and joyous motifs in the King's reign."[57] The triumphant close of the play celebrates the birth of Elizabeth. That is obviously where Shakespeare wanted to end rather than to pursue and develop later events in Henry's reign. What Shakespeare omits indicates his desire to present a sympathetic portrait of the king.

Had he wanted to, Shakespeare could have developed his material along the lines of Rowley's *When You See Me* (first published in 1605 and reissued in 1613, the latter printing perhaps calculated to reap benefits from Shakespeare's play). Rowley's play sprawls over thirty years of Henry's reign, 1514–44. The title page of the 1605 quarto says that it was performed by Prince Henry's Men. This information and the content of the play lead Bullough to suggest that it was performed for Prince Henry in 1604, indeed intended to honor him (IV, 438). Scene x, Bullough says, "indicates that the play was for performance before the boy Prince Henry" (439). In this scene, Edward and his tutor Cranmer are together, and there is much ado about Edward's love of tennis and his failure to study. Certainly the play's emphasis on the birth of Prince Edward and his development corresponds to the status of Prince Henry. We hear King Henry's praise of Edward: "I tell thee *Cranmer* he is all our hopes, / That what our age shall leaue vnfinished, / In his faire raigne shall be accomplished" (sc. ix, 1557–59).[58] Cranmer adds his own praise at the end of scene x: "Health to your Highnesse, God increase your dayes: / The hope of *England*, and of learnings praise" (2103–4).

Such comments resound with the kind of hope expressed for James's royal son, Henry. Assuming that the play was performed for Henry by his actors, one can readily see in Prince Edward the representation of Henry. By 1613, Shakespeare would, however, view things differently: Henry has died, and Elizabeth has married in February. Clearly the center of interest had shifted to her. I think that *Henry VIII* embodies and builds on that interest. Like the other

Romances, the emphasis will be on the royal father and daughter and succession through the female line.

Shakespeare will differ from Rowley's at times farcical drama, which is full of propaganda. Clearly, Rowley's text finds its place in Shakespeare's imagination. Indeed, Shakespeare apparently spells out his differences from Rowley in the Prologue to *Henry VIII*, which begins: "I come no more to make you laugh . . ." (Pro. 1). The speaker asserts: "Only they / That come to hear a merry bawdy play, / . . . Will be deceiv'd" (13–14, 17). Shakepeare's play purports to offer the "truth." As Shakespeare had done with much Jacobean comedy in writing the Romances, so he does with Rowley's play: he turns his back on this text, differs from it, though hearing its faint echoes.

Act IV of *Henry VIII* reveals, to me at least, the other two texts working in the play: the preceding Romances and the Stuart royal family. I suggest that this moment in the play represents the turning point in the drama as it moves from the "winter's tale" of Acts I–III to the celebration of coronation and royal birth. The First Gentleman signals the change in the play: "But that time offer'd sorrow, / This general joy" (IV.i.6–7). The citizens, the Second Gentleman observes, demonstrate "their royal minds / . . . In celebration of this day with shows, / Pageants and sights of honour" (8, 10–11). Shakespeare's "royal mind" is at work also, capturing in the coronation of Anne Boleyn, on 1 June 1533, the flavor of the court festivities for Princess Elizabeth's wedding eighty years later.

Shakespeare gives the "Order of the Coronation," a fairly accurate rendition of the actual procession in 1533. The Gentlemen who are spectators and commentators doubtless embody the scores of spectators lining the streets for such civic pageants whether in Tudor or Stuart England. The Second Gentleman, for example, comments: "A royal train, believe me: these I know; / Who's that that bears the sceptre?" (37–38). So the conversation goes until he sees Ann Boleyn: "Sir, as I have a soul, she is an angel; / Our king has all the Indies in his arms . . ." (44–45), an image appreciated by Donne. As in V.ii of *The Winter's Tale*, the Third Gentleman enters to describe the offstage coronation. He launches his description in response to the question "How was it?" (60), to which he replies: "Well worth the seeing" (61).

If not exactly the reunion of Leontes and Perdita, the scene described does capture the color, festivity, and joy of the moment. As the Third Gentleman says: "Such joy / I never saw before" (75–76).

206

When the people saw Anne, "such a noise arose / As the shrouds make at sea in a stiff tempest . . ." (71–72). The Third Gentleman follows this with a description of the rite of coronation, noting that the Queen "had all the royal makings of a queen" (87) given to her: "holy oil, Edward Confessor's crown, / The rod, and bird of peace and all such emblems . . ." (88–89). Any performance of *Henry VIII* in 1613 would have immediately struck a responsive chord in spectators who would see in Anne's coronation festivity a re-presentation of Princess Elizabeth's wedding celebration.

The Jacobean court was *en fête* for days before and after Elizabeth's wedding on Sunday, 14 February: masques, plays, fireworks displays, and sea battles on the Thames contributed to the celebration. All eyes focused on the royal family. As discussed earlier in this chapter, both *The Winter's Tale* and *The Tempest* were performed. The royal entry into London in 1604, the investiture festivities in 1610, and now the wedding celebration constitute the most obvious, the most public, displays of the royal family. Accounts of the 1613 festivities occupy nearly one hundred pages in Nichols, *Progresses of James*, volume 2. An anonymous report captures the splendor of the royal family at the wedding.

Elizabeth proceeded to the chapel, walking between her brother Charles and the Earl of Northampton. Her wedding attire was stunning,

> upon her head a crown of refined golde, made Imperiall by the pearles and diamonds thereupon placed, which were so thicke beset that they stood like shining pinnacles upon her amber-coloured haire, dependantly hanging playted downe over her shoulders to her waste; between every plaight a roll or liste of gold-spangles, pearles, rich stones, and diamonds; and, withall, many diamonds of inestimable value, embrothered upon her sleeves, which even dazzled and amazed the eies of the beholders.[59]

The Second Gentleman of *Henry VIII* might have commented that Elizabeth seemed "all the Indies." James wore a "sumptuous blacke suit, with a diamond in his hatte of a wonderfull great value; close unto him came the Queen, attired in white satin, beautified with much embrothery and many diamonds" (Nichols, *Progresses*, 2:544). One has to remind oneself that this is not a masque but the real thing. Such dazzling and opulent display belies the state of the royal treasury.

In the center of the chapel at Whitehall a "stage," some five feet high and twenty feet in length, stood waiting for its occupants, the royal family. I quote in full the 1613 description of the family as it stationed itself on this stage:

> On the stage, in the chair upon the right hand sate the King, most richly arraied, his jewells being esteemed not to be less worth than six hundred thousand pounds, the Earl of Arundell, bearing the Sword, stood close by the chair. Next below the Sword sate the Bridegroom upon a stool; and after him Prince Charles upon another stool; and by him stood Prince Henry, who was brother to Count Maurice of Nassau, and uncle to the Palatine. On the other opposite side sate the Queen in a chair most gloriously attired; her jewels were valued at four hundred thousand pounds. Near unto her sate the Bride on a stool; the Lady Harington her Governesse stood by her, bearing up her train; and no others ascended this place. (Nichols, *Progresses*, 2:546)

Upon a stage, for all the world to see, were the royal performers. This moment in 1613 makes literal a metaphor that James himself had used in *Basilicon Doron:* "A King is as one set on a stage, whose smallest actions and gestures, all the people gazinglie doe beholde."[60] Just as the anonymous Gentlemen watch the processions and coronation of Anne in IV.i, so citizens and courtiers beheld the spectacle of Elizabeth's wedding, excited and amazed, knowing that this moment was, as the Third Gentleman says in the play, "Well worth the seeing."

The obverse side of this royal coin is Katherine, whose moment in Act IV identifies the play with the Romances, those plays yet so fresh in Shakespeare's mind. The motto for much of *Henry VIII* could be the Shepherd's comment in *The Winter's Tale* that he and his son meet with things dying and with things new-born. We learn in the coronation scene that the divorce of Henry from the ill Katherine is final. Scene ii of Act IV presents Katherine near death and accompanied by her servant Patience, Shakespeare's unhistorical creation. (Patience is, of course, one of the principal themes throughout the play.) Coming from the other Romances, we are not startled to confront a dramatic character named Patience, given all the symbolic characters and events in those plays.

Nearly half the scene (IV.ii) recounts the death of Wolsey, his death in a sense thereby foreshadowing Katherine's, just as their lives frequently echo one another. Even though the larger play has turned in a hopeful direction, a winter's tale waits to be heard, just as the problems in *The Winter's Tale* do not suddenly evaporate in the sunshine of the sheep-shearing festival in Act IV. Griffith's report and praise of Wolsey help soften Wolsey's portrait and make him sympathetic. Indicating the changing perspective, Katherine remarks: "Whom I most hated living, thou hast made me, / With thy religious truth and modesty, / Now in his ashes honour: peace be with him" (IV.ii.73–75). The rarer action lies in virtue, as Prospero has told us: characters in the Romances become capable of forgiving their enemies and of reconciling with them. In this benign state Katherine is ready for her wondrous vision.

The vision that appears to Katherine links her with Pericles and the appearance of Diana, with Posthumus and the apparitions of his family and Jupiter, with Antigonus and the visionary appearance of Hermione in a dream, and with all those who witness the magical illusions of Prospero. Katherine orders the musicians to play a "sad note" while she sits "meditating / On that celestial harmony" to which she will go (79–80). The stage directions describe what appears to her:

> Enter solemnly tripping one after another, six personages, clad in white robes, wearing on their heads garlands of bays, and golden vizards on their faces, branches of bays or palm in their hands. They first congee unto her, then dance: and at certain changes, the first two hold a spare garland over her head, at which the other four make reverent curtsies.

The other figures repeat the pattern.

As by inspiration, Katherine "*makes (in her sleep) signs of rejoicing, and holdeth up her hands to heaven. And so in their dancing vanish, carrying the garland with them.*" She cries out: "Spirits of peace, where are ye? are ye all gone?" (83). No one has seen these spirits; like Pericles, who presumably hears the music of the spheres, Katherine has had a solitary vision. Incredulous, Katherine asks: "Saw you not even now a blessed troop / Invite me to a banquet, whose bright faces / Cast thousand beams upon me, like the sun? / They promis'd me eternal happiness . . ." (87–90). But all that Griffith can say is that he delights that "such good dreams" possess Katherine's fancy (93–94).

This beatific vision, unlike anything that one finds in the history plays, argues forcefully that the texts of the Romances permeate Shakespeare's imagination here. Griffith and Patience believe that Katherine is dying: "Do you note," Patience asks, "How much her grace is alter'd on the sudden?" (95–96). But Katherine rouses herself to greet Lord Capuchius, whom she recognizes as an ambassador "from the emperor, / My royal nephew . . ." (109–10). Much in the last part of this scene focuses on Katherine's royal heritage and the royal family. Capuchius has in fact brought greetings from King Henry, who "grieves much for your weakness . . ." (117). But about the commendations from her former royal husband, Katherine says: ". . . 'Tis like a pardon after execution; / That gentle physic, given in time, had cur'd me . . ." (121–22). In a letter prepared for Henry, Katherine emphasizes her concern for those who will remain, beginning with Mary, their royal daughter, "The model of our chaste loves . . ." (132). The image "The dews of heaven fall thick in blessings on her" (133) echoes comments made by Cymbeline and Hermione as they reunite with their daughters. Mary is "young and of a noble modest nature" (135); Katherine hopes that Henry will provide her "virtuous breeding" (134) and love her "for her mother's sake, that lov'd him, / Heaven knows how dearly" (137–38).

After calling attention to her serving women and men and after asking Henry's care for them, Katherine readies herself for death, desirous that all the world should know her as "a chaste wife" (170). Her instructions focus on her heritage: "embalm me, / Then lay me forth; although unqueen'd, yet like / A queen, and daughter to a king inter me" (170–72). Though having had a rare vision, Katherine closes her final appearance in the play by emphasizing her link to the royal family as wife, mother, and daughter to a king. This process of identification strengthens her character and underscores the magnitude of what Henry has done to her. Like Hermione who was the daughter of the emperor of Russia, Katherine has a royal genealogy. Both the wondrous vision and the emphasis on the royal family recall the Romances.

I turn now to explore more fully the text of the Jacobean royal family which is at work in and through *Henry VIII*. Did Shakespeare perceive some connection between the reigns of Henry and James?[61] In all likelihood; of course, all that I can do is to suggest parallels that I see. We do have, however, in Cranmer's final speech an explicit reference to James, something not in the other Romances. At least we know that Shakespeare saw the familial link between the two sovereigns, James being an immediate descendant of Margaret, Henry VIII's sister who married James IV of Scotland. Henry produced the offspring who carried the Tudor name into the beginning of the seventeenth century; James and his progeny reigned for most of that century. Henry had three children who survived; so did James until the end of 1612, when Shakespeare may have begun to contemplate such a play. In the twenty-third year of his marriage to Katherine, Henry divorced her and married Anne Boleyn. At a comparable point in their marriage, James and Anne prepared for the wedding of their daughter. Henry's only surviving son, Edward, died at the age of sixteen; Prince Henry was eighteen when he died, his sister Elizabeth being at that time sixteen.

Henry VIII, noted for his indulgence in pleasure, such as hunting, left the affairs of state to others—hence the power of one like Wolsey. Certainly, as I indicated in chapter 2, precisely the same can be said of James. The death of Robert Cecil in 1612 may have prompted Shakespeare to think about the role of a prominent and powerful adviser to the king. Wolsey's power and enemies find a parallel in Cecil, on whom James depended though he heaped abuse on him. Wolsey's downfall and death and Cecil's death brought forth much rejoicing from their enemies. Henry's knowledge of and interest in theology find their counterpart in James, who, from the Hampton Court conference in 1604 to the publication of the new authorized Bible in 1611, demonstrated great fascination with religious matters. Henry's attacks on Luther led to Henry's designation as ''Defender of the faith'' by the pope, though his marital problems ultimately led to his excommunication. Religious problems occupy much attention during both reigns. Peace with the French in 1520 led to considerable scoffing and disagreement, as did peace with the Spanish achieved in 1604.

Prince Henry carried on the name of his forebear, the last English sovereign to have that name. If Rowley's 1605 play may be said to include a representation of Henry in Prince Edward, then by 1613, after the prince's death, Shakespeare would need to shift the focus. So the attention moves to the birth of Elizabeth at the end of *Henry VIII*. As I suggested above, much in the play recalls the elaborate festivities for the royal wedding of 1613; Foakes argues persuasively for the links between this occasion and the play (see his Introduction in the Arden edition). Queen Elizabeth, whose birth is celebrated, was of course the namesake for James's daughter, just as she had been the godmother for Prince Henry. A comment by Thomas Ross in 1608 links the two women: ''. . . whatever was excellent or lofty in Queen Elizabeth, is all compressed in the tender age of this virgin princess, and if God spare her to us, will be found there accumulated.''[62] For Ross and many others, Princess Elizabeth was a representation of Queen Elizabeth. As the play demonstrates the emerging Protestant spirit in England, so Princess Elizabeth's marriage represents a triumph of Protestantism, her father having resisted Catholic overtures from France and Spain. In February 1613, Elizabeth married a solidly Protestant German prince, following the rite of the Book of Common Prayer and the well-established Church of England—the first royal child in English history to have such a wedding. Not in a hundred years in England had there been a royal daughter married in the full presence of the royal father and other family members.

Most of these connections or parallels are the happy accident of history; but I think that Shakespeare saw in his knowledge of Henry VIII a re-presentation of the Stuart royal family, not a duplication but another rendering. In this case, as distinct from the other Romances, the family of history *becomes* the family of art. No longer are we in some exotic part of the Mediterranean world or in first century A.D. Britain; we are in the midst of a living national history whose successors possess the English throne. Shakespeare holds the mirror up not to nature but to English history, seeing therein reflected the inevitable web of politics and royal family. What, one supposes, went through the minds of James, Anne, Elizabeth, or Charles as they watched *Henry VIII*, as I think they probably did? They and the audience around them no longer look at a Pericles, Cymbeline, Leontes, or Prospero—those other royal fathers—but at the flesh and blood of English history: their own ancestral royal family. The audience sees the smallest actions and gestures of this king and his family on a stage. I argue that Shakespeare moved from the living text of the Stuart royal family, occasioned by the festivities of 1613, to dramatize part of Henry VIII's reign. The familiar issues of succession through the female line, royal genealogy, and interpretation permeate this play. The Prologue urges: "Think ye see / The very persons of our noble story / As they were living" (25–27). I suggest that we do indeed see them through the re-presentation of the Jacobean royal family. Shakespeare's "noble story" interprets Henry VIII's reign as it also interprets James's family.

As we examine the play in more detail, I offer a metaphor that describes for me much of the play: it is a banquet—at first a "broken banquet," as Wolsey calls his interrupted festivity in I.iv; then a "banquet," as Katherine describes the experience of her vision when the spirits invite her to a banquet (IV.ii.88). This movement in the play culminates in the christening feast for Elizabeth at which Cranmer, called an "oracle," speaks, much as inspired voices do in the other Romances. Banquet implies communal or familial gatherings. The last one in the drama leads Henry to call it a "Holy-day" (V.iv.76)—the final word of the play.

The broken banquet of Acts I–III implies strife, especially but not exclusively in the royal family; the banquet of Acts IV–V depicts new familial life, as Henry marries Anne and she later gives birth to Elizabeth. The old order, Buckingham, Wolsey, and Katherine, has passed away. A process of substitution takes place: Cranmer for Wolsey, Anne for Katherine, Elizabeth for Mary. The final speeches about Elizabeth, no matter how exaggerated or propagandistic, point clearly in the direction of hope for the new royal child, much as in the other late plays. Is this Shakespeare's personal visionary or revisionary view of the first sovereign he knew? We cannot be certain, but we do know that it flatters James, who is Shakespeare's official patron. Removed from the shadowy mists of the long ago or faraway, Shakespeare here makes more explicit than anywhere else praise of James and his royal issue.

The play begins with a "banquet," a stunning report of the pageant of the Field of the Cloth of Gold that took place in France in June 1520, when Henry and Francis met near Calais. Foakes is right to suggest that the description "may have brought to mind for a 1613 audience the festivities at the wedding of Princess Elizabeth . . ." (p. 9n.26). Like the later coronation in Act IV, we get a report, an interpretation of the occasion. Norfolk captures the vivid scene:

> To-day the French,
> All clinquant all in gold, like heathen gods
> Shone down the English; and to-morrow they
> Made Britain India: every man that stood
> Show'd like a mine. (I.i.18–22)

One day a masque is deemed "incomparable," but the next night another masque makes the first "a fool and beggar" (28). Like those who witnessed the spectacle of the Jacobean royal family at Princess Elizabeth's wedding and recounted the event, so here in the play those present at the spectacle near Calais offer an interpretation of this royal occasion. Their "fabulous story" (36) taxes the skill of "a good discourser" (40). This opening scene repeatedly emphasizes the need for interpretation, Shakespeare's way of calling attention to what he himself is doing.

Buckingham breaks the spell of this banquet by his cynical questioning of the purpose and the instigator of this scene, namely

Wolsey. He asks: "What did this vanity / But minister communication of / A most poor issue?" (85–87). Norfolk agrees that the beautiful trappings only belie the consequences of the presumed peace, which is itself broken. Buckingham, able to "read in's [Wolsey's] looks / Matter against me" (125–26), interprets the significance of the storm that followed the lavish pageant: ". . . this tempest / Dashing the garment of this peace, aboded [i.e., foreshadowed] / The sudden breach on't" (92–94). After the tempest the garment of peace is not fresher than before. Nevertheless, pageantry, celebration, and diplomacy all inhere in the Cloth of Gold experience; so, too, in Elizabeth's wedding. In the play the political brokenness between countries will also be manifest in the conflict in England, first with Buckingham, who is arrested, tried, and executed, and then with Wolsey, whose overreaching brings his collapse. No longer will Wolsey offer sumptuous banquets and masques; he will die humbly in a monastery far from the seat of power.

The first stage image of Henry and Katherine implies their love and familial devotion. She enters in I.ii and kneels before the king: "King *riseth from his state, takes her up, kisses and placeth her by him*" (S.D.). Katherine has come to plead in behalf of their subjects upon whom grievous exactions have been placed—by Wolsey. Henry answers her: ". . . you have half our power, / The other moiety ere you ask is given . . ." (I.ii.11–12). "Moiety" is the word that Hermione uses to describe her rights as queen in Sicily in her trial in *The Winter's Tale*; it implies both a political and a familial relationship. At some length and with great persuasive force, Katherine outlines the noxious practice of the exactions, which compel each subject to give the "sixth part of his substance, to be levied / Without delay . . ." (58–59). Henry finally says: "By my life, / This is against our pleasure" (67–68). Wolsey, of course, claims that his intentions have been misunderstood by his subordinates; he then rushes to take advantage of the King's revocation, urging his secretary to noise it abroad that by his intervention "this revokement / And pardon comes" (106–7). Katherine also pleads in behalf of Buckingham, but futilely.

Though I know of no instances of Queen Anne's public boldness in behalf of certain political issues, there can be little doubt that on occasion she tried to influence James—about the destiny and care of the royal children, about a favorable policy toward Spain, about the marriages of Henry and Elizabeth, about leniency toward Catholics. She was not, however, a potent political force. Katherine uses her family position to argue a political cause. She cannot be persuasive about Buckingham because Henry sees in him a challenge to the throne (Buckingham is a descendant of Edward III's son, Thomas of Woodstock). The Surveyor summarizes the threat of Buckingham: ''. . . if the king / Should without issue die, he'll carry it so / To make the sceptre his'' (133–35). Here we face again the problem that every royal father has confronted in the Romances: political vulnerability about his royal issue and heir. Henry has a royal child, Mary, but of course he desires a son. History's ironic twist is that Henry's son Edward, about whom Rowley writes, sick and weak, dies at age sixteen, a few years after becoming king.

In what may have been the scene whose action set the Globe on fire, I.iv, Henry meets Anne Boleyn at Wolsey's banquet and masque and is himself set on fire for her. With the sounding of drum and trumpet and the discharging of cannons, Henry enters with others, *''habited like shepherds* . . .'' (I.iv.63 S.D.). Wolsey says to his guests: ''You have now a broken banquet; but we'll mend it'' (61). As a metaphor, the broken banquet foreshadows Wolsey's fall and his inability to ''mend'' the situation, and it epitomizes the broken royal family, once Henry begins his pursuit of Anne. An inverse proportional relationship exists between the fortunes of Anne and Wolsey, demonstrating again the inextricable link of family and politics. Henry, dressed as if ready for Act IV of *The Winter's Tale*, seizes on the beauty of Anne: ''The fairest hand I ever touch'd: O beauty, / Till now I never knew thee'' (75–76). Not since *Pericles* have we seen a royal prince falling in love. The harmony of the music and dance arrests a moment of peace before it belies the change and destruction that will come.

Buckingham's trial and execution (II.i) are the first tangible signs of altering political fortunes, though for the moment they represent another triumph for Wolsey, whom Henry characterizes as a ''cure fit for a king . . .'' (II.ii.75). Buckingham's final speech rehearses his political past, with special emphasis on his family. He praises his noble father and cites the action of Henry VII, who ''like a most royal prince'' (II.i.113) restored Buckingham to the family's honors. But now Henry VIII, Buckingham says, has taken ''life, honour, name and all / That made me happy, at one stroke . . .'' (116–17). Though forgiving his enemies, Buckingham does note the fickle nature of friends who, ''when they once perceive / The least rub in your fortunes, fall away / Like water from ye . . .'' (128–30). The fall of the noble Buckingham prepares the way for Katherine's fall in the last scene of Act II, her trial scene.

Three different but related matters are under way in Act II: Buckingham's destruction, increasing complaints about Wolsey that will eventually bear fruit, and Katherine's trial—all form part of the broken banquet of Acts I–III. Each seems to carry seeds of the other: for example, at the end of Buckingham's scene, we learn about the separation of Henry from Katherine and about Wolsey's hand in the whole matter. Meanwhile, Henry has bestowed on Anne the title of "Marchioness of Pembroke" (II.iii.63). Clearly the royal family is undergoing serious challenges and changes in Act II, the events of which will lead to a new definition of this family, much as Cymbeline's substitute family dissolved and was replaced.

The trial of Katherine in II.iv has several parallels to Hermione's trial in *The Winter's Tale*, though the circumstances differ. Like the scene in the earlier play, this one in *Henry VIII* has two basic parts: the formal trial of the wife and then the informal trial of the husband. Also on trial are the definition and structure of the royal family; this scene makes a perfect example of the politics of the family—domestic life moved to the public arena. As such, it is also the obverse of the coronation that occurs in IV.i; each demonstrates the politics of the royal family but in quite a different way. In Act II the royal family is dissolving, threatened by the destruction of the husband/wife relationship; in Act IV the royal family receives new life, a banquet, as husband and wife embark on a new course. The ceremony and formality of the trial mock the chaos that will result; the ceremony of the coronation implies an emergent ordered and peaceful society. In the Jacobean court the ritual of Prince Henry's funeral masks the dashed hopes and grief of a shocked nation; the ceremony and festivities of Princess Elizabeth's wedding imply an ever-renewing social and familial order.

Katherine's defense against unspecified charges moves vigorously as she eschews the formal help of Wolsey in her behalf. Like Hermione, Katherine is alone, cut off from family. Like Hermione, she begins by establishing her ethos, by insisting that she is "a most poor woman . . ." (II.iv.13), a point to which she returns as she closes. But in the middle she presses her claim as a royal figure, daughter of a sovereign and wife to a king. She answers her own question: "In what have I offended . . . ?" (17). She insists that she has been faithful and obedient in the nearly twenty years of their marriage; further, she has "been blest / With many children by you"

(34–35), though only one survives, of course. Defending the legality of their marriage, Katherine notes that Henry's father "was reputed for / A prince most prudent, of an excellent / And unmatch'd wit and judgment" (43–45) and that her father Ferdinand, king of Spain, "was reckon'd one / The wisest prince that there had reign'd by many / A year before" (46–48). How is it possible then that these two, "Who deem'd our marriage lawful" (51), could have been wrong? The sanction of royal fathers should settle the issue.

Moved to the point of weeping, Katherine reminds herself: "We are a queen . . . certain / The daughter of a king"; therefore, "my drops of tears / I'll turn to sparks of fire" (69–71). Her angry fire lashes out at Wolsey about whom she says bluntly: "You are mine enemy . . ." (75). She begins her peroration: "My lord, my lord, / I am a simple woman . . ." (103). Speaking to Wolsey, she says: ". . . I do refuse you for my judge, and here / Before you all, appeal unto the Pope, / . . . to be judg'd by him" (116–19). This echoes Hermione's appeal to Apollo. In this scene Shakespeare heeds several texts: the historical chronicles, which he follows closely; *The Winter's Tale*, specifically Hermione's trial; and the Stuart royal family, in which Anne's public identity is defined by her heritage as daughter of a king, her position as wife to a king, and as mother of the royal issue. Katherine is, I think, a representation of these three texts working in Shakespeare's imagination.

Henry heaps praise on Katherine when she departs, finding in her such rare qualities as "sweet gentleness," "meekness saintlike," and "wife-like government" (II.iv.135–36). The marriage to Katherine nevertheless troubles him, and he goes to some length to explain his position, a defense in his own "trial." The key word for Henry is "conscience," first pricked as he began marriage negotiations for his daughter Mary to the duke of Orleans. The word "conscience" appears more often in this play than in any other Shakespeare play; it carries with it both the sense of moral duty and private knowledge of oneself, consciousness.[63] Like King James, Henry VIII remains both known and unknown to his subjects, a text subject to interpretation. Certainly Wolsey's constant jockeying for position reflects his on-going attempt to interpret the king. But some things about a king are private. Shakespeare illustrates this point well in II.ii where the stage directions indicate that *"the King draws the curtain and sits reading pensively"* (61 S.D.). The King, a reader of texts, is himself a text—so with James. In his private thoughts Henry contemplates his "wounded conscience" (74); and he cries out: "But conscience,

conscience; / O 'tis a tender place, and I must leave her" (II.ii.142–43). Though "her" presumably refers to Katherine, his sweet "bedfellow," may it not also refer to his conscience, the private part of himself that he must leave in order to confront the public duty of Katherine's trial?

In the second part of that trial, the trial of Henry's own conscience, he says that the question of the legitimacy of his marriage affects his potential heir: "Whether our daughter were legitimate / Respecting this our marriage with the dowager, / Sometimes our brother's wife" (II.iv.177–79). The heart of the issue may or may not be Henry's troubled conscience, but it is surely the question of having no male heir. Henry really seeks the cause of the effect, that is, an answer to why he has no male child. He recalls that the males born to Katherine "died where they were made, or shortly after / This world had air'd them" (190–91). This he construes as a possible judgment on him because of his marriage to Katherine, for surely his kingdom is "Well worthy the best heir o'th'world . . ." (193).

The political implications for the state are clear to Henry: "I weigh'd the danger which my realms stood in / By this my issue's fail, and that gave to me / Many a groaning throe" (195–97). In a male-dominated society, no sovereign can feel entirely secure without a male heir. One recalls that despite considerable and justifiable pride in Queen Elizabeth as ruler, there was much relief when James, complete with family, ascended the English throne: no more women or children for sovereigns, George Marcelline noted in 1610. Such a context helps explain the outpouring of grief and dismay when the heir apparent, Prince Henry, died in 1612, leaving Charles, a sickly child, as possible male heir. King Henry orders the court: "Prove but our marriage lawful," and he will be content "To wear our mortal state" with Katherine (224, 226). In the play, at least, the statement rings hollow as Henry busies himself in proving the opposite. He sounds a bit like Othello.

Though Katherine at first resists, she eventually accepts the counsel of Wolsey and Campeius in III.i. She defines her position in familial and political terms. Henry, she observes, "has banish'd me his bed already, / His love, too long ago" (III.i.119–20). Being cut off from the royal bed carries a heavy price in both politics and self-esteem, as Hermione also understood. Katherine can find no counsel in England, for no one dares oppose the king by offering her help (83–85). The metaphor that she uses to describe her plight recalls the Romances; she is, she says, "Shipwrack'd upon a kingdom where no pity, / No friends, no hope, no kindred weep for me, / Almost no grave allow'd me" (149–51). Indulging in some self-pity, she radically alters the image: "like the lily / That once was mistress of the field and flourish'd, / I'll hang my head and perish" (151–53). Katherine stands on a darkling plain, cut off from the royal husband she has loved and from the resources and strength of her kindred. Like the lily, her political strength has perished.

But in that she is not alone, as III.ii makes ironically clear; for Wolsey overreaches himself and meets his downfall in a scene that functions as his trial. Shakespeare in fact alters his historical text in order to bring the falls of Katherine and Wolsey closer together and to link them closely in time to Henry's marriage to Anne. Norfolk, Suffolk, and Surrey are instrumental in setting up Wolsey's fall. Suffolk announces that the order has gone out for Anne's coronation. He adds: ". . . from her, / Will fall some blessing to this land, which shall / In it be memoriz'd" (III.ii.50–52)—a foreshadowing of the last act and of Cranmer's prophecy. Among Wolsey's complaints about Anne Boleyn is that she is a "spleeny Lutheran, and not wholesome to / Our cause . . ." (99–100). Interestingly, the Venetian ambassador, we recall, thought that James's Queen Anne was a Lutheran, when, of course, she was apparently a Catholic. Wolsey also chafes at the idea that Cranmer has "crawl'd into the favour of the king / And is his oracle" (103–4). Certainly he has that function at the end.

Henry's "performance" with Wolsey in III.ii is just that; it explicitly calls attention to the king as actor on a stage—in this case also the dramatist. Though Henry will be an opaque text to Wolsey, he is clear to Norfolk, Surrey, and Suffolk. Henry tells them state secrets: he has found in Wolsey's papers an inventory, documenting Wolsey's considerable personal wealth. What he has found, "on my conscience put unwittingly" (123), damns Wolsey. The king's inward knowledge now translates into outward action. The state papers will be interpreted by the king, much as James successfully fathomed documents that came to him in the Gunpowder Plot of 1605. The image of Henry's rule is one of the ruling images of James's absolutist view of his reign: the king knows, possesses, and interprets state secrets. Henry takes a seat both to watch and to participate in Wolsey's performance; each, of course, is a performer, but the king has hidden knowledge. Henry toys with Wolsey, finds him an emblem of obedience ("A loyal, and obedient subject is / Therein illustrated" [180–81]), knowing all the while of Wolsey's treachery and greed. Professing to be pleased with Wolsey's responses, Henry says: "... he has a loyal breast, / For you have seen him open't" (200–201). But Henry gives Wolsey something tangible to open: the papers that reveal his inventory of wealth. Henry commands simply: "Read o'er this, / And after, this, and then to breakfast with / What appetite you have" (201–3); then Henry exits. All that is left is the catastrophe: as in *The Winter's Tale*, the scroll of the oracle has been opened and the truth revealed. Wolsey now has an answer to his question, "What should this mean?" (160); he understands: "This paper has undone me" (210).

Norfolk, Surrey, and Suffolk pronounce sentence on Wolsey, enumerating the charges against him; they make explicit what is implicit in Henry's gesture. Wolsey correctly sums up his extensive self-analysis when he remarks to Cromwell: "Had I but serv'd my God with half the zeal / I serv'd my king, he would not in mine age / Have left me naked to mine enemies" (455–57). Wolsey has found peace: "The king has cur'd me" (380), an ironic reversal of his role as healer of the king. A humble and contrite spirit links Wolsey to someone like Leontes who also learned at great cost the price of pride; a re-creative process begins in Wolsey, too. With Wolsey fallen, Henry energizes his plan for the politics of family by ordering Anne's coronation, the beginning of the banquet experience of the play's final two acts.

As Act V opens, we learn that Anne is in labor; by the end of V.i, the Old Lady brings news of the birth. The king asks: "Is the queen deliver'd? / Say ay, and of a boy" (V.i.162–63). The Old Lady wittily answers that the child is a boy, "a girl / Promises boys hereafter" (165–66). Sounding like Paulina before Leontes, the Old Lady observes: "... 'tis as like you / As cherry is to cherry" (168–69). Beneath this banquet of good news runs the conspiracy against Cranmer, all of which comes into focus in V.ii, the "trial" of Cranmer. Cranmer survives the experience because Henry has given him a ring, emblem of the king's trust and authority in him. This episode provides clear evidence of the power-in-absence of Henry VIII. Cromwell's image sums up the plight of Cranmer's accusers: "... Ye blew the fire that burns ye" (147); the fire of Cranmer's honesty consumes them. Henry reaffirms his faith in Cranmer by insisting that "... a fair young maid that yet wants baptism; / You must be godfather, and answer for her" (195–96). Political squabbles set aside, the court moves to celebrate the birth of the royal child, confirming as a nation the political stability that the royal issue brings to the kingdom. Such a point, we remember, pervades the Romances.

Recalling the fate of the other newborn children in the Romances—Marina and Perdita—we can appreciate the contrasting tranquility and expectation of the young Elizabeth's christening. Not tossed ingloriously on the seas or left on hostile seacoasts of Bohemia, the princess Elizabeth rests secure amidst the full display of power, ceremony, and authority of the royal father. The politics of the royal family operates fully. The Duchess of Norfolk, as one of the godmothers, bears *"the child richly habited in a mantle"* (V.iv. S.D.) in a full procession, reminding us of the other public festivities in this play. Garter speaks: "Heaven, from thy endless goodness, send prosperous life, long and ever happy, to the high and mighty princess of England, Elizabeth" (V.iv.1–3). No one hearing those words in 1613 could resist the connection to the other Princess Elizabeth, James's daughter. King Henry offers his own benediction as he kisses the infant: "With this kiss take my blessing: God protect thee, / Into whose hand I give thy life" (10–11). Cranmer's long speech follows.

Cranmer is, as Henry calls him, the "oracle of comfort" (66), a prophet new-inspired like John of Gaunt in *Richard II*, or a Gonzalo in *The Tempest*, who envisions an ideal commonwealth and who at the end urges everyone to rejoice beyond a common joy. Cranmer speaks not flattery but truth—the play's presumed purpose. With rich images he enumerates the good fortune that shall come to the kingdom in Elizabeth's reign: "Upon this land a thousand thousand blessings, / Which time shall bring to ripeness" (19–20)—a time of fulness in the fulness of time. Those about Elizabeth, Cranmer says, "From her shall read the perfect ways of honour . . ." (37)—a transparent text of honor. Cranmer especially celebrates peace. The speech closes with a conscious reference to Elizabeth's successor, James, "As great in admiration as herself," "as great in fame as she was" (42, 46). All the virtues associated with Elizabeth will gravitate to James. He shall have the additional advantage of royal children. Cranmer prophesies:

> He shall flourish,
> And like a mountain cedar, reach his branches
> To all the plains about him: our children's children
> Shall see this, and bless heaven. (52–55)

James will not be of an age but for all time.

The self-reflexive nature of all this is quite wonderful, as well as being heady praise indeed. The Stuart royal family, watching this play along with other members of the audience, can know that

Cranmer's prophecy is fulfilled: the flesh-and-blood James, Elizabeth, and Charles confirm the veracity of what Cranmer says. The royal succession is secure; the royal genealogy, legitimate. The country's destiny will derive from that issue and genealogy. In this instance the energizing reality of what Cranmer prophesies flows from the royal audience to the play and then back. At such a moment we see the Stuart royal family *presented* in the audience and *re-presented* in the play. The wide gap between the family of history and the family of art blurs, making *Henry VIII*, whether by design or accident, the perfect culmination of the use of the text of the Jacobean royal family in the Romances.

In this play several texts are held in solution, but the play closes with a conscious emphasis on the Stuart royal family. *Henry VIII* makes explicit what has been implicit throughout the Romances. The final flattering image of Henry reflects the image of James and his family—here concrete but in the other Romances more oblique. The birth of the royal female child reminds the theater audience that their sovereign is himself king by virtue of the female line. The long road that Shakespeare has traveled in the Romances from London to Edinburgh and back is now complete.

5

Epilogue

The web of our life," the Second Lord says in *All's Well That Ends Well*, "is of a mingled yarn, good and ill together" (IV.iii. 66–67). Such a statement could serve as a description of the Romances, those interwoven plays of tragedy and comedy, hope and despair, things dying and things new–born. The Lord's comment also describes Shakespeare's technique of bringing together several different sources and his own imagination to create a web of drama. The mingled yarn that constitutes the web of life also functions as a definition for a text, "text" literally meaning that which is woven, a web. What I have been suggesting in the preceding pages is that James's family constitutes a text that Shakespeare weaves into the fabric of the Romances, its good and ill together, its private and political life. The bright thread of the Stuart royal family accents the politics of these plays. The story of James's family provides good yarn for the Romances.

Affecting our understanding of dramatic texts is the recognition that the radical of theatrical literature of the English Renaissance is its collaborative nature, as Stephen Orgel notes.[1] Despite our best efforts, we still know relatively little about the texts that playwrights presented to acting companies. With the exception of *Pericles*, the only texts that we have for the Romances are the ones printed in the 1623 Folio. But surely, from their documented performances to their first printing, a wide gap exists in which many changes may have occurred in the text. I raise this point to underscore the possibility that all kinds of forces—theatrical, political, and social—could have affected the eventual text. Hence, the presence of the royal family and certain events in its public and private life collaborate in shaping the Romances. I am not saying that King James ordered Shakespeare to do anything. But as the King's Men readied *The Winter's Tale*, *The Tempest*, *Henry VIII*, and perhaps the others, for court performances, did they take into account the royal family before whom they would perform? The texts of *The Winter's Tale* and *The Tempest* performed for the wedding festivities in 1613 may, for example, have differed from earlier versions. I am not urging that we fling wide the doors of speculation but only that we realize the limitations of our knowledge of Shakespeare's text and that we acknowledge the possible intervention of historical and topical events into the texture of the texts.

The intermingled nature of the Romances suggests that we can also see them as paintings, full of contrasting hues, tones, and subject matter. Indeed, some seventeenth-century paintings depict precisely the intertextual quality that I have analyzed. The much-commented-on Velázquez painting *Las Meninas* (1656) certainly offers an image of representation, as we see the king and queen reflected in a mirror.[2] I direct attention to *The Concert* (c. 1664), painted by the Dutch artist Johannes Vermeer (1632–75); the picture now hangs in the Isabella Stewart Gardner Museum in Boston.

The black-and-white tile floor in the painting suggests a mingling of contrasts, but at first glance everything appears completely serene and harmonious as two women and one man perform music. Typical of Vermeer's paintings, light enters from somewhere at the left side of the painting, casting a warm glow on the pleasant scene. In addition to the harpsichord that one woman plays, other musical instruments lie about the room, perhaps anticipating other performers. The lid on the harpsichord has a genial landscape on it that seems duplicated in a picture hanging on the left side of the wall. Indeed, the lid of the harpsichord almost touches the landscape painting, only to dip away from the picture on the right. The top of the lid also intersects the two paintings almost at their midpoint. The hues of color on the harpsichord serve as a transition or bridge between the two pictures.

I am particularly interested, however, in the other picture that hangs on that same wall, offering as it does a contrast to the rest of Vermeer's painting. Edward Snow observes that the contrast between the two wall paintings is that between "erotic interaction and imaginative solitude."[3] The sensual subject matter of the wall painting on the right sets it apart from the rest of the scene, but Vermeer intends that it be an integral part of the whole picture. At least four pictures compose Vermeer's painting: the two on the wall, the one on the harpsichord, and the total panorama that includes all the discrete parts (i.e., *The Concert*).

224

Johannes Vermeer, *The Concert* (c. 1664). Courtesy of Isabella Stewart Gardner Museum, Boston

We know the name of the sensual wall picture because in it Vermeer has deliberately, consciously imitated a 1622 picture by Dirck van Baburen (c. 1595–1624), entitled *The Procuress*, which today hangs in the Boston Museum of Fine Arts. In *The Concert*, Vermeer provides a faithful rendering of Baburen's picture. Vermeer had himself earlier painted a picture called *The Procuress* (1656), itself indebted to Baburen, but he avoids his own work and instead represents Baburen's version of the subject. Documentary evidence suggests that Vermeer's mother-in-law may have owned the Baburen picture.[4]

Certainly Vermeer's fascination with this picture continued to the end of his career, when he also included it in his *Lady Seated at a Virginal*, again in a wall painting.

As one looks at *The Concert*, one sees the intertextual relationship of several scenes in this one picture. Obviously Vermeer has "read" the "text" of Baburen's painting and has decided to weave it into the fabric of his pictorial text. *The Procuress* in the midst of *The Concert* demonstrates again the mingled nature of life and texts. For me it is an image of what Shakespeare was doing in the Romances as he brought together several sources to create his fictional world. As in Vermeer's painting, we can discern some identifiable texts within Shakespeare's last plays: Greene's *Pandosto*, Gower's *Confessio Amantis*, Holinshed's *Chronicles*, and, as I have argued, the Stuart royal family. Like the landscape wall picture in Vermeer's *The Concert*, other parts, other texts, also exist in the Romances, which we recognize but cannot identify.

The text of the Stuart royal family helps raise a question that surges through the Romances with relentless urgency, that voiced by the Surveyor in *Henry VIII*: ". . . if the king / Should without issue die . . ." (I.ii.133–34). In Tyre, Sicily, Milan, and ancient Britain, such a question resounds through the domestic and public life of the royal family. The Dedication to King James of the new Authorized Bible in 1611 celebrates what James has accomplished through his family. The writers of the Dedication, having acknowledged the "thicke and palpable cloudes of darkenesse" that shrouded the land at Elizabeth's death, emphasize the brightness of James's arrival to the English throne, his sun dispelling "those supposed and surmised mists." The "exceeding cause of comfort" grew "especially when we beheld the gouernment established in your HIGHNESSE, and your hopefull Seed, by an undoubted Title, and this also accompanied with Peace and tranquillitie, at home and abroad" (London, 1611, sig. A2). These writers interpret the meaning of James's succession and the legitimacy of his royal genealogy; so does Shakespeare. Such political issues are not, however, a matter of any significance in the majority of Jacobean comedies, as I demonstrated in chapter 3. Shakespeare generally situates himself at odds with most of his fellow comic dramatists. He becomes fascinated with the politics of the royal family in a comic mode at a time when the children of James are achieving prominence. He pursues these questions of politics and family with an intensity and emphasis not found in the usually acknowledged sources for the last plays.

Dirck van Baburen, *The Procuress* (1624), oil on canvas; Purchase, M. Theresa B. Hopkins Fund, 1950; courtesy, Museum of Fine Arts, Boston.

By placing the theater under royal patronage, James, whatever his motivation, endowed the theater with stability and security, making it possible, among other things, for dramatists to be self-conscious about their artistry in a way alien to Elizabethan drama. Similarly, I think James's solution to the succession problem by having living heirs freed Shakespeare to explore this political-familial matter through his fiction, dramatizing both the vulnerability and the possible stability that the kingdom experiences. Audiences seeing the

227

Romances in the aftermath of Prince Henry's death must have sensed a special immediacy in their topicality.

James believed that a king is as one set on a stage whose every gesture the public gazingly beholds. Certainly at the great public events for his family, the concept, no longer a metaphor, becomes a reality. In his families of art Shakespeare re-presents this experience of the family of history. When the royal family was present for performances of the Romances, they, too, could watch a king and a royal family. At such moments the audience's delight would multiply by seeing the presentation and the re-presentation of the Stuart royal family. In many ways James and his family constituted a drama, a public spectacle but also a hidden mystery: an opaque and a transparent text.

"Our revels now are ended," Prospero says in Act IV; but the play continues. This investigation of Shakespeare and the Stuart royal family ends, even as I am sure that it will continue. Cymbeline says: "Let's quit this ground, / And smoke the temple with our sacrifices" (V.v.398–99). The rising smoke, he notes later, will be "crooked"—perhaps because imperfect. That image captures, it seems to me, the position of the critic, struggling against the "sweet smoke of rhetoric" that Armado refers to in *Love's Labour's Lost* and yet trying to make an adequate sacrifice, even if with crooked smoke. What I have attempted coincides with Charles Frey's suggestion that dramatic criticism "will be satisfied with—in fact, will aim at— nothing less than a kind of failure, a conviction of having brought the reader or spectator not to the completion of the journey but only to its beginning."[5] In the end of this particular journey resides its beginning. I have opened the text of the Stuart royal family, the book of kings, have read from it, and have interpreted it. In now closing that text, I hope that we will spy many new possibilities.

Notes

CHAPTER 1
INTRODUCTION

1. Ralph Winwood, *Memorials of Affairs of State in the Reigns of Q. Elizabeth and K. James I*, ed. Edmund Sawyer, 3 vols. (London, 1725), 2:54.

2. Friederich Ludwig Georg von Raumer, *History of the Sixteenth and Seventeenth Centuries*, 2 vols. (London: John Murray, 1835), 2:219-220.

3. Jonathan Goldberg, *James I and the Politics of Literature: Jonson, Shakespeare, Donne, and Their Contemporaries* (Baltimore, Md., and London: Johns Hopkins University Press, 1983), p. 150.

4. Gary Schmidgall, *Shakespeare and the Courtly Aesthetic* (Berkeley, Los Angeles, and London: University of California Press, 1981), p. 100.

5. C. L. Barber, "The Family in Shakespeare's Development: Tragedy and Sacredness," in *Representing Shakespeare: New Psychoanalytic Essays*, ed. Murray M. Schwartz and Coppélia Kahn (Baltimore, Md.: Johns Hopkins University Press, 1980), pp. 188-202. Such interest continues; see, for example, Sarup Singh, *Family Relationships in Shakespeare and the Restoration Comedy of Manners* (Delhi: Oxford University Press, 1983); and David Sundelson, *Shakespeare's Restorations of the Father* (New Brunswick, N.J.: Rutgers University Press, 1983).

6. Louis Adrian Montrose, " 'The Place of a Brother' in *As You Like It*: Social Process and Comic Form," *Shakespeare Quarterly* 32 (1981): 28-54.

7. Maynard Mack, *Rescuing Shakespeare*, International Shakespeare Association Occasional Papers no. 1 (Oxford: University Press for the International Shakespeare Association, 1979), pp. 5-6.

8. S. Schoenbaum, *William Shakespeare: A Compact Documentary Life* (London and New York: Oxford University Press, 1977).

9. R. E. Gajdusek, "Death, Incest, and the Triple Bond in Shakespeare," *American Imago* 31 (1974): 133. The essay is found on pp. 109-58.

10. Charles K. Hofling, "Notes on Shakespeare's *Cymbeline*," *Shakespeare Studies* 1 (1965): 128. The essay appears on pp. 118-36.

11. *The Letters and the Life of Francis Bacon*, ed. James Spedding, vol. 4 (London: Longmans, Green, Reader & Dyer, 1868), p. 307.

12. Thomas Fuller, *The Church-History of Britain* (London, 1655), bk. 10, p. 67.

13. *The Letters of John Keats 1814–1821,* ed. Hyder E. Rollins (Cambridge: Harvard University Press, 1958), vol. 2, p. 67.

14. Josephine Waters Bennett, *Measure for Measure as Royal Entertainment* (New York and London: Columbia University Press, 1966). A more recent attempt to make the case for a topical interpretation is Arthur Melville Clark's *Murder under Trust: or, The Topical Macbeth and Other Jacobean Matters* (Edinburgh: Scottish Academic Press, 1981). In his brief introductory chapter, "Shakespeare and Topicality," pp. 1–6, Clark does not touch on the Romances, nor does he examine any recent studies of the issue of topicality.

15. Richard Levin, *New Readings vs. Old Plays* (Chicago: University of Chicago Press, 1979), pp. 171–93.

16. Frances Yates, *Majesty and Magic in Shakespeare's Last Plays* (Boulder, Colo.: Shambhala, 1978); published in 1975 in England under the title *Shakespeare's Last Plays: A New Approach* (London: Routledge & Kegan Paul, 1975)—a most interesting, perhaps revealing, change in title.

17. Glynne Wickham, *"The Winter's Tale:* A Comedy with Deaths," in his *Shakespeare's Dramatic Heritage* (London: Routledge & Kegan Paul, 1969), p. 265.

18. Glynne Wickham, "Shakespeare's Investiture Play: The Occasion and Subject of 'The Winter's Tale,' " *TLS,* 18 Dec. 1969, p. 1456. This brief piece was later expanded and appeared as "Romance and Emblem: A Study in the Dramatic Structure of *The Winter's Tale,"* in *Elizabethan Theatre III,* ed. David Galloway (Toronto: Macmillan, 1973), pp. 82–99. These early pieces by Wickham were attacked by Hallett Smith in his *Shakespeare's Romances: A Study of Some Ways of the Imagination* (San Marino, Calif.: Huntington Library, 1972), in app. B, "The Topicality of *Cymbeline* and *The Winter's Tale,"* pp. 211–21. Thus far Wickham has not responded to such criticism.

19. Glynne Wickham, "From Tragedy to Tragi-Comedy: 'King Lear' as Prologue," *Shakespeare Survey* 26 (1973): 33–48.

20. Wallace Notestein, *The House of Commons 1604–1610* (New Haven, Conn., and London: Yale University Press, 1971), p. 256.

21. Glynne Wickham, "Riddle and Emblem: A Study in the Dramatic Structure of *Cymbeline,"* in *English Renaissance Studies Presented to Dame Helen Gardner,* ed. John Carey (Oxford: Clarendon Press, 1980), p. 100. The essay is on pp. 94–113.

22. Glynn Wickham, "Masque and Anti-masque in 'The Tempest,' " *Essays and Studies* 28 (1975): 9.

23. M. C. Bradbrook, "Shakespeare and the Multiple Theatres of Jacobean London," *Elizabethan Theatre VI,* ed. G. R. Hibbard (Toronto: Macmillan, 1978), p. 101.

24. Rosalie L. Colie, *Shakespeare's Living Art* (Princeton, N.J.: Princeton University Press, 1974), pp. 25–26.

25. Maynard Mack, *King Lear in Our Time* (Berkeley and Los Angeles: University of California Press, 1972), p. 49.

26. Jonathan Goldberg, " 'Upon a publike stage': The Royal Gaze and Jacobean Theater," *Research Opportunities in Renaissance Drama* 24 (1981): 19.

27. Howard Felperin, *Shakespearean Representation: Mimesis and Modernity in Elizabethan Tragedy* (Princeton, N.J.: Princeton University Press, 1977), p. 8.

28. Goldberg, *James I*, p. 147.

29. Jonathan Culler, *The Pursuit of Signs: Semiotics, Literature, Deconstruction* (Ithaca, N.Y.: Cornell University Press, 1981), p. 110.

30. Norman Rabkin, *Shakespeare and the Problem of Meaning* (Chicago and London: University of Chicago Press, 1981), p. 124.

31. Northrop Frye, *The Secular Scripture: A Study of the Structure of Romance* (Cambridge: Harvard University Press, 1976), p. 53.

32. Peter Laslett, *The World We Have Lost*, 2d ed. (London: Methuen, 1971), p. 22.

33. L. P. Hartley, *The Go-Between* (London: Hamilton, 1953), p. 9. I am indebted to Maynard Mack's lecture for this reference.

CHAPTER 2
THE ROYAL FAMILY

1. *The Basilicon Doron of King James VI*, ed. James Craigie, Scottish Text Society (Edinburgh and London: Blackwood, 1944), p. 25.

2. *The Political Works of James I*, ed. Charles H. McIlwain (Cambridge: Harvard University Press, 1918), p. 272.

3. George Marcelline, *The Triumphs of King James the First* (London, 1610), pp. 50–51.

4. Leon Battista Alberti, *The Albertis of Florence: Leon Battista Alberti's "Della Famiglia,"* trans. Guido A. Guarino (Lewisburg, Pa.: Bucknell University Press, 1971), p. 188.

5. Phillipe Ariès, *Centuries of Childhood*, trans. Robert Baldick (London: Jonathan Cape, 1962), p. 353. Originally published in Paris in 1960 with the title *L'Enfant et la vie familiale sous l'ancien régime*.

6. Lawrence Stone, *The Family, Sex and Marriage in England 1500–1800* (London: Weidenfeld & Nicolson, 1977), p. 55. The abridged version was published in 1979.

7. Lynda E. Boose, "The Father and the Bride in Shakespeare," *PMLA* 97 (1982): 325.

8. Gordon J. Schochet, *Patriarchalism in Political Thought* (Oxford: Basil Blackwell, 1975), p. 65. See also Jonathan Goldberg's discussion "Fatherly Authority: Politics of the Family," in his *James I and the Politics of Literature* (Baltimore, Md., and London: Johns Hopkins University Press, 1983), pp. 85–112.

9. George Puttenham, *The Arte of English Poesie*, ed. Gladys Doidge Willcock and Alice Walker (Cambridge: Cambridge University Press, 1936), bk. 1, chap. 25, p. 49.

10. William McElwee, *The Wisest Fool in Christendom: The Reign of King James I and VI* (New York: Harcourt Brace, 1958), p. 123.

11. *The Works of Francis Bacon*, ed. James Spedding, Robert Ellis, and Douglas Heath, vol. 6 (London: Longmans, 1878), p. 276.

12. *The Letters and the Life of Francis Bacon*, ed. James Spedding, vol. 4 (London: Longmans, Green, Reader & Dyer, 1868), p. 307.

13. In John Nichols, *The Progresses, Processions, and Magnificent Festivities of King James the First*, 4 vols. (London: J. B. Nichols, 1828), 1:*122.

14. *Calendar of State Papers Venetian 1603–1607* (London: HMSO, 1900), vol. 10, p. 139.

15. Gilbert Dugdale, *The Time Triumphant* (London, 1604), sig. A3. See my discussion "Gilbert Dugdale and the Royal Entry of James I (1604)," *Journal of Medieval and Renaissance Studies* 13 (1983): 111–25.

16. Thomas Fuller, *The Church-History of Britain* (London, 1655), bk. 10, p. 21.

17. *The Autobiography of Phineas Pett*, ed. W. G. Perin (London: Navy Records Society, 1918), p. 80.

18. Ralph Winwood, *Memorials of Affairs of State in the Reigns of Q. Elizabeth and K. James I*, ed. Edmund Sawyer, 3 vols. (London, 1725), 2:57.

19. Nichols, *Progresses*, 1:505.

20. Ethel Carleton Williams, *Anne of Denmark: Wife of James VI of Scotland: James I of England* (London: Longman, 1970), p. 104.

21. P. M. Handover, *Arbella Stuart: Royal Lady of Hardwick and Cousin to King James* (London: Eyre & Spottiswoode, 1957), p. 214.

22. *Calendar of the Manuscripts of the Marquess of Salisbury, . . . Hatfield House* (London: HMSO, 1965), pt. 19, p. 308.

23. McElwee, *Wisest Fool in Christendom*, p. 169. Other studies of James to consult are: G. P. V. Akrigg, *Jacobean Pageant or the Court of King James I* (London: Hamish Hamilton, 1962); Caroline Bingham, *James I of England* (London: Weidenfeld & Nicolson, 1981); Antonia Fraser, *King James VI of Scotland I of England* (New York: Knopf, 1975); Samuel R. Gardiner, *History of England from the Accession of James I to the Outbreak of the Civil War 1603–1642*, 10 vols. (1894–96; reprint, New York: AMS Press, 1965); S. J. Houston, *James I* (London: Longman, 1973); David Mathew, *James I* (London: Eyre & Spottiswoode, 1967); Otto J. Scott, *James I* (New York: Mason Charter, 1976); Alan G. R. Smith, ed., *The Reign of James VI and I* (London: Macmillan, 1973); Charles Williams, *James I* (1934; reprint, London: Arthur Barker, 1951); D. Harris Willson, *King James VI and I* (London: Jonathan Cape, 1956).

24. Antonia Fraser, *Queen of Scots* (New York: Delacorte Press, 1969), p. 456. Fraser's Chapter 23, "Mother and Son," pp. 455–74, offers a convenient summary of the relationship between Mary and James.

25. On this point see Scott, *James I*, p. 87.

26. Goldberg, *James I*, p. 16; for a discussion of James's relationship with Mary see pp. 12–17.

27. William Sanderson, *A Compleat History of the Lives and Reigns of Mary Queen of Scotland and of Her Son and Successor, James* (London, 1656), p. 366.

28. Anthony Weldon, *The Court and Character of King James* (London, 1651), p. 173.

29. *Memoirs of Sir James Melville of Halhill 1535–1617*, ed. A. Francis Steuart (London: Routledge, 1929), p. 346.

30. In Friederich Ludwig Georg von Raumer, *History of the Sixteenth and Seventeenth Centuries*, 2 vols. (London: Murray, 1835), 2:197.

31. *Memorials of the Holles Family 1493–1656*, ed. A. C. Wood, Camden 3d ser., vol. 55 (London: Camden Society, 1937), p. 100.

32. *Calendar of the Manuscripts of the Marquess of Salisbury,* pt. 16, p. 220.

33. For a good account of their battle over the upbringing of Prince Henry see J. W. Williamson, *The Myth of the Conqueror: Prince Henry Stuart: A Study of 17th Century Personation* (New York: AMS Press, 1978), pp. 14–21.

34. Francis Osborne, *Traditional Memoirs,* in *Secret History of the Court of James the First,* ed. Sir Walter Scott, 2 vols. (Edinburgh: Ballantyne, 1811), 1:196.

35. Harleian MS. 6986.106, British Library.

36. Godfrey Goodman, *The Court of King James the First,* ed. John S. Brewer, 2 vols. (London: Richard Bentley, 1839), 1:168.

37. Edward Peyton, *The Divine Catastrophe of the Kingly Family of the House of Stuarts,* in *Secret History,* 2:346. Originally published in 1652.

38. *The Letters of John Chamberlain,* ed. Norman E. McClure, 2 vols. (Philadelphia: American Philosophical Society, 1939), 1:404.

39. Gardiner, *History of England,* 2:73.

40. Elkin Calhoun Wilson, *Prince Henry and English Literature* (Ithaca, N.Y.: Cornell University Press, 1946); Williamson, *Myth of the Conqueror.* I have added information not in Wilson's study in my "Prince Henry and English Civic Pageantry," *Tennessee Studies in Literature* 13 (1968): 109–16.

41. Charles Cornwallis, *The Life and Death of our late most incomparable and Heroique Prince Henry* (London, 1641), in John Somers, *A Collection of Scarce and Valuable Tracts* (hereafter cited as *Tracts*), 2d ed., ed. Walter Scott, vol. 2 (London, 1809), pp. 226–27.

42. Henry Peacham, *Minerva Britanna* (London, 1612), p. 17.

43. For a good summary of Henry as patron of the arts see Graham Parry, *The Golden Age Restor'd: The Culture of the Stuart Court, 1603–42* (Manchester: Manchester University Press, 1981), pp. 64–94.

44. W. H., *The True Picture and Relation of Prince Henry* (Leyden, 1634), p. 31. This anonymous account is extraordinarily rich in anecdotal examples about Henry.

45. In Thomas Birch, *The Life of Henry Prince of Wales* (London, 1760), p. 370.

46. James Maxwell, *The Laudable Life, and Deplorable Death, of our late peerlesse Prince Henry* (London, 1612), sig. B2^v.

47. Charles Cornwallis, *A Discourse of the most Illustrious Prince Henry, late Prince of Wales* (London, 1641), in Somers, *Tracts,* 2:222.

48. Harleian MS. 6986.103. British Library.

49. Cornwallis, *Discourse,* in Somers, *Tracts,* 2:223.

50. W. H., *True Picture,* p. 9.

51. *Letters of John Chamberlain,* 1:390.

52. Weldon, *Court and Character of King James,* p. 78.

53. For a convenient summary of the theories of Henry's death see Williamson, *Myth of the Conqueror,* pp. 166–69. Seventeenth-century writers, such as Edward Peyton and Arthur Wilson, fanned the flames of speculation about the possibility that Henry had been poisoned. The idea grows from a cryptic note sent by Sir Walter Ralegh, who, though imprisoned, was implored by Anne to prepare a cordial for her dying son. With the medicinal potion came the claim from Ralegh that this would surely cure Henry "except

in case of poison.'' Ralegh's note is, of course, a slim basis on which to suggest poisoning; after all, Ralegh puts himself in a good position, as he doubtless also gets even with James for imprisoning him. More credible is the recognition that the symptoms for typhoid fever, presumably the cause of Henry's death, and certain kinds of poisoning are identical. The last serious medical analysis and review of Henry's death was done in the late nineteenth century; perhaps time is ripe for another look at the medical evidence. Williamson rather accepts the idea of poisoning and surveys several possible perpetrators, especially Carr and James himself. That both Carr and James may have desired Henry's star to wane a bit is undeniable, but whether they were prompted to have him poisoned can only be speculation. Indeed, as I have shown, much in James's response suggests that he was genuinely touched by the death of his son, even if the mourning period was cut a bit short in order to get on with the betrothal of Elizabeth and Frederick. Like a famous fictional character, James, with an eye on his depleted treasury, may have decided to use the funeral meats ''to furnish forth the marriage tables''—thrift, thrift.

54. For studies of and information about Elizabeth see: Elizabeth Ogilvy Benger, *Memoirs of Elizabeth Stuart, Queen of Bohemia,* 2 vols. (London: Longman, Green, 1825); Alice Buchan, *A Stuart Portrait* (London: Peter Davies, 1934); Carola Oman [Lenanton], *Elizabeth of Bohemia* (London: Hodder & Stoughton, 1938); *The Letters of Elizabeth Queen of Bohemia,* ed. L. M. Baker (London: Bodley Head, 1953); Mary Anne Everett Green, *Elizabeth Electress Palatine and Queen of Bohemia,* revised by S. C. Loman (1855; reprint, London: Methuen, 1909); Marie Hay, *The Winter Queen Being the Unhappy History of Elizabeth Stuart* (London: Constable, 1910); Jessica Gorst-Williams, *Elizabeth the Winter Queen* (London: Abelard, 1977).

55. Thomas Ross, *Idae sive De Jacobi* (London, 1608), pp. 322–23. An enumeration of the several virtues of James's family may be found on pp. 240–330. The translation of this passage about Elizabeth is from Green, *Elizabeth,* pp. 15–16.

56. John Harington, *Nugae Antiquae,* 3 vols. (London, 1779), 2:239–40.

57. Lansdowne MS. 90, art. 77, recorded in Green, *Elizabeth,* p. 17.

58. Harleian MS. 6986.52, British Library.

59. *Report on the Manuscripts of the Duke of Portland,* ed. R. F. Isaacson, vol. 9 (London: HMSO, 1923), p. 26.

60. Parry, *Golden Age Restor'd,* p. 106. Parry has a chapter on the wedding festivities, pp. 95–107. He rightly calls Elizabeth and Frederick the ''most distinguished refugees of the Thirty Years' War'' (p. 106).

61. *The Memoirs of Robert Carey,* ed. F. H. Mares (Oxford: Clarendon Press, 1972), p. 68.

62. Harleian MS. 6986.85, British Library.

63. Akrigg, *Jacobean Pageant,* p. 116.

64. These and other events in Arbella's life are discussed by David N. Durant, *Arbella Stuart: A Rival to the Queen* (London: Weidenfeld & Nicolson, 1978), and by P. M. Handover, *Arbella Stuart;* see also Ian McInnes, *Arabella: The Life and Times of Lady Arabella Seymour, 1575–1615* (London: Allen, 1968).

65. Claude Lévi-Strauss, "The Family," in *Man, Culture, and Society,* ed. Harry L. Shapiro, rev. ed. (London: Oxford University Press, 1971), p. 356.

66. *Wentworth Papers 1597–1628,* ed. J. P. Cooper, Camden 4th ser., vol. 12 (London: Royal Historical Society, 1973), p. 82.

67. Lancelot Andrewes, *Ninety-six Sermons,* vol. 4 (Oxford: J. H. Parker, 1853), p. 217.

CHAPTER 3

FAMILY, SEX, AND MARRIAGE IN JACOBEAN COMEDY

1. *The Plays of George Chapman: The Comedies,* gen. ed. Allan Holaday (Urbana: University of Illinois Press, 1970).

2. Edward Sharpham, *The Fleire* (London, 1607), Act II, sig. D1^v.

3. For a standard discussion of satire see Alvin Kernan, *The Cankered Muse: Satire of the English Renaissance* (New Haven, Conn.: Yale University Press, 1959).

4. Clifford Geertz, "Centers, Kings, and Charisma: Reflections on the Symbolics of Power," in his *Local Knowledge: Further Essays in Interpretive Anthropology* (New York: Basic Books, 1983), p. 143.

5. *The Works of Francis Bacon,* ed. James Spedding et al., vol. 6 (London: Longmans, 1878), p. 397. I am indebted to George R. Hibbard's essay "Love, Marriage and Money in Shakespeare's Theatre and Shakespeare's England," in *Elizabethan Theatre VI,* ed. G. R. Hibbard (Toronto: Macmillan, 1978), p. 134, for this reference and several other ideas.

6. See Alexander Leggatt, *Citizen Comedy in the Age of Shakespeare* (Toronto: University of Toronto Press, 1973), chap. 5, pp. 78–98, for a discussion of marriage.

7. *The Dramatic Works in the Beaumont and Fletcher Canon,* gen. ed. Fredson Bowers, vol. 1 (Cambridge: Cambridge University Press, 1966). *The Coxcomb* is edited by Irby B. Cauthen, Jr.; I quote from this edition.

8. *Ben Jonson: Three Comedies,* ed. Michael Jamieson (Baltimore, Md.: Penguin, 1966). All quotations from *Volpone* will be from this edition.

9. *Epicoene or The Silent Woman,* ed. L. A. Beaurline (Lincoln: University of Nebraska, 1966). All quotations are from this edition. For a good discussion of this play on the subject of marriage see Leggatt, *Citizen Comedy in the Age of Shakespeare,* pp. 87–90. We share similar views about the play.

10. Louis Adrian Montrose, " 'The Place of a Brother' in *As You Like It:* Social Process and Comic Form," *Shakespeare Quarterly* 32 (1981): 28–54.

11. *The Dramatic Works of Thomas Heywood,* ed. R. H. Shepherd, vol. 6 (1874; reprint, New York: Russell & Russell, 1964). All quotations are from this edition.

12. *The Dramatic Works of Thomas Dekker,* ed. Fredson Bowers, vol. 1 (Cambridge: Cambridge University, 1955).

13. *The Dramatic Works in the Beaumont and Fletcher Canon,* gen. ed. Fredson Bowers, vol. 4 (Cambridge: Cambridge University Press, 1979). Bowers is the editor of *The Woman's Prize.* All quotations will be from this edition.

14. *The Fawn,* ed. Gerald A. Smith (Lincon: University of Nebraska Press, 1965).

15. *Cupids Whirligig* (London, 1616). I quote from this edition. The first quarto edition was in 1607. There is only one modern edition of the play, that edited by Allardyce Nicoll for the Golden Cockerel Press, 1926.

16. *The Plays of George Chapman. The Widow's Tears* is edited by Robert Ornstein. All quotations are from this edition.

17. *The Works of Thomas Middleton,* ed. A. H. Bullen, vol. 3 (Boston: Houghton, Mifflin, 1885). All quotations for this play are from the Bullen edition.

18. As Kernan notes in *The Cankered Muse,* Elizabethans, in their confused understanding of the etymology of the word "satire," thought that it might derive from the Arabic word for "spear" (p. 55). Perhaps Middleton has that in mind here.

19. *Michaelmas Term,* ed. Richard Levin (Lincoln: University of Nebraska Press, 1966). All quotations will be from this Regents Renaissance Drama text.

20. Hibbard, "Love, Marriage and Money in Shakespeare's Theatre and Shakespeare's England," p. 144. See his excellent discussion of *A Chaste Maid,* pp. 144–50. Ruby Chatterji has also explored the theme of family in "Theme, Imagery, and Unity in *A Chaste Maid in Cheapside,*" *Renaissance Drama* 8 (1965): 105–26. I have also touched on family relationships in my essay "Middleton's Moral Landscape: *A Chaste Maid in Cheapside* and *The Triumphs of Truth,*" in *"Accompaninge the players": Essays Celebrating Thomas Middleton, 1580–1980,* ed. Kenneth Friedenreich (New York: AMS Press, 1983), pp. 133–46.

21. *A Chaste Maid in Cheapside,* ed. R. B. Parker (London: Methuen, 1969). Quotations will be from this Revels edition. Parker in his introduction also discusses the commercial nature of marital and family relationships.

22. John Day, *Humour out of Breath* (London, 1608), sig. H2^v.

23. John Day, *Law-Tricks,* ed. John Crow (Oxford: Malone Society, 1950). All quotations will be from this edition.

24. William Rowley, *A Shoo-maker a gentleman* (London, 1638). All quotations are from this original text.

25. *The Dramatic Works in the Beaumont and Fletcher Canon,* gen. ed. Fredson Bowers, vol. 2 (Cambridge: Cambridge University Press, 1970). *A King and No King* is edited by George Walton Williams. I quote from this edition.

26. For a discussion of this question and other pertinent issues see *Philaster,* ed. Andrew Gurr (London: Methuen, 1969), "Introduction," pp. xix–lxxxiv.

27. *The Dramatic Works in the Beaumont and Fletcher Canon,* gen. ed. Fredson Bowers, vol. 1 (Cambridge: Cambridge University Press, 1966). *Philaster* is edited by Robert K. Turner, Jr. I quote from this edition.

CHAPTER 4
SHAKESPEARE'S ROMANCES

PERICLES
1. Stephen Greenblatt, "The Cultivation of Anxiety: King Lear and His Heirs," *Raritan* 2 (1982): 102.

2. C. L. Barber, "'Thou that beget'st him that did thee beget': Transformation in 'Pericles' and 'The Winter's Tale,'" *Shakespeare Survey* 22 (1969): 61.

3. Jonathan Goldberg, *James I and the Politics of Literature* (Baltimore, Md.: Johns Hopkins University Press, 1983), p. 119.

4. D. W. Harding, "Shakespeare's Final View of Women," *TLS*, 30 Nov. 1979, p. 61.

5. Gary Schmidgall, *Shakespeare and the Courtly Aesthetic* (Berkeley, Los Angeles, and London: University of California Press, 1981), p. 114.

6. Carol Gesner, *Shakespeare & the Greek Romance: A Study of Origins* (Lexington: University Press of Kentucky, 1970).

7. *Pericles*, ed. F. David Hoeniger, Arden edition (London: Methuen, 1963). All quotations will be from this edition.

8. Howard Felperin, *Shakespearean Romance* (Princeton, N.J.: Princeton University Press, 1972), p. 155.

9. Gerard A. Barker, "Themes and Variations in Shakespeare's *Pericles*," *English Studies* 44 (1963): 407.

10. Geoffrey Bullough, ed. *Narrative and Dramatic Sources of Shakespeare*, vol. 6 (London: Routledge & Kegan Paul; New York: Columbia University Press, 1966). All citations will be to the texts included in Bullough's volume.

11. *The Political Works of James I*, ed. Charles Howard McIlwain (Cambridge: Harvard University Press, 1918), p. 271.

12. Harding, "Shakespeare's Final View of Women," p. 60.

CYMBELINE

13. G. Wilson Knight, *The Crown of Life* (1947; reprint, New York: Barnes & Noble, 1966), p. 129.

14. J. P. Brockbank, "History and Histrionics in *Cymbeline*," *Shakespeare Survey* 11 (1958): 42–49.

15. Robin Moffet, "*Cymbeline* and the Nativity," *Shakespeare Quarterly* 13 (1962): 207–18.

16. See my "*Cymbeline*: Shakespeare's Last Roman Play," *Shakespeare Quarterly* 31 (1980): 31–41.

17. Emrys Jones, "Stuart Cymbeline," *Essays in Criticism* 11 (1961): 84–99. Paul A. Jorgenson, in his *Shakespeare's Military World* (Berkeley and Los Angeles: University of California Press, 1956), had, in fact, in chapter 5, "War and Peace," pp. 169–207, discussed the connection of *Cymbeline* with James's policy of pacifism (see especially pp. 199–203). Jorgenson suggests that "*Cymbeline* provides a more sustained mirroring of Jacobean policy" (p. 201).

18. Bernard Harris, "'What's past is prologue': 'Cymbeline' and 'Henry VIII,'" in *Later Shakespeare*, ed. J. R. Brown and Bernard Harris, Stratford-upon-Avon Studies 8 (London: Arnold, 1966; New York: St. Martin's, 1967), pp. 202–33.

19. Philip Edwards, *Threshold of a Nation: A Study in English and Irish Drama* (Cambridge: Cambridge University Press, 1979), p. 94.

20. Glynne Wickham, "Riddle and Emblem: A Study in the Dramatic Structure of *Cymbeline*," in *English Renaissance Studies Presented to Dame Helen Gardner*, ed. John Carey (Oxford: Clarendon Press, 1980), pp. 94, 103.

21. *Narrative and Dramatic Sources of Shakespeare*, ed. Geoffrey Bullough, vol. 8, (London: Routledge & Kegan Paul; New York: Columbia University Press, 1975), p. 43.

22. See my essay "Sexuality in *Cymbeline*," *Essays in Literature* 10 (1983): 159–68.

23. Anthony Munday, *Triumphs of Re-United Britannia* (London, 1605), sig. B2.

24. Anthony Munday, *Londons Love to the Royal Prince Henrie* (London, 1610), sig. C2.

25. *Cymbeline*, ed. James Nosworthy (1959; rpt. London: Methuen, 1966). All quotations will be from this Arden edition.

26. *Political Works of James I*, p. 306.

27. Meredith Skura, "Interpreting Posthumus' Dream from Above and Below: Families, Psychoanalysts, and Literary Critics," in *Representing Shakespeare: New Psychoanalytic Essays*, ed. Murray M. Schwartz and Coppélia Kahn (Baltimore, Md., and London: Johns Hopkins University Press, 1980), p. 207. Skura's essay is an excellent investigation of families in *Cymbeline*.

28. See my essay "Sexuality in *Cymbeline*."

29. At least one critic has explored a connection between Guiderius and King James. James Dauphiné in "Le Secret de *Cymbeline*," *Études Anglaises* 32 (1979): 129–42, suggests that these two share the same zodiac sign of their birth (p. 140). He adds also that the cedar and lion, so important in the play, were associated with James as traditional emblems of royalty. On the whole this seems slight evidence indeed for connecting James with the play.

THE WINTER'S TALE

30. *The Winter's Tale*, ed. J. H. P. Pafford (London: Methuen, 1963). All quotations will be from this Arden edition.

31. Hallett Smith, *Shakespeare's Romances: A Study of Some Ways of the Imagination* (San Marino, Calif.: Huntington Library, 1972), p. 221. Other critics do, however, see the relevance of historical events for the play; consider Frederick W. Sternfeld, "Le Symbolisme musical dans quelques pièces de Shakespeare présentées à la Cour d'Angleterre," in *Les Fêtes de la Renaissance*, ed. Jean Jacquot (Paris: Centre National de la Recherche Scientifique, 1956), pp. 319–33. Sternfeld touches on the marriage negotiations for the royal children.

32. Charles Barber, "*The Winter's Tale* and Jacobean Society," in *Shakespeare in a Changing World*, ed. Arnold Kettle (New York: International, 1964), p. 251. The essay is on pp. 233–52. This essay is incorrectly attributed to C. L. Barber in Bullough's *Narrative and Dramatic Sources*, vol. 8.

33. Peter B. Erickson, "Patriarchal Structures in *The Winter's Tale*," *PMLA* 97 (1982): 819. The essay is on pp. 819–29.

34. Mack, *Rescuing Shakespeare*, p. 11.

35. I have surveyed critical opinions about possible revision of *The Winter's Tale* in my essay "Hermione's Restoration in *The Winter's Tale*," in *Shakespeare's Romances Reconsidered*, ed. Carol McGinnis Kay and Henry E. Jacobs (Lincoln: University of Nebraska Press, 1978), pp. 125–33. See especially W. W. Greg, *The Shakespeare First Folio* (Oxford: Clarendon Press, 1955), pp. 415–17. Knowledge of E. A. J. Honigmann's *The Stability of Shakespeare's Text* (Lincoln: University of Nebraska Press, 1965) gives one pause about many textual issues, including the matter of revision.

36. Bullough, *Narrative and Dramatic Sources of Shakespeare*, 8:116–55.

37. There is an interesting scriptural analogy found in Luke's gospel. In his early ministry Jesus of Nazareth went to the synagogue. "He stood up to read the lesson and was handed the scroll of the prophet Isaiah. He opened the scroll and found the passage. . . . He rolled up the scroll, gave it back to the attendant, and sat down; and all eyes in the synagogue were fixed on him. He began to speak: 'Today,' he said, 'in your hearing this text has come true' " (Luke 4:17–21, New English Bible).

38. For two excellent essays on the women in this play see Carol Thomas Neely, "Women at Issue in *The Winter's Tale*," *Philological Quarterly* 56 (1978): 181–94; and Patricia Southard Gourlay, " 'O my most sacred lady': Female Metaphor in *The Winter's Tale*," *English Literary Renaissance* 5 (1975): 375–95. On the matter of fathers and daughters see Cyrus Hoy, "Fathers and Daughters in Shakespeare's Romances," in *Shakespeare's Romances Reconsidered*, ed. Carol McGinnis Kay and Henry E. Jacobs (Lincoln: University of Nebraska Press, 1978), pp. 77–90. On the role of men see Coppélia Kahn, *Man's Estate: Masculine Identity in Shakespeare* (Berkeley, Los Angeles, London: University of California Press, 1981), pp. 214–20.

THE TEMPEST

39. For discussion of the sources see Bullough, *Narrative and Dramatic Sources of Shakespeare*, 8:237–74. For further discussion of the travel pamphlets and the play see Philip Brockbank, "*The Tempest*: Conventions of Art and Empire," in *Later Shakespeare*, ed. John Russell Brown and Bernard Harris, Stratford-upon-Avon Studies 8 (New York: St. Martin's, 1967), pp. 182–201.

40. Christopher Morris, *Political Thought in England: Tyndale to Hooker* (London: Oxford University Press, 1953), p. 107.

41. Glynne Wickham, "Masque and Anti-masque in 'The Tempest,' " *Essays and Studies* 28 (1975): 1–14. I discuss this essay in chapter 1.

42. Schmidgall, *Shakespeare and the Courtly Aesthetic*, p. 154. In the same year as Schmidgall's book, Paul Cantor published an essay that examines the political nature of *The Tempest*: "Prospero's Republic: The Politics of Shakespeare's *The Tempest*," in *Shakespeare as Political Thinker*, ed. John Alvis and Thomas G. West (Durham, N.C.: Carolina Academic Press, 1981), pp. 239–55. Cantor does not comment on the politics of the family; instead, he focuses on Prospero's growth as a ruler, as one who comes to understand the need to rule. Cantor interestingly links the play and its political problems to the tragedies. He sees Prospero as finally joining the issues of wisdom and power, though the solution remains problematical.

43. Goldberg, *James I and the Politics of Literature*, p. 238.

44. Harding, "Shakespeare's Final View of Women," p. 61.

45. *The Tempest*, ed. Frank Kermode (London: Methuen, 1964). All references will be to this Arden edition.

46. See my essay "The Tempest / *The Tempest*," *Essays in Literature* 7 (1980): 6.

47. McIlwain, *Political Works of James I*, p. 272.

48. Lancelot Andrewes, *Ninety-six Sermons*, vol. 1 (Oxford: J. H. Parker, 1856), pp. 60–61.

49. John B. Bender, "The Day of *The Tempest*," *ELH* 47 (1980): 235–58. On the general relationship of liturgy to the drama see R. Chris Hassel, Jr.,

Renaissance Drama and the English Church Year (Lincoln and London: University of Nebraska Press, 1979). See especially his chapter "The Epiphany Plays," pp. 77–93; he does not, however, mention *The Tempest*.

50. Andrewes, *Ninety-six Sermons*, 4:214. Andrewes may himself be recalling Daniel 3:27.

51. Jacqueline E. M. Latham, "*The Tempest* and King James's *Daemonologie*," *Shakespeare Survey* 28 (1975): 117–23.

52. David Young, "Where the Bee Sucks: A Triangular Study of *Doctor Faustus, The Alchemist,* and *The Tempest*," in *Shakespeare's Romances Reconsidered*, eds. Carol McGinnis Kay and Henry Jacobs (Lincoln: University of Nebraska Press, 1978), pp. 149–66. In this same collection see also Joan Hartwig's "Cloten, Autolycus, and Caliban: Bearers of Parodic Burdens," pp. 91–103, for an examination of Caliban's parodic function.

53. Samuel Daniel, *The Vision of the Twelve Goddesses*, ed. Joan Rees, in *A Book of Masques in Honour of Allardyce Nicoll*, ed. T. J. B. Spencer and S. W. Wells (Cambridge: Cambridge University Press, 1967), pp. 26, 28.

54. See, for example, Norman Louis Morgan, "King James, Magic, the Masque, and *The Tempest*," in *Literature and Iconoclasm: Shakespeare*, ed. Brian Caraher and Irving Massey (Buffalo, N.Y.: SUNY at Buffalo Occasional Papers no. 2, 1976), pp. 18–27.

HENRY VIII

55. Quoted in *King Henry VIII*, ed. R. A. Foakes (London: Methuen, 1968), p. xxviii. All quotations from the play will be from this Arden edition.

56. Knight, *Crown of Life*, p. 257.

57. Geoffrey Bullough, *Narrative and Dramatic Sources of Shakespeare*, vol. 4 (London: Routledge & Kegan Paul; New York: Columbia University Press, 1962), p. 443; see pp. 435–51 for Bullough's discussion of the sources.

58. Samuel Rowley, *When You See Me, You Know Me*, ed. F. W. Wilson (Oxford: Malone Society, 1952). All quotations are from this edition.

59. Nichols, *Progresses of James*, 2:542–43. Quotations will be from this edition.

60. *The Basilicon Doron of King James VI*, ed. James Craigie (Edinburgh and London: Blackwood, 1944), p. 163.

61. The connections between the reigns of Henry VIII and James I have been pursued by William M. Baillie, "*Henry VIII*: A Jacobean History," *Shakespeare Studies* 12 (1979): 247–66. Baillie sums up his purpose: "It is the purpose of this essay to demonstrate that Jacobean issues and events of the months immediately preceding the play's premiere are reflected in basic features of the dramatic design; these topical motifs include the birth of a new Protestant optimism, the expansion of the monarch's personal authority in relation to the law, the sudden fall of a court favorite, and a divorce" (p. 248). I agree that the play reflects the Jacobean court, but Baillie and I disagree about the nature of the topicality. He does not accept, for example, that the play may have been written for the wedding festivities. Baillie assumes that the late-June performance in 1613 was the first. His main emphasis is on the Frances Howard/Earl of Essex divorce proceedings in 1613. But on this matter I find him least persuasive. He assumes that the King's Men would undertake a drama about divorce in order to "appeal both to the general

public and to the special power centers at court upon whom the company's still rising fortunes most closely depended" (p. 259). He says that the King's Men "were growing increasingly dependent on court patronage" (p. 258). I know of no evidence to support this idea. For further and more recent discussion of the play's link to Jacobean court life see Stuart M. Kurland, "The Drama of Politics: Shakespeare's *Henry VIII* and Jacobean England" (Ph.D. diss., University of Chicago, 1984).

Shakespeare's link between a Tudor monarch and the first Stuart sovereign had been anticipated in the magnificent royal entry for James into London in March 1604. The second triumphal arch device, prepared by the Italian merchants in London, included a picture of Henry VII and James. Dekker describes the scene on the arch: "In a large Square erected aboue these, King *Henry* the seuenth was royally seated in his Imperiall Robes, to whome King *James* (mounted on horsebacke) approches, and receyues a Scepter" (Dekker, *Dramatic Works,* 2:262). One of the dominant figures on the arch was Peace—another obvious connection between the first Tudor and the first Stuart monarch. My point is that Shakespeare's seeing in Henry VIII a Jacobean relevance is not at all far-fetched; it is indeed already established in the public imagination.

62. Thomas Ross, *Ilae siue De Jacobi* (London, 1608), pp. 322–23. The translation is from Mary Anne Everett Green, *Elizabeth,* pp. 15–16.

63. For an illuminating discussion of the term and its application to James see Jonathan Goldberg, chap. 3, "The Theater of Conscience," pp. 113–63, in *James I and the Politics of Literature.* Also examining the question of "conscience" and the larger matter of the play's "truth," and its relationship of fact and fiction, is Judith Anderson in *Biographical Truth: The Representation of Historical Persons in Tudor-Stuart Writing* (New Haven, Conn., and London: Yale University Press, 1984), chap. 8, pp. 124–54.

EPILOGUE

1. Stephen Orgel, "What Is a Text?" *Research Opportunities in Renaissance Drama* 24 (1981): 3–6.

2. For discussion of this painting consult Michel Foucault, *The Order of Things* (New York: Vintage, 1973), pp. 3–16 (originally published in France in 1966); John R. Searle, "*Las Meninas* and the Paradoxes of Pictorial Representation," *Critical Inquiry* 6 (1980): 477–88; Schmidgall, *Shakespeare and the Courtly Aesthetic,* pp. 263–71.

3. Edward A. Snow, *A Study of Vermeer* (Berkeley, Los Angeles, and London: University of California Press, 1979), p. 82.

4. Albert Blankert, *Vermeer of Delft: Complete Edition of the Paintings* (Oxford: Phaidon, 1978), p. 27. I am indebted to Professor Linda Stone of the Kress Foundation Department of Art History, University of Kansas, for introducing me to the works of Vermeer.

5. Charles Frey, *Shakespeare's Vast Romance: A Study of the Winter's Tale* (Columbia: University of Missouri Press, 1980), p. 49.

Bibliography

PRIMARY SOURCES

British Library Manuscripts
    Additional MS. 28032
    Harleian MS. 38
    Harleian MS. 366
    Harleian MS. 852
    Harleian MS. 6986
    Lansdowne MS. 1236
Alberti, Leon Battista. *The Albertis of Florence: Leon Battista Alberti's "Della Famiglia."* Translated by Guido A. Guarino. Lewisburg, Pa.: Bucknell University Press, 1971.
Andrewes, Lancelot. *Ninety-six Sermons.* 5 vols. Oxford: John Henry Parker, 1843–61.
Bacon, Francis. *The Letters and the Life of Francis Bacon.* Edited by James Spedding. Vols. 3 and 4. London: Longmans, Green, Reader & Dyer, 1868.
———. *The Works of Francis Bacon.* Edited by James Spedding, Robert Ellis, and Douglas Heath. 14 vols. London: Longmans, 1868–90.
Beaumont, Francis; and Fletcher, John. *The Dramatic Works in the Beaumont and Fletcher Canon.* General editor Fredson Bowers. 5 vols. Cambridge: Cambridge University Press, 1966–82.
Birch, Thomas. *The Court and Times of James the First.* 2 vols. London: Henry Colburn, 1849.
———. *The Life of Henry Prince of Wales.* London, 1760.
A Book of Masques in Honour of Allardyce Nicoll. Edited by T. J. B. Spencer and S. W. Wells. Cambridge: Cambridge University Press, 1967.
Bromley, George. *A Collection of Original Royal Letters.* London: John Stockdale, 1787.
Buccleuch, Duke of. *Report on the Manuscripts of the Duke of Buccleuch: The Montagu Papers.* Vols. 1 and 2. London: HMSO, 1899, 1926.
Bullough, Geoffrey, ed. *Narrative and Dramatic Sources of Shakespeare.* 8 vols. London: Routledge & Kegan Paul; New York: Columbia University Press, 1957–75.

Calendar of State Papers Domestic 1603–1610. London: Longman, Brown, Green, Longmans, & Roberts, 1857.

Calendar of State Papers Venetian 1603–1607, 1607–1610, 1610–1613. Vols. 10–12. London: HMSO, 1900–1905.

Carey, Robert. *The Memoirs of Robert Carey.* Edited by F. H. Mares. Oxford: Clarendon Press, 1972.

Chamberlain, John. *The Chamberlain Letters: A Selection of the Letters of John Chamberlain concerning Life in England from 1597 to 1626.* Edited by Elizabeth McClure Thomson. London: John Murray, 1966.

———. *The Letters of John Chamberlain.* Edited by Norman E. McClure. 2 vols. Philadelphia: American Philosophical Society, 1939.

Chapman, George. *The Plays of George Chapman: The Comedies.* General editor Allan Holaday. Urbana: University of Illinois Press, 1970.

Clifford, Lady Anne. *The Diary of the Lady Anne Clifford.* Introduction by V. Sackville-West. London: Heinemann, 1923.

Cornwallis, Charles. *A Discourse of the most Illustrious Prince Henry, Late Prince of Wales* (London, 1641). In *A Collection of Scarce and Valuable Tracts,* edited by Lord John Somers. Vol. 2. London, 1809.

———. *The Life and Death of our late most incomparable and Heroique Prince Henry* (1641). In Somers, *Tracts.* Vol. 2. London, 1809.

Day, John. *Humour out of Breath.* London, 1608.

———. *Law-Tricks.* Edited by John Crow. Oxford: Malone Society, 1950.

Dekker, Thomas. *The Dramatic Works of Thomas Dekker.* Edited by Fredson Bowers. 4 vols. Cambridge: Cambridge University Press, 1953–61.

D'Ewes, Sir Simonds. *The Autobiography and Correspondence of Sir Simonds D'Ewes, Bart., During the Reigns of James I and Charles I.* Edited by James O. Halliwell. 2 vols. London: Richard Bentley, 1845.

Dugdale, Gilbert. *The Time Triumphant.* London, 1604.

Elizabeth, Queen of Bohemia. *The Letters of Elizabeth Queen of Bohemia.* Edited by L. M. Baker. London: Bodley Head, 1953.

England as Seen by Foreigners in the Days of Elizabeth and James the First. Edited by William Brenchley Rye. London: J. R. Smith, 1865.

Englands Wedding Garment. London, 1603.

Fuller, Thomas. *The Church-History of Britain.* London, 1655.

Goodman, Godfrey. *The Court of King James the First.* Edited by John S. Brewer. 2 vols. London: Richard Bentley, 1839.

Greville, Fulke. *The Five Yeares of King James.* London, 1643.

H., W. *The True Picture and Relation of Prince Henry.* Leyden, 1634.

Hailes, David Dalrymple. *Memorials and Letters Relating to the History of Britain in the Reign of James the First.* 2d ed. Glasgow, 1766.

Harington, John. *The Letters and Epigrammes of Sir John Harington.* Edited by Norman E. McClure. Philadelphia: University of Pennsylvania Press, 1930.

———. *Nugae Antiquae.* 3 vols. London, 1779.

Harris, William. *An Historical and Critical Account of the Life and Writings of James the First, King of Great Britain.* London, 1753.

Harrison, G. B., ed. *A Jacobean Journal . . . 1603–1606.* New York: Macmillan, 1941.

————. *A Second Jacobean Journal . . . 1607 to 1610.* London: Routledge & Kegan Paul, 1958.

Herbert, Edward, Lord. *The Autobiography of Edward, Lord Herbert of Cherbury.* Introduction by Sidney Lee. London: John Nimmo, 1886.

Heywood, Thomas. *The Dramatic Works of Thomas Heywood.* Edited by R. H. Shepherd. 1874. Reprint. New York: Russell & Russell, 1964.

Hoby, Lady Margaret. *Diary of Lady Margaret Hoby 1599–1605.* Edited by Dorothy M. Meads. London: Routledge, 1930.

Holles, Gervase. *Memorials of the Holles Family 1493–1656.* Edited by A. C. Wood. London: Camden Society, 1937.

James I. *The Political Works of James I.* Edited by Charles H. McIlwain. Cambridge: Harvard University Press, 1918.

James VI. *The Basilicon Doron of King James VI.* Edited by James Craigie. Scottish Text Society. 2 vols. Edinburgh and London: Blackwood, 1944.

————. *The Workes of the most high and mightie prince, James.* London, 1616.

Jesse, John Heneage. *Memoirs of the Court of England During the Reign of the Stuarts.* 3 vols. London: Bohn, 1857.

Jonson, Ben. *Ben Jonson: Three Comedies.* Edited by Michael Jamieson. Baltimore, Md.: Penguin, 1966.

————. *Epicoene or The Silent Woman.* Edited by L. A. Beaurline. Lincoln: University of Nebraska Press, 1966.

Letters to King James the Sixth. Edited by Alexander MacDonald. Edinburgh: Maitland Club, 1835.

Mar, Earl of. *Report on the Manuscripts of the Earl of Mar and Kellie.* London: HMSO, 1904.

Marcelline, George. *The Triumphs of King James the First.* London, 1610.

Marston, John. *The Fawn.* Edited by Gerald A. Smith. Lincoln: University of Nebraska Press, 1965.

Maxwell, James. *The Laudable Life, and Deplorable Death, of our late peerlesse Prince Henry.* London, 1612.

Melville, James. *Memoirs of of Sir James Melville of Halhill 1535–1617.* Edited by A. Francis Steuart. London: Routledge & Sons, 1929.

Middleton, Thomas. *A Chaste Maid in Cheapside.* Edited by R. B. Parker. London: Methuen, 1969.

————. *Michaelmas Term.* Edited by Richard Levin. Lincoln: University of Nebraska Press, 1966.

————. *The Works of Thomas Middleton.* Edited by A. H. Bullen. Boston: Houghton Mifflin, 1885.

Munday, Anthony. *Londons Love to the Royal Prince Henrie.* London, 1610.

————. *The Triumphs of Re-United Britannia.* London, 1605.

Nichols, John. *The Progresses, Processions, and Magnificent Festivities of King James the First.* 4 vols. London: J. B. Nichols, 1828.

Osborne, Francis. *Traditional Memoirs* (1658). In *Secret History of the Court of James the First,* edited by Sir Walter Scott. 2 vols. Edinburgh: Ballantyne, 1811.

Papers Relative to the Marriage of King James the Sixth of Scotland, with the Princess Anna of Denmark. Edinburgh: Bannatyne Club, 1828.

Peacham, Henry. *Minerva Britanna*. London, 1612.

Pett, Phineas. *The Autobiography of Phineas Pett*. Edited by W. G. Perrin. London: Navy Records Society, 1918.

Peyton, Edward. *The Divine Catastrophe of the Kingly Family of the House of Stuarts* (1652). In *Secret History of the Court of James the First*, edited by Sir Walter Scott. 2 vols. Edinburgh: Ballantyne, 1811.

Puttenham, George. *The Arte of English Poesie*. Edited by Gladys Doidge Willcock and Alice Walker. Cambridge: Cambridge University Press, 1936.

Raumer, Friederich Ludwig Georg von. *History of the Sixteenth and Seventeenth Centuries*. 2 vols. London: John Murray, 1835.

Ross, Thomas. *Idae sive De Jacobi*. London, 1608.

Rowley, Samuel. *When You See Me, You Know Me*. Edited by F. W. Wilson. Oxford: Malone Society, 1952.

Rowley, William. *A Shoo-maker a gentleman*. London, 1638.

Rutland, Duke of. *The Manuscripts of the Duke of Rutland at Belvoir Castle*. London: HMSO, 1905.

Sackville, Major-General Lord. *Calendar of the Manuscripts of Major-General Lord Sackville: Cranfield Papers 1551–1612*. 2 vols. London: HMSO, 1940, 1966.

Salisbury, Marquess of. *Calendar of the Manuscripts of the Marquess of Salisbury, Hatfield House*. Parts 15–24. London: HMSO, 1930–76.

Sanderson, William. *A Compleat History of the Lives and Reigns of Mary Queen of Scotland and of Her Son and Successor, James*. London, 1656.

Secret History of the Court of James the First. Edited by Sir Walter Scott. 2 vols. Edinburgh: Ballantyne, 1811.

Shakespeare, William. *The Complete Works*. General editor Alfred Harbage. Baltimore, Md.: Penguin, 1969.

———. *Cymbeline*. Edited by James Nosworthy. 1955. Reprint. London: Methuen, 1966.

———. *King Henry VIII*. Edited by R. A. Foakes. London: Methuen, 1968.

———. *Pericles*. Edited by F. David Hoeniger. London: Methuen, 1963.

———. *The Tempest*. Edited by Frank Kermode. London: Methuen, 1964.

———. *The Winter's Tale*. Edited by J. H. P. Pafford. London: Methuen, 1963.

Sharpham, Edward. *Cupids Whirligig*. London, 1616.

———. *The Fleire*. London, 1607.

Sparke, Michael. *The Narrative History of King James, for the first fourteen years*. London, 1651.

Stow, John. *Annales or a Generall Chronicle of England*. London, 1631.

Weldon, Anthony. *The Court and Character of King James*. London, 1651.

Wentworth Papers 1597–1628. Edited by J. P. Cooper. Camden 4th ser., vol. 12. London: Royal Historical Society, 1973.

Whitaker, Thomas Dunham. *The Life and Original Correspondence of Sir George Radcliffe*. London: John Nichols, 1810.

Wilson, Arthur. *The History of Great Britain, Being the Life and Reign of King James the First*. London, 1653.

Winwood, Ralph. *Memorials of Affairs of State in the Reigns of Q. Elizabeth and K. James I*. Edited by Edmund Sawyer. 3 vols. London, 1725.

Wotton, Sir Henry. *The Life and Letters of Sir Henry Wotton.* Edited by Logan Pearsall Smith. 2 vols. 1907. Reprint. Oxford: Clarendon Press, 1966.

SECONDARY SOURCES

Aikin, Lucy. *Memoirs of the Court of King James the First.* 2 vols. London: Longman, Brown, & Green, 1823.

Akrigg, G. P. V. *Jacobean Pageant or the Court of King James I.* London: Hamish Hamilton, 1962.

Anderson, Judith. *Biographical Truth: The Representation of Historical Persons in Tudor-Stuart Writing.* New Haven Conn., and London: Yale University Press, 1984.

Ariès, Phillipe. *Centuries of Childhood.* Translated by Robert Baldick. London: Jonathan Cape, 1962. Originally published as *L'Enfant et la vie familiale sous l'ancien régime.* Paris, 1960.

Baillie, William M. *"Henry VIII:* A Jacobean History." *Shakespeare Studies* 12 (1979): 247–66.

Barber, C. L. "The Family in Shakespeare's Development: Tragedy and Sacredness." In *Representing Shakespeare: New Psychoanalytic Essays,* edited by Murray M. Schwartz and Coppélia Kahn, pp. 188–202. Baltimore, Md.: Johns Hopkins University Press, 1980.

———. " 'Thou that beget'st him that did thee beget': Transformation in 'Pericles' and 'The Winter's Tale.' " *Shakespeare Survey* 22 (1969): 59–67.

Barber, Charles. *"The Winter's Tale* and Jacobean Society." In *Shakespeare in a Changing World,* edited by Arnold Kettle, pp. 233–52. New York: International, 1964.

Barker, Gerard A. "Themes and Variations in Shakespeare's *Pericles." English Studies* 44 (1963): 401–14.

Bender, John B. "The Day of *The Tempest." ELH* 47 (1980): 235–58.

Benger, Elizabeth Ogilvy. *Memoirs of Elizabeth Stuart, Queen of Bohemia.* 2 vols. London: Longman, Green, 1825.

Bennett, Josephine Waters. *Measure for Measure as Royal Entertainment.* New York and London: Columbia University Press, 1966.

Bergeron, David M. *"Cymbeline:* Shakespeare's Last Roman Play." *Shakespeare Quarterly* 31 (1980): 31–41.

———. "Gilbert Dugdale and the Royal Entry of James I (1604)." *Journal of Medieval and Renaissance Studies* 13 (1983): 111–25.

———. "Hermione's Restoration in *The Winter's Tale."* In *Shakespeare's Romances Reconsidered,* edited by Carol McGinnis Kay and Henry E. Jacobs, pp. 125–33. Lincoln: University of Nebraska Press, 1978.

———. "Middleton's Moral Landscape: *A Chaste Maid in Cheapside* and *The Triumphs of Truth."* In *"Accompaninge the players": Essays Celebrating Thomas Middleton, 1580–1980,* edited by Kenneth Friedenreich, pp. 133–46. New York: AMS Press, 1983.

———. "Prince Henry and English Civic Pageantry." *Tennessee Studies in Literature* 13 (1968): 109–16.

———. "Sexuality in *Cymbeline." Essays in Literature* 10 (1983): 159–68.

———. "The Tempest / *The Tempest." Essays in Literature* 7 (1980): 3–9.

247

Bingham, Caroline. *James I of England*. London: Weidenfeld & Nicolson, 1981.

Blankert, Albert. *Vermeer of Delft: Complete Edition of the Paintings*. Oxford: Phaidon, 1978.

Boose, Lynda E. "The Father and the Bride in Shakespeare." *PMLA* 97 (1982): 325–47.

Bowen, Catherine Drinker. *The Lion and the Throne: The Life and Times of Sir Edward Coke (1552–1634)*. Boston: Little, Brown, 1956.

Bradbrook, M. C. "Shakespeare and the Multiple Theatres of Jacobean London." In *Elizabethan Theatre VI*, edited by G. R. Hibbard, pp. 88–104. Toronto: Macmillan, 1978.

Bradley, E. T. *Life of the Lady Arabella Stuart*. 2 vols. London: Bentley, 1889.

Brockbank, J. P. "History and Histrionics in *Cymbeline*." *Shakespeare Survey* 11 (1958): 42–49.

Brockbank, Philip. "*The Tempest*: Conventions of Art and Empire." In *Later Shakespeare*, edited by John Russell Brown and Bernard Harris, pp. 182–201. Stratford-upon-Avon Studies 8. New York: St. Martin's Press, 1967.

Buchan, Alice. *A Stuart Portrait*. London: Peter Davies, 1934.

Cantor, Paul. "Prospero's Republic: The Politics of Shakespeare's *The Tempest*." In *Shakespeare as Political Thinker*, edited by John Alvis and Thomas G. West, pp. 239–55. Durham, N.C.: Carolina Academic Press, 1981.

Chatterji, Ruby. "Theme, Imagery, and Unity in *A Chaste Maid in Cheapside*." *Renaissance Drama* 8 (1965): 105–26.

Clark, Arthur Melville. *Murder under Trust, or, The Topical Macbeth and Other Jacobean Matters*. Edinburgh: Scottish Academic Press, 1981.

Colie, Rosalie L. *Shakespeare's Living Art*. Princeton, N.J.: Princeton University Press, 1974.

Culler, Jonathan. *The Pursuit of Signs: Semiotics, Literature, Deconstruction*. Ithaca, N.Y.: Cornell University Press, 1981.

Dauphiné, James. "Le Secret de *Cymbeline*." *Etudes Anglaises* 32 (1979): 129–42.

Davies, Godfrey. *The Early Stuarts 1603–1660*. 2d ed. Oxford: Clarendon Press, 1959.

Disraeli, Isaac. *An Inquiry into the Literary and Political Character of James the First*. London: John Murray, 1816.

Durant, David N. *Arbella Stuart: A Rival to the Queen*. London: Weidenfeld & Nicolson, 1978.

Edwards, Philip. *Threshold of a Nation: A Study in English and Irish Drama*. Cambridge: Cambridge University Press, 1979.

Erickson, Peter B. "Patriarchal Structures in *The Winter's Tale*." *PMLA* 97 (1982): 819–29.

Felperin, Howard. *Shakespearean Representation: Mimesis and Modernity in Elizabethan Tragedy*. Princeton, N.J.: Princeton University Press, 1977.

———. *Shakespearean Romance*. Princeton, N.J.: Princeton University Press, 1972.

Flandrin, Jean-Louis. *Families in Former Times: Kinship, Household and Sexuality*. Translated by Richard Southern. Cambridge: Cambridge University Press, 1979.

Bibliography

Foakes, R. A. *Shakespeare: The Dark Comedies to the Last Plays: From Satire to Celebration.* Charlottesville: University Press of Virginia, 1971.
Fraser, Antonia. *King James VI of Scotland I of England.* New York: Knopf, 1975.
———. *Mary Queen of Scots.* New York: Delacorte Press, 1969.
Frey, Charles. *Shakespeare's Vast Romance: A Study of the Winter's Tale.* Columbia: University of Missouri Press, 1980.
Frye, Northrop. *The Secular Scripture: A Study of the Structure of Romance.* Cambridge: Harvard University Press, 1976.
Gajdusek, R. E. "Death, Incest, and the Triple Bond in Shakespeare." *American Imago* 31 (1974): 109–58.
Gardiner, Samuel R. *History of England from the Accession of James I to the Outbreak of the Civil War 1603–1642.* 10 vols. 1894–96. Reprint. New York: AMS Press, 1965.
Geertz, Clifford. "Centers, Kings, and Charisma: Reflections on the Symbolics of Power." In *Local Knowledge: Further Essays in Interpretive Anthroplogy,* pp. 121–46. New York: Basic Books, 1983.
Gesner, Carol. *Shakespeare & the Greek Romance: A Study of Origins.* Lexington: University Press of Kentucky, 1970.
Goldberg, Jonathan. *James I and the Politics of Literature: Jonson, Shakespeare, Donne, and Their Contemporaries.* Baltimore, Md., and London: Johns Hopkins University Press, 1983.
———. " 'Upon a publike stage': The Royal Gaze and Jacobean Theater." *Research Opportunities in Renaissance Drama* 24 (1981): 17–21.
Goody, Jack. *The Character of Kinship.* Cambridge: Cambridge University Press, 1973.
Goody, Jack; Thirsk, Joan; and Thompson, E. P., eds. *Family and Inheritance: Rural Society in Western Europe, 1200–1800.* Cambridge: Cambridge University Press, 1976.
Gorst-Williams, Jessica. *Elizabeth the Winter Queen.* London: Abelard, 1977.
Gourlay, Patricia Southard. " 'O my most sacred lady': Female Metaphor in *The Winter's Tale.*" *English Literary Renaissance* 5 (1975): 375–95.
Green, Mary Anne Everett. *Elizabeth Electress Palatine and Queen of Bohemia.* Revised by S. C. Loman. 1855. Reprint. London: Methuen, 1909.
Greenblatt, Stephen. "The Cultivation of Anxiety: King Lear and His Heirs." *Raritan* 2 (1982): 92–114.
———. "Invisible Bullets: Renaissance Authority and Its Subversion." *Glyph* 8 (1981): 40–61.
———. *Renaissance Self-Fashioning: From More to Shakespeare.* Chicago and London: University of Chicago Press, 1980.
Greg, W. W. *The Shakespeare First Folio.* Oxford: Clarendon Press, 1955.
Handover, P. M. *Arbella Stuart: Royal Lady of Hardwick and Cousin to King James.* London: Eyre & Spottiswoode, 1957.
Harding, D. W. "Shakespeare's Final View of Women." *TLS,* 30 Nov. 1979, pp. 59–61.
Hardy, B. C. *Arbella Stuart: A Biography.* London: Constable, 1913.
Harris, Bernard. " 'What's past is prologue': 'Cymbeline' and 'Henry VIII.' " In *Later Shakespeare,* edited by John Russell Brown and Bernard Harris, pp. 202–33. Stratford-upon-Avon Studies 8. London: Arnold, 1966; New York: St. Martin's, 1967.

249

Hartwig, Joan. "Cloten, Autolycus, and Caliban: Bearers of Parodic Burdens." In *Shakespeare's Romances Reconsidered*, edited by Carol McGinnis Kay and Henry E. Jacobs, pp. 91–103. Lincoln: University of Nebraska Press, 1978.

———. *Shakespeare's Tragicomic Vision*. Baton Rouge: Louisiana State University Press, 1972.

Hassel, R. Chris, Jr. *Renaissance Drama and the English Church Year*. Lincoln: University of Nebraska Press, 1979.

Hay, Marie. *The Winter Queen Being the Unhappy History of Elizabeth Stuart*. London: Constable, 1910.

Henderson, Thomas F. *James I and VI*. Paris, London, and New York: Goupil, 1904.

Hexter, J. H. *Reappraisals in History: New Views on History and Society in Early Modern Europe*. 2d ed. Chicago and London: University of Chicago Press, 1979.

Hibbard, George R. "Love, Marriage and Money in Shakespeare's Theatre and Shakespeare's England." In *Elizabethan Theatre VI*, edited by G. R. Hibbard, pp. 134–55. Toronto: Macmillan, 1978.

Hill, Christopher. *Change and Continuity in Seventeenth-Century England*. London: Weidenfeld & Nicolson, 1974.

Hofling, Charles K. "Notes on Shakespeare's *Cymbeline*." *Shakespeare Studies* 1 (1965): 109–58.

Honigmann, E. A. J. *The Stability of Shakespeare's Text*. Lincoln: University of Nebraska Press, 1965.

Houston, S. J. *James I*. London: Longman, 1973.

Hoy, Cyrus. "Fathers and Daughters in Shakespeare's Romances." In *Shakespeare's Romances Reconsidered*, edited by Carol McGinnis Kay and Henry E. Jacobs, pp. 77–90. Lincoln: University of Nebraska Press, 1978.

Hunt, David. *Parents and Children in History: The Psychology of Family Life in Early Modern France*. New York: Basic Books, 1970.

James, David. *The Dream of Prospero*. Oxford: Clarendon Press, 1967.

Javitch, Daniel. *Poetry and Courtliness in Renaissance England*. Princeton, N.J.: Princeton University Press, 1978.

Jones, Emrys. "Stuart Cymbeline." *Essays in Criticism* 11 (1961): 84–99.

Jorgenson, Paul A. *Shakespeare's Military World*. Berkeley and Los Angeles: University of California Press, 1956.

Kahn, Coppélia. *Man's Estate: Masculine Identity in Shakespeare*. Berkeley, Los Angeles, and London: University of California Press, 1981.

Kernan, Alvin. *The Cankered Muse: Satire of the English Renaissance*. New Haven, Conn.: Yale University Press, 1959.

Knight, G. Wilson. *The Crown of Life*. 1947. Reprint. New York: Barnes & Noble, 1966.

Kurland, Stuart M. "The Drama of Politics: Shakespeare's *Henry VIII* and Jacobean England." Ph.D. diss., University of Chicago, 1984.

Laing, R. D. *The Politics of the Family and Other Essays*. New York: Random House, 1971.

Laslett, Peter. *Family Life and Illicit Love in Earlier Generations: Essays in Historical Sociology*. Cambridge: Cambridge University Press, 1977.

————. *Household and Family in Past Time.* Cambridge: Cambridge University Press, 1972.

————. *The World We Have Lost.* 2d ed. London: Methuen, 1971.

Latham, Jacqueline E. M. "*The Tempest* and King James's *Daemonologie.*" *Shakespeare Survey* 28 (1975): 117–23.

Leggatt, Alexander. *Citizen Comedy in the Age of Shakespeare.* Toronto: University of Toronto Press, 1973.

[Lenanton], Carola Oman. *Elizabeth of Bohemia.* London: Hodder & Stoughton, 1938.

Levin, Richard. *New Readings vs. Old Plays.* Chicago: University of Chicago Press, 1979.

Lévi-Strauss, Claude. "The Family." In *Man, Culture, and Society,* edited by Harry L. Shapiro, pp. 333–57. Rev. ed. London: Oxford University Press, 1971.

McElwee, William. *The Wisest Fool in Christendom: The Reign of King James I and VI.* New York: Harcourt Brace, 1958.

McInnes, Ian. *Arabella: The Life and Times of Lady Arabella Seymour, 1575–1615.* London: Allen, 1968.

Mack, Maynard. *King Lear in Our Time.* Berkeley and Los Angeles: University of California Press, 1972.

————. *Rescuing Shakespeare.* International Shakespeare Association Occasional Papers no. 1. Oxford: Oxford University Press, for the International Shakespeare Association, 1979.

Marcus, Leah Sinanoglou. *Childhood and Cultural Despair: A Theme and Variations in Seventeenth-Century Literature.* Pittsburgh, Pa.: University of Pittsburgh Press, 1978.

Mathew, David. *James I.* London: Eyre & Spottiswoode, 1967.

Moffet, Robin. "*Cymbeline* and the Nativity." *Shakespeare Quarterly* 13 (1962): 207–18.

Montrose, Louis Adrian. " 'The Place of a Brother' in *As You Like It:* Social Process and Comic Form." *Shakespeare Quarterly* 32 (1981): 28–54.

Morgan, Norman Louis. "King James, Magic, the Masque, and *The Tempest.*" In *Literature and Iconoclasm: Shakespeare,* edited by Brian Caraher and Irving Massey, pp. 18–27. Buffalo, N.Y.: SUNY at Buffalo Occasional Papers no. 2, 1976.

Morris, Christopher. *Political Thought in England: Tyndale to Hooker.* London: Oxford University Press, 1953.

Mowat, Barbara A. *The Dramaturgy of Shakespeare's Romances.* Athens: University of Georgia Press, 1976.

Neely, Carol Thomas. "Women at Issue in *The Winter's Tale.*" *Philological Quarterly* 56 (1978): 181–94.

Notestein, Wallace. *The House of Commons 1604–1610.* New Haven, Conn., and London: Yale University Press, 1971.

Orgel, Stephen. *The Illusion of Power: Political Theater in the English Renaissance.* Berkeley, Los Angeles, and London: University of California Press, 1975.

————. "What Is a Text?" *Research Opportunities in Renaissance Drama,* 24 (1981): 3–6.

Orgel, Stephen; and Strong, Roy. *Inigo Jones: The Theatre of the Stuart Court.* 2 vols. Berkeley and Los Angeles: University of California Press, 1973.

Parry, Graham. *The Golden Age Restor'd: The Culture of the Stuart Court, 1603–42.* Manchester: Manchester University Press, 1981.

Paul, Henry N. *The Royal Play of Macbeth.* New York: Macmillan, 1950.

Peterson, Douglas. *Time, Tide, and Tempest: A Study of Shakespeare's Romances.* San Marino, Calif.: Huntington Library, 1973.

Pettet, E. C. *Shakespeare and the Romance Tradition.* London and New York: Staples, 1949.

Pinchbeck, Ivy; and Hewitt, Margaret. *Children in English Society.* Vol. 1: *From Tudor Times to the Eighteenth Century.* London: Routledge & Kegan Paul; Toronto: University of Toronto Press, 1969.

Poster, Mark. *Critical Theory of the Family.* New York: Seabury, 1978.

Rabb, Theodore K; and Rothberg, Robert I. eds. *The Family in History: Interdisciplinary Essays.* New York: Octagon, 1976.

Rabkin, Norman. *Shakespeare and the Problem of Meaning.* Chicago and London: University of Chicago Press, 1981.

Raumer, Friedrich Ludwig Georg von. *The Political History of England during the 16th, 17th, and 18th Centuries.* London: Richter, 1837.

Rosenberg, Charles E., ed. *The Family in History.* Philadelphia: University of Pennsylvania Press, 1975.

Rowse, A. L. *Simon Forman: Sex and Society in Shakespeare's Age.* London: Weidenfeld & Nicolson, 1974.

Schmidgall, Gary. *Shakespeare and the Courtly Aesthetic.* Berkeley, Los Angeles, and London: University of California Press, 1981.

Schochet, Gordon J. *Patriarchalism in Political Thought.* Oxford: Basil Blackwell, 1975.

Schoenbaum, S. *William Shakespeare: A Compact Documentary Life.* London and New York: Oxford University Press, 1977.

Scott, Otto J. *James I.* New York: Mason Charter, 1976.

Sharpe, Kevin. *Sir Robert Cotton 1586–1631: History and Politics in Early Modern England.* Oxford: Oxford University Press, 1979.

Shorter, Edward. *The Making of the Modern Family.* New York: Basic Books, 1975.

Singh, Sarup. *Family Relationships in Shakespeare and the Restoration Comedy of Manners.* Delhi: Oxford University Press, 1983.

Skura, Meredith. "Interpreting Posthumus' Dream from Above and Below: Families, Psychoanalysts, and Literary Critics." In *Representing Shakespeare,* edited by Murray M. Schwartz and Coppélia Kahn, pp. 203–16. Baltimore, Md., and London: Johns Hopkins University Press, 1980.

Smith, Alan G. R., ed. *The Reign of James VI and I.* London: Macmillan, 1973.

Smith, Hallett. *Shakespeare's Romances: A Study of Some Ways of the Imagination.* San Marino, Calif.: Huntington Library, 1972.

Smith, Warren D. "Cloten with Caius Lucius." *Studies in Philology* 49 (1952): 185–94.

Snow, Edward A. *A Study of Vermeer.* Berkeley, Los Angeles, and London: University of California Press, 1979.

Sternfeld, Frederick W. "Le Symbolisme musical dans quelques pièces de Shakespeare présentées à la Cour d'Angleterre." In *Les Fêtes de la Renaissance,* edited by Jean Jacquot, pp. 319–33. Paris: Centre National de la Recherche Scientifique, 1956.

Stone, Lawrence. *The Family, Sex and Marriage in England 1500-1800.* London: Weidenfeld & Nicolson, 1977.

Strong, Roy. *Britannia Triumphans: Inigo Jones, Rubens and Whitehall Palace.* London: Thames & Hudson, 1980.

————. *The English Icon: Elizabethan and Jacobean Portraiture.* London: Routledge & Kegan Paul; New York: Pantheon, 1969.

Sundelson, David. *Shakespeare's Restorations of the Father.* New Brunswick, N.J.: Rutgers University Press, 1983.

Tawney, R. H. *Business and Politics under James I: Lionel Cranfield as Merchant and Minister.* Cambridge: Cambridge University Press, 1958.

Thomas, Keith. "Age and Authority in Early Modern England." *Proceedings of the British Academy* 62 (1976): 205-48.

Tillyard, E. M. W. *Shakespeare's Last Plays.* London: Chatto & Windus, 1938.

Traversi, Derek. *Shakespeare: The Last Phase.* London: Hollis & Carter, 1954.

Uphaus, Robert W. *Beyond Tragedy: Structure and Experience in Shakespeare's Romances.* Lexington: University Press of Kentucky, 1981.

Vaughan, Robert. *The History of England under the House of Stuart.* London: Baldwin & Cradock, 1840.

Wickham, Glynne. "From Tragedy to Tragi-comedy: 'King Lear' as Prologue." *Shakespeare Survey* 26 (1973): 33-48.

————. "Masque and Anti-masque in 'The Tempest.'" *Essays and Studies* 28 (1975): 1-14.

————. "Riddle and Emblem: A Study in the Dramatic Structure of *Cymbeline*." In *English Renaissance Studies Presented to Dame Helen Gardner*, edited by John Carey, pp. 94-113. Oxford: Clarendon Press, 1980.

————. "Romance and Emblem: A Study in the Dramatic Structure of *The Winter's Tale*." In *Elizabethan Theatre III*, edited by David Galloway, pp. 82-99. Toronto: Macmillan, 1973.

————. "Shakespeare's Investiture Play: The Occasion and Subject of 'The Winter's Tale.'" *TLS*, 18 Dec. 1969, p. 1456.

————. "*The Winter's Tale*: A Comedy with Deaths." In his *Shakespeare's Dramatic Heritage*, pp. 249-56. London: Routledge & Kegan Paul, 1969.

Williams, Charles. *James I.* 1934. Reprint. London: Arthur Barker, 1951.

Williams, Ethel Carleton. *Anne of Denmark: Wife of James VI of Scotland: James I of England.* London: Longman, 1970.

Williamson, J. W. *The Myth of the Conqueror: Prince Henry Stuart: A Study of 17th Century Personation.* New York: AMS Press, 1978.

Willson, D. Harris. *King James VI and I.* London: Jonathan Cape, 1956.

Wilson, Elkin Calhoun. *Prince Henry and English Literature.* Ithaca, N.Y.: Cornell University Press, 1946.

Yates, Frances. *Majesty and Magic in Shakespeare's Last Plays.* Boulder, Colo.: Shambhala, 1978,

Young, David. "Where the Bee Sucks: A Triangular Study of *Doctor Faustus, The Alchemist*, and *The Tempest*." In *Shakespeare's Romances Reconsidered*, edited by Carol McGinnis Kay and Henry E. Jacobs, pp. 149-66. Lincoln: University of Nebraska Press, 1978.

Index